Developing
Critical Thinkers

Developing
Critical Thinkers

Challenging Adults
to Explore Alternative Ways
of Thinking and Acting

STEPHEN D. BROOKFIELD

Open University Press

Milton Keynes

Open University Press
Celtic Court
22 Ballmoor
Buckingham
MK18 1XW, England

First published in 1987 by Open University Press
Reprinted 1993

Published simultaneously in the United States by
Jossey-Bass Publishers, Inc.
433 California Street
San Francisco, California 94104
USA

ISBN 0 335 15551 0

Printed and bound in Great Britain by
Biddles Ltd, Guildford and King's Lynn

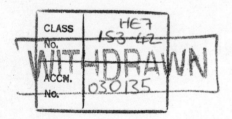

Contents

Preface

Learning to think critically is one of the most significant activities of adult life. When we become critical thinkers we develop an awareness of the assumptions under which we, and others, think and act. We learn to pay attention to the context in which our actions and ideas are generated. We become skeptical of quick-fix solutions, of single answers to problems, and of claims to universal truth. We also become open to alternative ways of looking at, and behaving in, the world. The ability to think critically is important for our lives in many different ways. When we are critical thinkers within our intimate relationships we learn to see our own actions through the eyes of others. At our workplaces we seek to exercise democratic control over workplace functions and organization and to take initiative in charting new directions and in designing the form and content of our activities. We become aware of the potential for distortion and bias in media depictions of our private and public worlds. Politically, we value freedom, we practice democracy, we encourage a tolerance of diversity, and we hold in check the demagogic tendencies of politicians.

As a dimension of learning, however, critical thinking in adulthood has been greatly neglected in the educational literature. Books on critical thinking tend to be written for students in higher education, rather than for adults living at the nexus of complex and conflicting pressures. Critical thinking is seen as a process applicable chiefly to the college classroom, as something undergraduates do in order to perform well on tests of reasoning abilities or to write persuasive academic essays. The ways in which people become critically reflective in the dimensions of their everyday lives—in their relationships, at their workplaces, with regard to the media, and as citizens—are generally excluded from these works. But the activities involved in thinking critically should not be restricted to the college classroom or to the undergraduate essay. Thinking critically—reflecting on the assumptions underlying our and others' ideas and actions, and contemplating alternative ways of thinking and living—is one of the important ways in which we become adults. When we think critically, we come to our judgments, choices, and decisions for ourselves, instead of letting others do this on our behalf. We refuse to relinquish the responsibility for making the choices that determine our individual and collective futures to those who presume to know what is in our own best interests. We become actively engaged in creating our personal and social worlds. In short, we take the reality of democracy seriously.

Developing Critical Thinkers has three central aims. The first is to help readers understand the phenomenon of critical thinking: to describe its essential components, to provide examples of how it can be observed in people's actions, and to set out the research and conceptual base for this activity. The second aim is to examine the various methods, techniques, and approaches that can be used by anyone seeking to help people develop better critical thinking skills. To this end, this work provides various case studies of successful practice and outlines specific exercises designed to foster critical thinking. The third aim is to explore the opportunities for people to become critical thinkers in four specific arenas, all of which are central to most adults' lives: in their intimate relationships, at their workplace, as part of their political involvements, and with regard to the mass media that influence their perceptions of the world.

The intended readers are all those professionals, managers, and educators who seek to understand, and develop, skills of critical thinking in their colleagues, clients, learners, and peers.

In terms of professional groups, this includes teachers in a wide range of educational settings, trainers and human resource developers, counselors, social workers, psychologists, therapists, and community activists. In terms of professional functions, the book will be useful for anyone who is trying to understand how people can be challenged to become more questioning and more involved in controlling their own lives, workplaces, and society. If you think that your intimates, colleagues, clients, or learners need to take a critical look at what they are doing, why they are doing it, what alternatives they might consider, and how they can learn from all this critical scrutiny, then this book is meant for you.

Overview of the Contents

The book is divided into three distinct parts. In the first part, I introduce the concept of critical thinking, set out its chief components, and indicate how it might be recognized. Chapter One considers what it means to think critically. Central features of the critical thinking process are identified, and the role of helpers in prompting others to begin the process is explored. Chapter Two describes in detail how the components of critical thinking can be recognized in people's actions. These components include such elements as being aware of the assumptions under which we and others live and act, challenging these assumptions, becoming aware of how context alters behavior, becoming skeptical of claims to universal truths or ultimate explanations, and considering and imagining alternatives to our current ways of thinking and living. The importance of critical thinking for personal development is discussed in Chapter Three, where I argue that the ability to be critically reflective is one significant criterion we use when judging whether a person is mature and whether a society is democratic. In Chapter Four the social importance of critical thinking is considered in more detail. A central theme is the need for people to connect their private lives with broader social forces. The risks and satisfactions of taking collective action as a result of becoming critically reflective in some sphere of our lives are discussed.

In the second part of the book the focus is on general ways in which people can be helped to become critical thinkers. The purpose of this section is to examine practical methods, techniques, and approaches for developing critical thinking. I provide case studies of successful practice in this area and suggest specific exercises that can be used in a range of settings by educators and helping professionals. Chapter Five opens with a general discussion of the roles and functions involved in developing critical thinkers. How helpers and educators might model the kinds of critically reflective behaviors they seek to encourage in others is also considered in this chapter. The tricky business of prompting people to identify and then critically examine the assumptions underlying their thoughts and actions is the focus of Chapter Six. A number of ways people can be helped to challenge assumptions such as criteria analysis, critical questioning, critical incidents, role play, and crisis-decision simulations are presented. Chapter Seven explores a range of techniques for encouraging people to imagine alternatives to their familiar ways of thinking and living. Here I examine a variety of approaches such as the futures invention technique, the development of preferred scenarios, and the use of esthetic triggers to help people break free from habitual ways of thinking and perceiving.

The final part of the book reviews opportunities for developing critical thinking in specific contexts. Chapter Eight explores how people can be helped to think critically at the workplace. Here I discuss the findings of organizational psychologists regarding the ways managers and workers develop their own private theories of practice. In particular, I look at the opportunities for developing critical thinking through attempts to democratize the workplace. Programs designed to foster political learning are reviewed in Chapter Nine. How adults develop political commitments and how these can be encouraged are examined through a review of case studies. In Chapter Ten I suggest a number of specific techniques that can help people to view television critically. Here I introduce the concept of media literacy and argue that the development of this new form of literacy is crucial if people are to become critical thinkers.

Critical thinking in intimate relationships such as those between parents and children, between lovers or spouses, and between friends is discussed in Chapter Eleven. The ways critical thinking can be recognized in these relationships are outlined, and suggestions are made concerning how people might be stimulated to think critically within these relationships.

Chapter Twelve summarizes and highlights the key arguments, ideas, and suggestions regarding the development of critical thinkers. In this chapter I present a theory in use of facilitating critical thinking—that is, a number of hunches, intuitions, and rules of thumb that guide my own attempts in this area and that I suggest others might like to keep at the forefront of their minds as they engage in this activity. The risks and rewards I have experienced in encouraging critical thinking are discussed in the Epilogue. Here, I give specific details regarding how I apply these rules of thumb in my own life. The chapter is a personal account, describing, as concretely as possible, my own attempts to model critical thinking.

Acknowledgments

A number of people have, both wittingly and unwittingly, helped me develop the analysis and exercises in this book. Clark Taylor and Alan Knox's comments on early drafts of the manuscript were invaluable in encouraging me to think through the organization and purpose of the book. Through her analysis of learning at the workplace, my colleague at Teachers College, Victoria Marsick, has contributed much to my thinking in Chapter Eight. By far the greatest debt, however, is the one I owe to Jack Mezirow, my colleague in the adult education program at Teachers College, Columbia University. In a very real sense this is his book as much as it is mine (though the errors are, of course, my own). Practically every page contains ideas developed in the course of my conversations with Jack. He has served as a model of a critical facilitator, continually challenging, suggesting alternatives, and being as critically questioning of the merits of his own ideas as he is of those of others. He has been crucial to my own intellectual development and this book is, in many ways, a direct result of my good fortune in being able to work with him over the last five years. For his intellectual mentorship and for his friendship I am deeply grateful.

This book is lovingly dedicated to my mother and father, Sybil and David Brookfield.

New York, New York   Stephen D. Brookfield
July 1987

The Author

Stephen D. Brookfield is associate professor in the department of higher and adult education and associate director of the Center for Adult Education at Teachers College, Columbia University, in New York City. He received his B.A. degree (1970) from Lanchester Polytechnic (Coventry) in modern studies, his M.A. degree (1974) from the University of Reading in sociology, and his Ph.D. degree (1980) from the University of Leicester in adult education. He also holds a postgraduate diploma in modern social and cultural studies (1971) from the University of London, Chelsea College, and a postgraduate diploma in adult education (1977) from the University of Nottingham.

Brookfield's main research activities have been in the fields of adult learning (particularly self-directed learning), community education, comparative adult education, the application of qualitative research approaches to studying adult learning and education, and political and philosophical aspects of adult and continuing education. He has been national chair of the Adult Education Research Conference of North America (1985), a founding member of the International League for Social Commitment in Adult Education and of the British and North American Network for Adult Education, and a member of the national executive committee of the Association for Recurrent Education (United Kingdom).

He serves on the editorial and advisory boards of *Adult Education Quarterly* (United States), the *Canadian Journal for Studies in Adult Education,* and *Studies in Continuing Education* (Australia).

Brookfield has been head of a community, social, and environmental development program at Malvern Hills College of Adult Education in Worcestershire, England, a professor of adult education at the University of British Columbia in Vancouver, Canada, and a research officer for the national Advisory Council for Adult and Continuing Education of England and Wales. In this last capacity he authored a national report entitled *Distance Learning and Adult Students* (1983). He has been a consultant and workshop leader on adult learning, education, and critical thinking for a wide range of organizations including television companies, banks, voluntary action centers, hospitals, health education centers, school districts, and many universities.

The American Association for Adult and Continuing Education awarded him the 1986 Cyril O. Houle World Award for Literature in Adult Education and the 1986 Imogene E. Okes Award for Outstanding Research in Adult Education for his book *Understanding and Facilitating Adult Learning: A Comprehensive Analysis of Principles and Effective Practices* (1986). His other books and monographs include *Independent Adult Learning* (1982), *Adult Learners, Adult Education and the Community* (1984), *Self-Directed Learning: From Theory to Practice* (1985), and *Learning Democracy: Eduard Lindeman on Adult Education and Social Change* (1987).

Developing
Critical Thinkers

∿ *Part 1* ∿

Understanding Critical Thinking in Adult Life

Critical thinking can be recognized in the contexts of our personal relationships, work activities, and political involvements. This activity entails much more than the skills of logical analysis taught in so many college courses on critical thinking. It involves calling into question the assumptions underlying our customary, habitual ways of thinking and acting and then being ready to think and act differently on the basis of this critical questioning. In this first part of the book, I describe the essential components of critical thinking and identify the ways these components might be recognized in people's behaviors.

Being a critical thinker is part of what it means to be a developing person, and fostering critical thinking is crucial to creating and maintaining a healthy democracy. Without critical thinking our personal relationships become atrophied, our workplaces remain organized as they were twenty years ago, and our political involvements dwindle to the point of total nonparticipation. Before examining how critical thinking can be fostered in these three contexts, it is important to understand the central components of this activity.

❧ 1 ❧

What It Means
to Think Critically

The need to develop critical thinkers is currently something of
a cause célèbre. The *New York Times* reports that "the public
schools have discovered the importance of critical thinking, and
many of them are trying to teach children how to do it" (Hechinger, 1987, p. 27). Educational journals regularly advertise conferences on critical thinking, and three recent major reports on
American education, *Involvement in Learning* (National Institute
of Education, 1984), *A Nation at Risk* (National Commission on
Excellence in Education, 1983), and *Higher Education and the
American Resurgence* (Newman, 1985), all call for the development of critical thinkers as a national priority for both civic
and economic reasons. Civically, a critically informed populace
is seen as more likely to participate in forms of democratic
political activity. Economically, a critically active and creative
work force is seen as the key to American economic resurgence
in the face of crippling foreign trade competition. Johnston
(1986, p. 4) observes that "it is generally agreed that nothing
is more important to the nation's ability to meet the competitive
challenge of the future than what Samuel Ehrenhalt (1983, p. 43)
of the Department of Labor has termed a 'flexible, adaptable
labor force.'" That the message contained in these reports is
having some practical effect is evident from case studies of education for critical thinking (Young, 1980; Gamson and Associates,

1984; Stice, 1987), from special issues being devoted to this topic in such journals as *Phi Delta Kappan* and *National Forum* in 1985, from a flow of grant monies for projects to research applications of critical thinking, and from a recent upsurge in conferences on critical thinking. There have been attempts to propose a new concept described as *critical literacy* (Kretovics, 1985) and to outline the foundations of a critical pedagogy (Greene, 1986; Livingstone, 1987) that would foster this capacity. As Sternberg (1985, p. 194) observes, "It would be difficult to read anything at all in the contemporary literature of education without becoming aware of this new interest in teaching critical thinking."

But critical thinking is an activity that can be observed in settings and domains very far removed from the school or college classroom. Indeed, there is no clear evidence that any of the skills of critical thinking learned in schools and colleges have much transferability to the contexts of adult life. Sternberg (1985) points out the lack of correspondence between what is required for critical thinking in adulthood and what is taught in school programs intended to develop critical thinking. He writes that "the problems of thinking in the real world do not correspond well with the problems of the large majority of programs that teach critical thinking. We are preparing students to deal with problems that are in many respects unlike those that they will face as adults" (p. 194). In adulthood, we are thinking critically whenever we question why we, or our partners, behave in certain ways within relationships. Critical thinking is evident whenever employees question the appropriateness of a certain technique, mode of production, or organizational form. Managers who are ready to jettison outmoded organizational norms or unwieldy organizational hierarchies, and who are prepared to open up organizational lines of communication in order to democratize the workplace and introduce participatory forms of management, are critical thinkers. Citizens who ask "awkward" questions regarding the activities of local, regional, and national government offices, who call for political leaders to account for their actions, and who are ready to challenge the legitimacy of existing policies and political structures are critical thinkers. Television viewers who are skeptical of the accuracy of media depictions of what are portrayed as "typical" families, or of the neutrality and objectivity of television's reporting of political events, are critical thinkers.

Recognizing Critical Thinking

What characteristics do we look for in critical thinkers? How can we recognize when critical thinking is happening? What are the chief capacities we are trying to encourage when we help people to become critical thinkers? What activities and processes are taking place when people are thinking critically? These questions, and others, are addressed in the nine critical thinking "themes" developed throughout this book.

1. Critical thinking is a productive and positive activity.
Critical thinkers are actively engaged with life. They see themselves as creating and re-creating aspects of their personal, workplace, and political lives. They appreciate creativity, they are innovators, and they exude a sense that life is full of possibilities. Critical thinkers see the future as open and malleable, not as closed and fixed. They are self-confident about their potential for changing aspects of their worlds, both as individuals and through collective action. Critical thinkers are sometimes portrayed as cynical people who often condemn the efforts of others without contributing anything themselves. Those who hold this view see being critical as somehow antisocial; it is seen as a belittling activity engaged in only by those with false assumptions of superiority. In fact, the opposite is true. When we think critically we become aware of the diversity of values, behaviors, social structures, and artistic forms in the world. Through realizing this diversity, our commitments to our own values, actions, and social structures are informed by a sense of humility; we gain an awareness that others in the world have the same sense of certainty we do—but about ideas, values, and actions that are completely contrary to our own.

2. Critical thinking is a process, not an outcome.

Being critical thinkers entails a continual questioning of assumptions. People can never be in a state of complete critical development. If we ever felt that we had reached a state of fully developed or realized critical awareness, we would be contradicting one of the central tenets of critical thinking—namely, that we are skeptical of any claims to universal truth or total certainty. By its nature, critical thinking can never be finished in some final, static manner.

3. Manifestations of critical thinking vary according to the contexts in which it occurs.

The indicators that reveal whether or not people are thinking critically vary enormously. For some people, the process appears to be almost wholly internal; very few external features of their lives appear to change. With these individuals, we can look for evidence of the critical process in their writing or talking. With others, critical thinking will manifest itself directly and vividly in their external actions. People who renegotiate aspects of their intimate relationships, managers who deliberately depart from their habitual ways of coming to decisions or solving problems, workers who reshape their workplace according to nonhierarchical organizational norms after establishing a worker cooperative, or citizens campaigning for a nuclear freeze after observing the effects of a radiation leak in their community are all examples of how critical thinking can prompt dramatic action.

4. Critical thinking is triggered by positive as well as negative events.

A theme common to many discussions of critical thinking is that this activity usually results from people having experienced traumas or tragedies in their lives. These events, so the argument goes, cause people to question their previously trusted assumptions about how the world works; and this questioning prompts a careful scrutiny of what were previously unquestioned ways of thinking and living. This often happens. It is also true, however, that critical thinking is triggered by a joyful, pleasing, or fulfilling event—a ''peak'' experience such as falling in love, being unexpectedly successful in some new workplace role, or finding that others place great store by abilities or accomplishments that we exhibit almost without being aware of them. In such circumstances we begin to reinterpret our past actions and ideas from a new vantage point. We begin to wonder if our old assumptions about our roles, personalities, and abilities were completely accurate. We begin to be aware of and to explore new possibilities with our intimates, at our workplace, and in our political involvements.

5. Critical thinking is emotive as well as rational.
    Critical thinking is sometimes regarded as a kind of pure, ascetic cognitive activity above and beyond the realm of feeling and emotions. In fact, emotions are central to the critical thinking process. As we try to think critically and help others to do so, we cannot help but become aware of the importance of emotions to this activity. Asking critical questions about our previously accepted values, ideas, and behaviors is anxiety-producing. We may well feel fearful of the consequences that might arise from contemplating alternatives to our current ways of thinking and living; resistance, resentment, and confusion are evident at various stages in the critical thinking process. But we also feel joy, release, relief, and exhilaration as we break through to new ways of looking at our personal, work, and political worlds. As we abandon assumptions that had been inhibiting our development, we experience a sense of liberation. As we realize that we have the power to change aspects of our lives, we are charged with excitement. As we realize these changes, we feel a pleasing sense of self-confidence. Critical thinkers and helpers ignore these emotions at their peril.

Components of Critical Thinking

1. Identifying and challenging assumptions is central to critical thinking.
    Trying to identify the assumptions that underlie the ideas, beliefs, values, and actions that we (and others) take for granted is central to critical thinking. Once these assumptions are identified, critical thinkers examine their accuracy and validity. They

ask awkward questions concerning whether the taken-for-granted, common-sense ideas about how we are supposed to organize our workplaces, act in our intimate relationships, become politically involved, and view television fit the realities of our lives. They are open to jettisoning old assumptions when these are clearly inappropriate (for example, "Workers are there to work, not to think"; "Decisions made by executive directors, parents, and presidents are infallible and inviolable"; "Women should be kept barefoot and pregnant") and to search for new assumptions that fit more closely their experiences of the world.

2. Challenging the importance of context is crucial to critical thinking.
     When we are aware of how hidden and uncritically assimilated assumptions are important to shaping our habitual perceptions, understandings, and interpretations of the world, and to influencing the behaviors that result from these interpretations, we become aware of how context influences thoughts and actions. Critical thinkers are aware that practices, structures, and actions are never context-free. What we regard as appropriate ways of organizing the workplace, of behaving toward our intimates, of acting politically, and of viewing television reflect the culture and time in which we live. In realizing this, critical thinkers are contextually aware.

3. Critical thinkers try to imagine and explore alternatives.
     Central to critical thinking is the capacity to imagine and explore alternatives to existing ways of thinking and living. Realizing that so many ideas and actions spring from assumptions that might be inappropriate for their lives, critical thinkers are continually exploring new ways of thinking about aspects of their lives. Being aware of how context shapes what they consider normal and natural ways of thinking and living, critical thinkers realize that in other contexts entirely different norms of organizing the workplace, behaving politically, interpreting media, and living in relationships are considered ordinary. These contexts are scrutinized for assumptions that might be adopted and integrated into their own lives.

4. Imagining and exploring alternatives leads to reflective skepticism.
          When we realize that alternatives to supposedly fixed belief
systems, habitual behaviors, and entrenched social structures
always exist, we become skeptical of claims to universal truth
or to ultimate explanations. In short, we exhibit what might
be called *reflective skepticism.* People who are reflectively skeptical do not take things as read. Simply because a practice or
structure has existed for a long time does not mean that it is
the most appropriate for *all* time, or even for this moment. Just
because an idea is accepted by everyone else does not mean that
we have to believe in its innate truth without first checking its
correspondence with reality as we experience it. Just because
a chief executive officer, executive director, prime minister,
president, religious leader, or parent says something is right or
good does not make it so. Critical thinkers become immediately
suspicious of those who say they have the answers to all of life's
problems. They are wary of the management consultant who
argues that "if only you will buy my training package and follow
these steps to executive development, your executives will double
the company's output in the next fiscal quarter." They distrust
the educator who purports to have a curriculum or model of
teaching appropriate for all learners or subjects. They scrutinize
carefully the therapist or counselor who argues that he or she
has discovered the key to resolving difficulties within intimate
relationships.

How Others Contribute to Critical Thinking

          On a very personal level, practically all adults function
in some way as critical thinkers. At some time or another, most
people decide that some aspect of their lives is unsatisfactory,
and decide of their own volition to change this. Such self-initiated
changes are often (though not always) connected to externally
imposed crises. Being fired or suffering crippling mental or
physical disability is not something we choose to happen. When
an intimate relationship dissolves, or a loved one dies, several
reactions are possible. We may be thrown into an apathetic

resignation to these changed circumstances, or we may deny this disappearance of a previously stable element in our life. We may well fluctuate between periods of acceptance of, and flight from, these changes. Energy alternates with apathy as we first scramble to deny or forget the changes forced upon us, and then become aware of their overwhelming reality. The rollercoaster turbulence of these changes is tiring and debilitating, and we describe ourselves as exhausted, burned out, or finished.

As people try to make sense of these externally imposed changes, they are frequently at teachable moments as far as the process of becoming critical thinkers is concerned. As people begin to look critically at their past values, common-sense ideas, and habitual behaviors, they begin the precarious business of contemplating new self-images, perspectives, and actions. Skilled helpers can support these first tentative stages in critical thought by listening empathetically to people's "travelers' tales" of their journeys into unexplored personal and political territories. Helpers act as sounding boards, providing reactions to people's experiences, pleasures, and anxieties. They help to make connections between apparently disparate occurrences and assist people in reflecting on the reasons for their actions and reactions. They encourage people to identify the assumptions underlying their behaviors, choices, and decisions. They help clients, learners, friends, and colleagues to recognize aspects of their situations that are of their own making and hence open to being changed by an act of will. They encourage skepticism of anyone claiming to have "the answer." They help people to realize that while actions are shaped by context, context can be altered to be more congruent with people's desires.

When helpers and educators work in these ways, they are encouraging critical thinking. Critical thinking is complex and frequently perplexing, since it requires the suspension of belief and the jettisoning of assumptions previously accepted without question. As people strive for clarity in self-understanding, and as they try to change aspects of their lives, the opportunity to discuss these activities is enormously helpful. By providing an opportunity for reflection and analysis, educators and other helpers, such as counselors, therapists, trainers, and friends, are crucial. They are sympathizers, empathizers, reactors, devil's advocates, initiators, and prompters. They help people to articulate and understand the assumptions underlying their actions. In short, they assist people to become critical thinkers.

Concepts of Critical Thinking

Phrases such as *critical thinking, critical analysis, critical awareness, critical consciousness*, and *critical reflection* are exhortatory, heady, and often conveniently vague. We can justify almost any action with a learner, client, friend, or colleague by claiming that it assists the process of critical thinking. Haranguing a friend who feels satisfied with life, forcing a learner to view things the way we do, and requiring that lovers re-evaluate their relationship or that colleagues change their work patterns may all be claimed (inaccurately) as examples of facilitating critical thinking. Central to developing critical thinkers must be some minimal level of consent on the part of those involved. Trying to force people to analyze critically the assumptions under which they have been thinking and living is likely to serve no function other than intimidating them to the point where resistance builds up against this process. We can, however, try to awaken, prompt, nurture, and encourage this process without making people feel threatened or patronized. These are the skills of critical helpers.

As a concept, critical thinking has been interpreted in a variety of ways. It has been equated with the development of logical reasoning abilities (Hallet, 1984; Ruggiero, 1975), with the application of reflective judgment (Kitchener, 1986), with assumption hunting (Scriven, 1976), and with the creation, use, and testing of meaning (Hullfish and Smith, 1961). Ennis (1962) lists twelve aspects of critical thinking, which include analytical and argumentative capacities such as recognizing ambiguity in reasoning, identifying contradictions in arguments, and ascertaining the empirical soundness of generalized conclusions. D'Angelo (1971) specifies ten attitudes that are necessary conditions for being critical, including curiosity, flexibility, skepticism, and honesty. As the central component of critical thinking, O'Neill (1985) proposes the ability to distinguish bias from

reason and fact from opinion. To Halpern (1984), critical
thought is a rational and purposeful attempt to use thought in
moving toward a future goal.

Critical thinking is generally conceptualized as an intellectual ability suitable for development by those involved in higher
education (Drake, 1976; Young, 1980; Meyers, 1986; Stice,
1987). Empirical studies of the development of critical thinking capacities focus on young adults (Kitchener, 1986; King,
Kitchener, and Wood, 1985) or college students (Perry, 1970,
1981). While this setting for critical thinking is undoubtedly
crucial, it is but one of the many settings in which critical thinking is practiced, particularly in adult life. This book takes the
concepts of critical thinking, analysis, and reflection out of the
classroom and places them firmly in the contexts of adults'
lives—in their relationships, at their workplaces, in their political
involvements, and in their reactions to mass media of communication. Critical thinking is not seen as a wholly rational,
mechanical activity. Emotive aspects—feelings, emotional responses, intuitions, sensing—are central to critical thinking in
adult life. In particular, the ability to imagine alternatives to
one's current ways of thinking and living is one that often entails a deliberate break with rational modes of thought in order
to prompt forward leaps in creativity.

One alternative interpretation of the concept of critical
thinking is that of *emancipatory learning*. The idea of emancipatory
learning is derived from the work of Habermas (1979), who
distinguished this as one of the three domains of learning (technical and communicative learning being the other two). As interpreted by adult educators (Collins, 1985; Hart, 1985; Apps,
1985), emancipatory learning is evident in learners becoming
aware of the forces that have brought them to their current situations and taking action to change some aspect of these situations. To Apps (1985, p. 151), "emancipatory learning is that
which frees people from personal, institutional, or environmental
forces that prevent them from seeing new directions, from gain-
ing control of their lives, their society and their world."

A second concept closely related to that of critical thinking is *dialectical thinking*. Dialectical thinking is viewed as a par-

ticular form of critical thinking that focuses on the understanding and resolution of contradictions. Morgan (1986, p. 266) writes that "dialectical analysis (thus) shows us that the management of organization, of society, and of personal life ultimately involves the management of contradiction." As proposed by Riegel (1973) and Basseches (1984), dialectical thinking is thinking in which elements of relativistic thought (for example, "Morality can be understood only in the context of the culture concerned") are fused with elements of universalistic thought (for example, "Moral conduct is recognizable in any society by certain innate features"). Dialectical thinkers engage in a continual process of making judgments about aspects of their lives, identifying the general rules implicit in these judgments, modifying the original judgments in light of the appropriateness of these general rules, and so on. To Deshler (1985, p. 6), "dialectical thinking is thinking which looks for, recognizes, and welcomes contradictions as a stimulus to development." Change is regarded as the fundamental reality, forms and structures are perceived as temporary, relationships are held to involve developmental transformations, and openness is welcomed. Hence, we are involved in a constant process of trying to create order in the world—to discover what elements are missing from our existing ordering and to create new orderings that include these. Daloz (1986, p. 141) echoes this idea in his belief that dialectical thinking "presumes change rather than a static notion of 'reality.' As each assertion is derived from the one before, truth is always emergent, never fixed; relative, not absolute."

Being a critical thinker involves more than cognitive activities such as logical reasoning or scrutinizing arguments for assertions unsupported by empirical evidence. Thinking critically involves our recognizing the assumptions underlying our beliefs and behaviors. It means we can give justifications for our ideas and actions. Most important, perhaps, it means we try to judge the rationality of these justifications. We can do this by comparing them to a range of varying interpretations and perspectives. We can think through, project, and anticipate the consequences of those actions that are based on these justifications. And we can test the accuracy and rationality of these justifications against some kind of objective analysis of the ''real'' world as we understand it.

Critical thinking, then, involves a reflective dimension. The idea of *reflective learning* is a third concept closely related to that of critical thinking. Boyd and Fales (1983, p. 100) define reflective learning as ''the *process* of internally examining and exploring an issue of concern, triggered by an experience, which creates and clarifies meaning in terms of self, and which results in a changed conceptual perspective.'' Boud, Keogh, and Walker (1985, p. 3) view reflection as ''a generic term for those intellectual and affective activities in which individuals engage to explore their experiences in order to lead to new understandings and appreciation.'' To Schlossberg (1981, p. 5), the outcome of these activities is ''a change in assumptions about oneself and the world'' requiring ''a corresponding change in one's behavior and relationships.''

Conclusion

Critical thinking is a lived activity, not an abstract academic pastime. It is something we all do, though its frequency, and the credibility we grant it, vary from person to person. Our lives are sufficiently complex and perplexing that it would be difficult to escape entirely from feeling that at times the world is not working the way we thought it was supposed to, or that there must be other ways of living. This book takes the capacity for critical thinking and places it at the heart of what it means to be a developed person living in a democratic society. I argue that the ability to think critically is crucial to understanding our personal relationships, envisioning alternative and more productive ways of organizing the workplace, and becoming politically literate. Before examining the personal and social importance of critical thinking, it is important that the two central components of this activity be clearly elaborated. The next chapter defines these components and provides examples of how they might be recognized.

2

Recognizing
Critical Thinking

Given that critical thinking is often thought of as an abstract academic activity that has little to do with the reality of adult life, it is important that this idea be dispelled by making clear the two activities central to critical thinking. As was indicated briefly in the first chapter these two activities—(1) identifying and challenging assumptions and (2) exploring and imagining alternatives—are directly observable on many occasions in adults' lives. They are normal and natural activities, very far removed from the artificial atmosphere of the college classroom. In this chapter, the various facets of the two central components of critical thinking are clearly specified. Examples of these activities are provided, and some typical intellectual and behavioral outcomes of thinking this way are discussed. For reasons of clarity and ease of understanding, these components and outcomes are presented as if they were all discrete and separate from each other. In reality, of course, the components of critical thought and action are interconnected in bewildering and idiosyncratic configurations according to the people and contexts involved.

Identifying and Challenging Assumptions

Identifying and challenging assumptions takes place when people probe their habitual ways of thinking and acting (and

those of others around them) for their underlying assumptions—
those taken-for-granted values, common-sense ideas, and stereotypical notions about human nature and social organization that
underlie our actions. When people reflect on why they habitually
behave toward their spouses or lovers in certain ways, or when
workers start to wonder what assumptions about worker motivation lie behind the way the workplace is organized, the first component of critical thinking is happening. The following are examples of how assumption recognition and analysis begins:

> Teachers who begin to wonder why certain
> educational methods (lecturing, discussion, com-
> puter-assisted instruction) are considered inherently
> suitable for certain objectives or for certain kinds
> of learners.
> Partners who speculate on what ideas lie
> behind the judgments they make concerning the
> division of labor (cooking, cleaning, house repair)
> in their marriage.
> Citizens who ask what reasons politicians
> would give for their portrayal of certain nations or
> groups as wholly good and others as wholly evil.
> Viewers who wonder what criteria and judg-
> ments inform producers of news broadcasts when
> they choose what they think are newsworthy stories.

A major outcome of identifying and challenging assumptions is the recognition of how important it is to understand the
context within which assumptions, and the actions that spring
from these, are formed. Being aware of the importance of context can be called *contextual awareness*. Such awareness is evident
when the assumptions undergirding our ideas and behaviors are
seen to be culturally and historically specific. When people realize
that actions, values, beliefs, and moral codes can be fully understood only when the context in which they are framed is appreciated, they become much more contextually aware. Assumptions of what are considered ''moral'' behaviors toward others,
or of what we believe to be ''just'' and ''equitable'' social struc-

tures, are considered in the context within which they originate. We come to realize that the assumptions governing the ways we behave toward friends, colleagues, parents, and lovers are, at least partly, the result of cultural factors. Contextual thinkers view their dearly held beliefs and values as, to some extent, social constructs. They understand that value systems and behavioral codes are socially transmitted as well as personally generated and sharpened by personal experiences. Public and private knowledge are seen as provisional, relative, and contextual. The following are examples of contextually aware thinkers:

> Workers who understand that the "normal" ways of working or organizing production at the workplace reflect the personal philosophy of the chief executive officer.
> Citizens who realize that what a government defines as "normal" unemployment or inflation reflects a particular political philosophy and set of party manifesto priorities.
> Adult sons or daughters who are aware that their parents' opposition to their marital or career choices is often grounded in cultural rules and expectations assimilated when these parents were themselves growing up.

Making the attitudinal shift to reinterpret as culturally induced what were initially held to be personally devised value systems, beliefs, and moral codes can be highly intimidating. To realize that the moral and behavioral codes we regard as our personal creations are, in fact, culturally induced is threatening to our sense of self. Identifying the culturally produced assumptions underlying our "common-sense" ideas is sometimes liberating, but it can also make us feel that we are entirely the product of social forces. This may be seen as demeaning to our capacity for original thought, and we may be depressed by the idea that our own personalities played a very minor role in developing our value systems, beliefs, and moral codes when compared to the overwhelming influence of cultural factors.

Having skilled helpers to whom we can turn at this stage in our development as critical thinkers is important, lest we become so depressed that we cease prematurely the process of critical thinking.

Exploring and Imagining Alternatives

The focus of this second component of critical thinking is on people realizing that alternatives exist to their current ways of thinking and living. Broughton (1977, p. 90) describes this as "the capacity to generate mentally a structure of possibilities extending beyond the empirically known world of the here and now." Central to the idea of critical literacy (Kretovics, 1985, p. 51) is "the need for students to develop a collective vision of what it might be like to live in the best of all societies and how such a vision might be made practical." We come to realize that every belief we hold, every behavior we cherish as normal, every social or economic arrangement we perceive as fixed and unalterable can be and is regarded by other people (in our own culture as well as in other cultures) as bizarre, inexplicable, and wholly irrational.

Realizing that alternatives exist to our present ways of thinking, and that those living these alternatives regard them as normal and self-evident, is both liberating and threatening. It is liberating, because it implies that if something is not as fixed as had previously been thought, we can replace unsatisfactory beliefs and behaviors with ones that are more congenial and meaningful. Similarly, it suggests that if we find economic or social arrangements to be obsolete, irrational, or oppressive, we can replace them with more effective, rational, or just alternatives. This realization is threatening, however, because it implies that we may have been taking on trust stereotypes and givens that are meaningless, obsolete, or harmful. As this suspicion begins to nudge at the perimeter of our consciousness, our immediate reaction may be to dismiss it as irrational and unfounded. If, however, the circumstances of our daily existence are such that suspicions and misgivings arise repeatedly, forcing themselves on our consciousness and destroying our prized and comfortable mental equilibrium, we are forced eventually to acknowledge them. The following are examples of people who are imagining and exploring alternatives in different aspects of their lives:

> The woman who finds that being married to Mr. Right, owning a home, and raising children is not the euphorically satisfying experience she had anticipated. Observing other women of her age returning to education, returning to work, or living as single-parent families, she begins to question the suitability of her life choices for her personality.

> The woman who has graduated from a university and carved out a successful career in a male-dominated work world but finds that single life and professional esteem still leave an emotional vacuum in her life. Talking to friends in similar positions, she finds that some of them feel the same gnawing discontent; to them, too, the family lifestyle they had previously unthinkingly rejected now appears appealing.

> The man who has presumed that wives should subordinate their own energies to nurturing their husbands' interests and careers, but who finds after several years of marriage that the persistent and slavish devotion of his wife has become irritating rather than satisfying. Observing colleagues whose wives challenge their husbands' expectations, and who exhibit independence of thought and action, he begins to feel envious and curiously dissatisfied with the marital relationship he has worked so hard to create.

> The teacher who initially regards a new colleague's classroom innovations (moving chairs into circles, encouraging first-name contact between students and teachers, diverging from standardized curricula, allowing conversation between pairs of

students during teacher-talk) as evidence of professional sloppiness. Finding out that attendance improves and that work is handed in on time in this apparently anarchic atmosphere, the more experienced colleague begins to ponder the possibility of introducing some of these innovations into her own classroom.

The executive who dismisses a union shop steward's claim of middle-management inflexibility as subversion or a maneuvering ploy. Being told at the monthly departmental meeting that production is falling and absenteeism increasing in the production unit within which the union organizer is employed, the executive starts to question the previously optimistic reports of satisfactory management-worker relations provided by the middle manager concerned.

The administrator who enrolls in a higher education program or a professional development workshop because only through such participation can he or she become eligible for a salary raise or promotion. Opening up channels of organizational communication as part of a course assignment, he or she finds that attendance at staff meetings increases and that some staff take the initiative in suggesting administrative improvements. The administrator begins to replace the attitude of cynical instrumentalism (''I'll suffer through this course for the promotion or salary increase'') with a suspicion that newfangled ideas of participatory management or workplace democracy might actually merit serious consideration.

Just as identifying and challenging assumptions results in a major shift in our way of thinking (developing our contextual awareness), so considering and imagining alternatives leads to the development of a particularly critical cast of mind, especially where any claims for the universal truth or validity of an idea or practice are concerned. We become suspicious of those who tell us that they have "the answer" to life or the solution to all our problems. In short, we develop *reflective skepticism*; we do not take for granted the universal truth of some statement, policy, or justification simply because of the authority ascribed to the source of this supposed truth. Reflective skepticism is evident when we refuse to accept as the justification for an action that "That's just the way it is" or "That's how things are." It is apparent when we are skeptical of "divinely ordained" givens, such as gender stereotypes, assumptions concerning ethnic groups other than our own, and assertions about the one, single way to truth. Reflective skepticism is present whenever individuals call into question the belief that simply because some idea or social structure has existed unchanged for a period of time, it therefore must be (a) right and (b) the best possible arrangement. Elbow (1973) calls this "playing the doubting game."

Critical thinkers are wary of individuals who claim either universal truth for themselves or access to some reified and otherwise inaccessible fount of wisdom. This is not to say that critical thinkers avoid commitment to beliefs or cease to develop allegiance to causes. We can commit ourselves wholeheartedly to an idea, social structure, or cause and still be critically aware. The point is that this commitment is informed; we have arrived at our convictions after a period of questioning, analysis, and reflection. We have examined these ideas, structures, and causes and decided that they are the closest to reality as we understand it. They are not taken on trust or taken as read. Being reflectively skeptical of universal rules or divinely ordained givens is not the same as being completely cynical about making any commitments in life. Pure skepticism entails a knee-jerk dismissal, on principle, of any and all claims to truth. Reflective skepticism, on the other hand, applies a cautious intelligence to grandiose claims regarding "ultimate" truth or "final" solutions. Commitments are made only after a period of critically reflective analysis, during which we establish the validity of the apparently ultimate or final truth by examining its congruence with reality as we perceive it. Examples of reflective skepticism can be seen in the following:

Partners challenging the stereotypical notions of female and male behavior within relationships— for example, that women's "natural" compassion and caring mean they are best fitted to nurturing children, or that men's emotional strength and ability to distance themselves personally mean that they are best suited to disciplining children.

Citizens regarding skeptically the idea that if enough money is devoted to building the ultimate weapons system, peace will be secured forever.

Television viewers questioning the reporting of arms negotiations in which the actions of one side are portrayed as motivated solely by a quest for pure truth and justice, and the actions of the other side are portrayed as motivated wholly by a cynical and evil desire for imperialistic expansion.

Teachers who are wary of a staff-development expert's assertion that if they adopt this new curriculum, that new instructional technique, or the other form of advanced technology, discipline problems will cease and grades rise.

Workers who challenge the idea that a new drafting of the institutional mission statement, or the introduction of a company song, will usher in productivity and collegiality at the workplace.

Citizens treating cautiously the claims of a political candidate to the effect that if he or she is elected, the major social ills of our era will automatically be eradicated.

Reflective skepticism is not outright cynicism, nor is it a contemptuous dismissal of all things new. It is, rather, the belief that claims for the universal validity and applicability of an idea or practice must be subject to a careful testing against each individual's experiences. It is being wary of uncritically accepting an innovation, change, or new perspective simply because it is new. It is not to be equated with resistance to change. It is, rather, a readiness to test the validity of claims made by others for any presumed givens, final solutions, and ultimate truths against one's own experience of the world. As such, it is a major affective outcome of critical thinking.

Critical Thinking as Analysis and Action

As a process, critical thinking is not purely passive. It involves alternating phases of analysis and action. The capacities outlined above are not exercised in a vacuum; they are developed and refined in active inquiry. This process of active inquiry combines reflective analysis with informed action. We perceive a discrepancy, question a given, or become aware of an assumption—and then we *act* upon these intuitions. As our intuitions become confirmed, refuted, or (most likely) modified through action, we hone and refine our perceptions so that they further influence our actions, become further refined, and so on. Critical thinking is a praxis of alternating analysis and action.

A common misconception about critical thinking is that it precludes commitment to any ideas, actions, or purposes. If we are continually questioning everything (so the argument goes), we become ensnared by the comforts of relativism; since everything can be viewed as culturally specific and bound by context, we need never commit ourselves to an idea, person, institution, or cause. This is a serious misunderstanding of critical thinking. In fact, the opposite is true. As critical thinkers we can still hold passionately to certain beliefs, actions, and causes. However, our commitment is not slavish or uninformed, the result of successful socialization. Instead, it is arrived at after skeptical scrutiny and after being repeatedly tested against reality as we understand it; and this commitment is all the more strong because it has passed through the fires of this critical analysis. Our commitment is informed and rational, balanced by a recognition of its possible falsity. This balance ensures that we do not fall prey to the dangers of demagoguery. If asked, we can justify our reasons for our commitment and point to evidence in its support. We reach a point at which we can identify our assumptions and recognize the contextuality of the world while still holding true to hard-won beliefs and commitments.

The Process of Critical Thinking

We can observe a common process in the development of the critical thinking capacities discussed in the previous section. For example, the beginnings of critical thinking are frequently seen in people perceiving a contradiction between how the world is supposed to work (according to assumptions acquired and trusted up to that point) and their own experiences of reality. This perception of anomalies or contradictions is seen as the first stage in various conceptualizations of critical thinking, such as perspective transformation (Mezirow, 1977), emancipatory learning (Apps, 1985), and reflective learning (D'Andrea, 1986; Boyd and Fales, 1983). Apps (1985, p. 157) describes the initial prompt to critical thinking as the person's "realizing that something is wrong, that there is a certain discomfort in one's life, that things could be better, that a societal situation could be different, that certain policies are not working properly." Mezirow (1977) writes of the disorienting dilemmas of adult life (such as the death of a mate, divorce, unemployment) that trigger self-examination. D'Andrea (1986) describes the first "attention" phase of reflective learning as one in which an unanticipated surprise is caused by discrepancies between one's expectations and one's perceptions of an occurrence. Boyd and Fales (1983) write of the inner discomfort—"an awareness that something does not fit, or does not sit right within them, or of unfinished business"—that initiates reflective thinking.

We can see that people are often prompted to become critical thinkers by an external circumstance or stimulus of some kind; only rarely does a change in thinking patterns happen because of a person's self-willed decision to become more critically reflective. At times this external stimulus or circumstance may be a deliberate human action—a lover pointing out to us the self-serving nature of what we fondly believe to be altruistic behaviors; the teacher who places before us alternative ways of thinking about an issue; the counselor who suggests other ways of communicating with intimates or work colleagues. At other times an unanticipated event comes tearing through the fabric of our well-ordered lives. When we are fired from what was thought of as a "safe" job, when our spouse or lover walks out without (to our conscious mind) any forewarning, or when we, or an intimate, suffer a serious disability or illness (cancer, AIDS, a heart attack, disfigurement in an auto accident), we are forced into a drastic reordering of priorities and assumptions.

The process of recognizing and exploring the discrepancies between our assumptions about how things should be and the way they really are is made easier and more congenial when accomplished in the company of others. When we realize that what were perceived as unique tragedies and difficulties are, in fact, shared by many others, there is an immediate reduction of self-doubt. The discrepancies will not immediately be resolved, but the perception that one is somehow singled out as the sole object of cosmic misfortune is dispelled. The period in which we might consider denying the existence of some anomaly or discrepancy is considerably reduced when we perceive others in similar circumstances admitting to the same anomalies and perplexities. For people in peer support groups such as are common in the women's movement, in gay and lesbian communities, or among alcoholics ready to admit to the actuality of their condition, belonging to a group in which one's experiences are recognized by others is a powerful pscyhological ballast. It makes the painful process of admitting that one is confused, uncertain, and not in control of every aspect of one's life a good deal less traumatic. When we hear our own experiences paralleled in accounts given by others, we realize that our private troubles are, to some extent, reflections of public issues. We know we are not alone.

Phases of Critical Thinking

Accounts of how people become critical thinkers portray those involved as passing through a number of identifiable and commonly experienced phases. Many different terms are used to describe these phases, but their essential components appear remarkably similar. Taken together they comprise the following pattern.

Trigger Event. Some unexpected happening prompts a sense of inner discomfort and perplexity. Examples typically cited include divorce, bereavement, unemployment, disability, forced job change, and geographical mobility. Interestingly, practically every theorist of critical awareness and reflective change emphasizes negative, disruptive triggers, rather than positive, affirming ones. Hopson and Adams (1977), for example, write of this transitional stage as one of shock and immobilization. Some examples of *positive* triggers to critical thinking are given at the end of this chapter.

Appraisal. A period of self-scrutiny and appraisal of the situation follows the trigger event. In this phase we alternate between minimization and denial (Hopson and Adams, 1977), and brooding on the exact nature of our perplexing contradiction. We identify and clarify the concern (Boyd and Fales, 1983), engage in self-examination (Mezirow, 1977), and begin looking for those confronting a similar contradiction.

Exploration. Having admitted to anomalies or discrepancies in some aspect of life, we begin to search for new ways of explaining these discrepancies or of living with them—ways that reduce our sense of discomfort. We may flirt with new identities and contemplate new role models. We are also likely to admit publicly that we are seeking change, perhaps through a public declaration (for example, to a spouse or to work colleagues) or by joining some new peer support group (for example, an Alcoholics Anonymous group, women's consciousness-raising group, community action group, or gay rights group). During this phase we test out new ways of thinking and acting that seem more congruent with our perceptions of what is happening in our lives. This phase is variously described as the consideration phase (D'Andrea, 1986), as testing options and searching for meaning (Hopson and Adams, 1977), as being open to new information (Boyd and Fales, 1983), and as exploring new ways of acting (Mezirow, 1977). Apps (1985, p. 158) summarizes it as "searching for new ways of doing things, new answers, new concepts, new ways of organizing one's world views."

Developing Alternative Perspectives. Arising out of the testing and exploring of alternatives come ways of thinking and acting that we feel "make sense" for our situations. We select from identities, role models, and philosophies we have explored those assumptions and activities that seem most satisfactory and congruent with our relationships and ways of living. We develop confidence in the new roles we wish to play and develop knowledge and skills for the actions we wish to take (Mezirow, 1977). In this phase, "the new insight or changed perspective is analyzed in terms of its operational feasibility" (Boyd and Fales, 1983, p. 112). Apps (1985) refers to this as the transition stage, during which the old is left behind and new ways of thinking and acting are developed.

Leaving behind a familiar but now inappropriate assumption or behavior is a wrenching experience. A common tendency is to hang on to the assumption or behavior, but to try to modify it to fit the situation more closely: This may be a perfectly appropriate response in some situations. We may decide that the benefits we derive from a relationship, work situation, or political arrangement are sufficiently valuable for us to consider protracted negotiation or compromise. In some instances (for example, a husband who "allows" a newly confident and emancipated wife to spend one evening each week attending her women's group meeting, but expects her to revert to a traditional wifely role for the other six evenings), modification is insufficient. At other times (for example, when a husband listens seriously to his wife's frustrations and makes a concerted effort to change the assumptions underlying the relationship up to that point), modification and negotiation ease the sense of perplexity induced by the trigger event.

Integration. Having decided on the worth, accuracy, and validity of new ways of thinking or living, we begin to find ways to integrate these into the fabric of our lives. Resolutions range from tenuous and tentative solutions to satisfactory negotiations of conflict. Sometimes this integration involves transforming attitudes and assumptions. At other times it entails confirming, with a renewed sense of conviction, existing stances. We may decide not to let the reaction of others to what they see as bizarre actions on our part (such as going to an adult education class unconnected to job advancement, or trying to live without owning

a car) cause feelings of guilt or embarrassment. We may decide
to commit to relationships previously characterized by ambivalence and ambiguity, to end relationships that are unsatisfactory,
to change jobs, to insist on changes in workplace organization,
or to press for political change.

In this stage, we achieve some sort of integration of our
conflicting feelings and ideas. The "actions" involved in this
phase may be externally observable, such as renegotiating relationships, joining advocacy or support groups, or proposing
workplace reforms. They may, however, be entirely internal;
we may repeatedly affirm to ourselves that an inability to exemplify textbook role models of "the good counselor" does not
mean that we are professional failures, or resolve to accept external criticism without retreating immediately into a defensive
posture of righteous indignation. Apps (1985, p. 162) describes
the integration stage as "becoming comfortable with and acting
on the new ideas, new assumptions, new ways of thinking that
have emerged from the transition stage." We have tested the
new roles entailed by our change in perspective (Mezirow, 1977),
and we have become reintegrated into society with our behavior
informed by this new perspective. Boyd and Fales (1983, p. 109)
see this as "the point at which people experience themselves
as having learned, or having come to a satisfactory point of
closure in relation to the issue." Cognitively, this stage represents
a "creative synthesis of various bits of the information previously
taken and the formation of a new 'solution' or change in the
self" (p. 110). Experientially, we feel the new solution to make
sense and to be personally meaningful. We have sufficient self-
confidence to view this subjective sense of "rightness" in the
solution as accurately representing our own reality.

Boyd and Fales (1983) report that surprise at the apparently
unconscious nature of the integration process is frequently felt by
those involved: "[Integration] appears to represent an unconscious
selection of previously assimilated information, which emerges in
consciousness as a full formulated integration" (p. 110). The resolution appears when the person is psychologically "ready," rather
than when it is actively being sought. Awareness of this integration is accompanied by a rush of self-affirmation and a sense of

pleasurable satisfaction at having reached this stage. In fact, the integration of cognitive and affective domains throughout these phases of critical thinking is an important consideration. As D'Andrea (1986, p. 258) notes in her study of reflective thinking among Canadian teachers, ''Emotions such as frustration, depression, love, shock, elation, hatred and fear interacted with cognitive components throughout the reflective process.''

The Role of Helpers

Helpers are all those people who assist us to become critical thinkers. Often they are professionals of some kind—educators, counselors, therapists, trainers, or human resource developers. Sometimes our colleagues at work function as helpers in our development of critical thinking skills. Frequently friends perform this function. Helpers are important to the development of our critical thinking capacities, because they assist us in breaking out of our own frameworks of interpretation. Trying to understand the motives for our actions or attempting to identify the assumptions undergirding our apparently objective, rational beliefs is like trying to catch our psychological tail. We twist and turn in a frantic attempt to grasp hold of ever more elusive suspicions about the reasons for our actions.

Attempting to understand our frameworks of understanding by using those very same frameworks is highly problematic. It is like trying to step outside of our physical body so that we can see how a new coat or dress looks from behind. In fact, the way we are able to judge the fit of new clothes is to use a combination of mirrors. We hold up a mirror to allow us to gain an unfamiliar vantage point on our body. Much the same mirroring process is used in trying to explore and understand assumptions, beliefs, and actions, except that the mirrors in this case are interpersonal. We hold up our behavior for scrutiny by others, and in their interpretation of our actions we are given a reflection, a mirroring of our own actions from an unfamiliar psychological vantage point. This is how critical helpers function; they are mirrors who help us interpret and question our ideas and actions from a new viewpoint.

As happens in a clothing store fitting room, what we see in the mirrors of others' perceptions of our actions is often both strange and oddly familiar. Seeing the back of our head, torso, and legs in a mirror provides a surprisingly different, but still recognizable, perspective on our body. Similarly, seeing our actions reflected in the mirror offered by others' perceptions is tantalizing yet unsettling. We recognize elements of congruence between their perceptions of what we were doing and our own. We are also struck by those instances in which actions that were self-evident to us are seen by those around us as ambiguous and contradictory to our stated intentions. Questioning the assumptions under which we have been acting, and exploring alternative ideas, is psychologically explosive. The effect can be appreciated by visualizing an explosives expert who lays dynamite charges at the base of a building requiring demolition. When these charges ignite at key points in the structure's foundation, the whole edifice comes crashing down. Beginning to question key assumptions is like laying down charges of psychological dynamite. When they explode, forcing us to realize that what we thought of as fixed, given ways of thinking and living are only options among a range of alternatives, the whole psychological structure of our framework of understanding comes crumbling down.

Educators and other helpers who encourage critical thinking are rather like psychological demolition experts. In saying this, it is important to remember that demolition is not the same as random, willful destruction. In fact, when done properly, demolition requires training and sensitivity. Demolition experts who blow up industrial chimney stacks or structurally unsound high-rise apartment buildings frequently have to bring these down in densely populated areas. The charges are laid carefully, based on the expert's knowledge of how structures can collapse in on themselves without flattening the surrounding area. Similarly, when helpers and educators assist people in questioning the assumptions underlying their structures of understanding, or in realizing alternatives to their habitual ways of thinking and living, they must act with care and sensitivity. They have to ensure that when the foundations of these structures are shaken, the framework of the individual's self-esteem is left relatively intact. Encouraging people to probe their assumptions, without taking them to the point at which this probing threatens their self-esteem, is a crucial helping task.

Positive Triggers to Critical Thinking

Ever since Dewey (1933) interpreted critical reflection as arising out of perplexity and doubt, and involving a search for material that would resolve this doubt, the emphasis in this area has been placed on what might be called *negative triggers* to critical thinking. As is evident from literature on adult transitions, perspective change, and transformational learning, the prompts to critical thinking most often identified are crises, disorienting dilemmas, and anomalies and discrepancies between expectations and actuality in people's lives. Belenky, Clinchy, Goldberger, and Tarule (1986, p. 227) note that "in the psychological literature concerning the factors promoting cognitive development, doubt has played a more prominent role than belief. People are said to be precipitated into states of cognitive conflict when, for example, some external event challenges their ideas and the effort to resolve the conflict leads to cognitive growth." They call these studies of dissonance and discrepancy *disequilibration studies*. The trigger events frequently mentioned in these studies are life-shaking incidents such as death, divorce, unemployment, conscription, or sudden disabling illness. These are all distressingly traumatic, involving great pain, anxiety, and self-doubt on the part of those seeking to make sense out of them.

It is a mistake to regard critical thinking as occasioned only by trauma. In groups where people have discussed the events occasioning their own critical analysis, it has surprised me to discover how frequently positive, joyful incidents are mentioned. Moments of sudden insight or self-awareness can, it seems, be triggered by events that are fulfilling rather than distressing. "Peak" experiences in which people feel a surprising but undeniable sense of rightness, a feeling that "things fit," can prompt a critically reflective evaluation of aspects of their ways of thinking and living. Suddenly realizing that one has found a work setting, relationship, political cause, or mode of artistic creation in which there is an overwhelming sense of ''coming home'' can lead to a fundamental rethinking of pri-- orities.

Belenky, Clinchy, Goldberger, and Tarule (1986) note the prevalence of positive triggers to critical thinking in their research into women's ways of knowing. They propose the concept of the midwife-teacher to describe the kinds of encouraging and nurturing behaviors of teachers who promote critical thought without threatening or paralyzing learners with the need to be critically sophisticated. The authors of this study observe that ''because so many women are already consumed with self-doubt, doubts imposed from outside seem at best redundant and at worst destructive, confirming the women's own sense of themselves as inadequate knowers. The doubting model, then, may be peculiarly inappropriate for women, although we are not convinced that it is appropriate for men, either'' (p. 228). In fact, the doubting model is probably damaging for any insecure individuals or groups who perceive themselves as somehow being in marginal or minority positions within their own culture.

In Musgrove's (1977) study of people whose critical reappraisals of themselves led them to change their lives in a dramatic manner, those who opted for positions of voluntary marginality (late entrants to the ministry, self-employed artists, Sufi and Hare Krishna commune members) were all people who had come to perceive a ''fit'' between their own selves and their new lifestyles. They did not seek change to escape frustration in their previous occupations. Upon discovering a group of people living in a markedly different way, these individuals felt a deep sense of recognition. Their joining the group was marked by a conviction of the utter rightness of their decisions.

Boud, Keogh, and Walker (1985, p. 19) also acknowledge that critical reflection can be prompted by positive experiences, such as successfully completing a task previously thought impossible. The resultant increase in self-confidence can prompt a decision to take action in areas formerly only contemplated. Spending a week or so substituting for a colleague at work, and finding that experience to be so enjoyable as to cause us to question the suitability of our current position, is an example of such a positive trigger. We may have had no previous thoughts of job change or any awareness of discomfort or contradiction in the workplace. Upon being asked, by chance, to fill in for a colleague taken ill unexpectedly, we may feel a sense of recognition, of fulfillment, of "coming home," that is entirely unlooked for. Much the same process occurs when we fall in love unexpectedly and find that a chance encounter has proved so intense that we begin to reassess all our other relationships in terms of the pleasure gained from being in the company of the new person. Up to that point we may have felt no sense of incompleteness or dissatisfaction in our lives; the impetus for reflection and change is derived solely from the joy felt in communicating with someone we feel to be "on our wavelength."

On a political level, community workers, social activists, union organizers, and political leaders can be positive change agents triggering critical thinking in people. They can do this by transmitting the sheer inspirational force of their vision of what might be. They can cause people to take seriously the idea that if enough of us are willing to work for the collective visions of change we share (a nuclear-free society, a crime-free neighborhood, a multiethnic school, a city in which housing and health facilities are available to all, a national minimum wage), these visions can become realities. They can make clear how such apparently idealized visions can be realized in terms of the specific actions we can take. They know how to dramatize issues—to personalize the political—making a broad social issue comprehensible through an individual case study. They can generate vivid images that inspire us with a sense of possibility about what can be achieved.

Through their enthusiastic presentation of alternative ideas, concepts, and interpretative frameworks, teachers and trainers can also serve as powerful motivators for critical thinking. Most adults, when asked to recall their most influential teachers, typically talk of the commitment and enthusiasm of teachers under whose influence they had fallen. Even though this commitment may have been manifested in rigorous grading

and a refusal to accept what the teacher regarded as substandard student efforts, the experience of having been under the influence of someone who cared enough about the ideas being explored to insist on their being taken seriously is remembered favorably.

Although counselors, therapists, and other helping professionals are often engaged in assisting people to make sense of, and negotiate, periods of traumatic change, they can also act as positive triggers for critical thinking. These helpers do not always work in crisis-management modes; a major part of their function is to build clients' self-worth. Central to this task is helping them to find their "authentic" voices—that is, to express aspirations and enthusiasms (as well as doubts and fears) that spring from their deeply felt sense of who they are. Counselors may help people to interpret the meaning of those "peak" experiences in which they feel they are realizing aspects of their essential selves.

Conclusion

Educators and helping professionals should not be thought of as professional doom-managers, appearing only in the event of tragedy to mitigate its worst effects. This is the "ambulance driver" concept of education (Boshier, 1984, p. 12), in which helpers "arrive at the scene of the psychological, social or international accident, after the damage is done." It condemns helpers and educators to fundamentally reactive modes of practice by calling them in only at times of crisis and then reducing them to performing a "mopping up" function when things have gone wrong. Helping people make sense of, and survive, traumas is an important function and should not be undervalued, but it is not the whole story. It is just as important to encourage people to explore ideas and activities they had not previously considered, but that appear to embody and reflect essential elements of their personalities or open new avenues for realization. How educators, counselors, trainers, and other helpers can prompt people to become critical thinkers without the necessity of experiencing major personal traumas is a central concern of this book.

❧ 3 ❧

Learning to Think Critically
in Adult Life

Why should we be critical thinkers? What's so important about critical thinking that it merits a book, or four years of an author's life? Isn't being critical tantamount to being negative, destructive, and blocking? Aren't critics people who make a parasitical living from tearing to pieces the accomplishments of others? Isn't criticizing others demeaning to them and destructive of their initiative and commitment? These are questions commonly asked of anyone advocating that people be encouraged to think critically. The image of a critical person that underlies these questions is hardly flattering. It is that of someone who is insensitive to others' feelings and who is destructively contemptuous of their accomplishments. Critical thinkers can be parodied either as disgruntled and bitter subversives or as elitist mockers of others' well-meant efforts. The pejorative associations surrounding the word *critical* have meant that advocating critical thinking is a form of social or educational bad taste. Being critical is seen to have harmful consequences, such as destroying others' motivation or causing irreparable harm to their self-image. Film, theater, and music critics are castigated by the artists who are the objects of their critical attentions as parasites unable to create their own original works and forced to ease their frustrations by demolishing the efforts of others. Within most circles then, being critical is regarded almost wholly as a negative activity.

35

The concept of critical thinking informing this book is directly contrary to that idea. It is important to emphasize that critical thinking involves elements of positive as well as negative appraisal. To ask, "Why are things as they are?" or "How might things be different?" does not necessarily entail the wholesale destruction of the ideas, institutions, or values under analysis. At times the result of a critical scrutiny will be a realization that, in an imperfect world, the idea, institution, or value under review is justified and the most acceptable that might be expected in the circumstances. We might be forced by an intimate to think seriously about the assumptions underlying a relationship and conclude that the relationship is strong and founded on realistic expectations. As workers, we might be worried about the grounds underlying a decision made by an employer (for example, the decision to introduce work sharing or three-day work weeks) but decide after reviewing the company's balance sheet that it was justified. Politically, we might question a government's decision (for example, the decision to hold wage increases for teachers to a predefined level) but after reflection accept that the policy was the least objectionable of several unpalatable options (including, for example, reducing overall staff levels or stopping all other public sector wage increases in order to satisfy the demands of one well-organized professional pressure group).

At other times, critical thinking will result in the modification of the practice or idea under scrutiny, to make it more congenial, humane, or effective. Partners in a troubled relationship might decide to stay together but resolve to accept and encourage each other's diverse interests rather than insist that each participate fully in the other's enthusiasms. Workers critical of poor management decisions might insist on worker representation on executive boards. They might prefer to replace the capitalist economic structure with worker ownership but be satisfied for the moment with a greater voice in company decisions. Public sector workers might organize to press for a reduction in the defense budget and a reallocation of resources to all public service employees and services.

Critical Thinking and Adulthood

Critical thinking as a process and activity seems to figure more strongly in adulthood than in childhood and adolescence. Because of the intensity and breadth of most adults' experiences, we expect men and women to have developed some capacity for critical reflection on their lives; we expect them to be able to identify discrepancies between ideals and their realization and to be skeptical of dualistic, black-and-white perceptions of the world. This childhood-adulthood difference is not a hard and fast distinction, however. Chronological age is not *necessarily* correlated with increased breadth and depth of experience. An adult's work life can be forty years in which one year's activities and experiences are repeated forty times. A ten-year marriage can be one year's habitual interactions repeated ten times. There are single teenage mothers living on the streets in my own neighborhood whose experiences of certain realities of life in New York are far more intense and varied than my own.

Critical thinking does happen in schools, and school teachers do try to develop critical capacities in their students. Thinking critically in the context of adult life is, however, a broader and deeper activity that involves our scrutinizing the stock of developed assumptions and habitual behaviors we have evolved during our lives. When we are learning new rules, knowledge, and assumptions (as happens in childhood), it is hard to be critically reflective, since we have no way of knowing the accuracy, validity, and efficacy of those norms. It is only after testing them through experience that we can begin to question their legitimacy. In adult life, the same holds true; as we enter a new skill or knowledge area, or as we explore a new way of interpreting ourselves and others around us, we are chiefly concerned with learning this new information, skill, or insight effectively. It is difficult to assess the use or accuracy of the learning at this stage, since we have had no opportunity to test its validity against our own experiences.

Generally, we expect adults to be able to reflect critically on the truth of general rules taught to them in childhood. As

Argyris, Putnam, and Smith (1985, p. 289) write, "In adulthood this early learning returns to roost, as the learning frames and strategies we developed in childhood begin to jeopardize the very growth and learning they were initially designed to ensure." Gould (1978, 1980, 1984) has studied the development of adult consciousness in psychiatric outpatients and nonpatients. He posits a "maturational push" throughout adult life to achieve a sense of inner freedom from inhibitions acquired in childhood. Hence, "during the adult years we strive to become more liberated from ideas that were generated in childhood and persevere in adulthood even though they constrain us. . . . We are continuously transforming ouselves—within a community, out of the past into the future, with and within a complex mind, trying always to gain a little more liberty to be what we are becoming" (1980, p. 237). Mezirow (1981, p. 7) describes this process as *perspective transformation:* "the learning process by which adults come to recognize their culturally induced dependency roles and relationships and the reasons for them and take action to overcome them."

We might be told in childhood that we should never lie, that honesty is the best policy, and that policemen should always be trusted. As we pass through adolescence and enter adulthood, we begin to question the accuracy and utility of such simple prescriptions. We decide to keep secret the fatal condition of someone we love until it becomes too obvious to deny that he or she has cancer or AIDS. We realize that it is sometimes in our own best interests to conceal our real intentions. We apply for other jobs without telling our employer. We artificially inflate our wage expectations (or falsify our current wage levels) when negotiating for a new job or a raise. After hearing of case after case of corruption among public officials or police, our first reactions on being arrested is to call a lawyer.

In adulthood, then, we are often prone to call into question the validity of norms, values, and beliefs that we were encouraged as children to accept as general rules. When faced with a situation in which our common-sense ideas and explanations do not fit, we find ourselves identifying, and then challenging the validity of, assumptions we learned in childhood. We begin to be aware of how the context of a situation affects how these childhood rules are applied. We become skeptical of anyone—therapist, friend, accountant, politician—who tells us that he or she has *all* the answers to our problems. We begin to think through the consequences for ourselves and those around us of blindly following these general rules. In short, we engage in critical analysis of the validity of norms we were socialized to accept uncritically in childhood.

These kinds of critically reflective capacities are frequently said to be indicative of an adult consciousness. According to developmental psychologists such as Kohlberg (1981), Loevinger (1976), Gilligan (1982), and Kegan (1982), an adult's increasing sophistication can be seen in his or her "coming to see one's own culture from a critical stance and establishing loyalties that go beyond one's immediate community" (Daloz, 1986, p. 47). Paterson (1979) points out that our culture expects increasing age and developing maturity to be correlated. Hence, "whereas we rightly expect a man of forty to display qualities of prudence, self-control, and perseverance, it would be quite unfair to expect a boy of ten to possess these qualities in anything like the same measure" (p. 13). To Levinson (1978, p. 53), the central task in managing the transitions of adult life is being able "to question and reappraise the existing structure, to search for new possibilities in self and world, and to modify the present structure enough so that a new one can be formed." In other words, the capacity to think critically can be seen as one of the chief markers by which we recognize adult qualities in an individual. As Daloz (1986, p. 154) puts it, "The struggle to be something more than the person others have made, to construct and then live up to a set of *our own* expectations, is one of the most compelling struggles of our adult lives."

The vision of adulthood as characterized by critical thinking is, of course, itself culturally bound. It is reflective of my own biography and the culture (university world) to which I currently belong. In other cultures, "adult" behaviors are conceived of in very different ways—in, for example, the demonstration of an unswerving loyalty to a political ideology or religious creed, or in the ability to produce and support a large extended family. In my own terms, the readiness to question stereotypes and the refusal to accept moral codes and value systems simply because they are "there" are examples of adult behavior. To others in this culture, these same characteristics might be viewed as evidence of immaturity rather than of maturity. As well as being culturally bound, this concept of adulthood is also prescriptive, not descriptive. There are, after all, many people who are chronologically adult but who think in highly dualistic, simplistic ways. Indeed, it has been argued (Usher, 1981) that the capacity to think dualistically might be seen by some as essential for political success. In the last volume of his *Strangers and Brothers* sequence of novels on British political life, C. P. Snow (1970, p. 243) describes successful leadership: "You had to believe the other side was a hundred percent wrong, and preferably evil, to be a hundred percent committed to your own."

In times of war, patriotism requires that citizens suspend their critical questioning of the merits of an opposing country's cause so that they can be utterly dedicated to the actions of their own government. Waging a war is hardly conducive to a critical examination of the moral or strategic rightness of a country's cause. Those who do engage in this questioning may be ostracized, imprisoned, or even executed for treason. Sometimes, as happened with the Vietnam War, there is an incremental build-up of public skepticism of the rightness of a government's action, resulting in a policy reversal. At other times (the 1982 British-Argentine war over the Falkland Islands, the 1983 American invasion of Grenada, and the 1986 American attack on Libya all come to mind), very little public questioning of a governmental action is apparent.

It can be argued that only those political leaders who are fired by the utter rightness of their actions, and who refuse to consider the validity of alternatives, can effect real change in their societies. Ronald Reagan and Margaret Thatcher are both remarkably successful political leaders in terms of their ability to gain and maintain power. Yet neither apparently exhibits the conditions of critical thinking as defined in this book. Rather than being skeptical of universal solutions, they believe with total certainty that they possess the one correct way to organize society and that their political values are innately superior to any others. In commenting on the Reagan administration, the *New York Times* put it this way: "At all times they are absolutely certain of their own rightness. It is never in need of a proof; it is, rather, taken as a premise" (Wieseltier, 1986, p. 45). Margaret Thatcher has been publicly admired by such left-wing opponents as Tony Benn for being a "conviction politician," utterly committed to a cause in which she believes, and unequivocally determined to advance the interests of the class her party represents. Rather than criticizing her for this, these same opponents urge that she be removed so that *they* can come into office and pursue the interests of *their* class with equal singlemindedness.

Acknowledging the culturally bound nature of critical thinking as a characteristic of adult life does not necessarily invalidate this concept. As long as the reasons critical thinking is considered so important are clearly stated, the necessary conditions for a dialogue have been established. If I am open to divergent interpretations of the concept of adulthood, and can treat seriously others' criticism of these ideas, I am engaged in an active analysis of my own experience. Such a probing and analysis is at the heart of critical thinking. Again, just because critical reflection is not empirically observable in every adult does not mean that we should not strive to develop this capacity. Critical thinking is like self-directedness in learning: both are capacities that are generally regarded as desirable, both are empirically observable (to very different degrees in different individuals), and both are seen as better open to development in adults than in children or adolescents.

The Importance of Critical Thinking

Why is the process of critical thinking outlined in Chapter Two so important? The answers to this question take up much of this book. At a very simple level, however, one useful approach is to imagine what it would mean *not* to be able to think critically. It would mean that we would be happy to reproduce in our marriages patterns of male-female domination we had observed in our parents' marriages. It would mean that we regarded as normal and natural the denial of certain economic and educational benefits to people because of their skin pigmentation. It would mean that we accepted massive disparities in wealth between social classes and ethnic groups as inevitable. It would mean our accepting as objective truth every justification that a politician gave for an action. It would mean accepting as accurate, statements by those in power: "Trees cause pollution," "All people who are out of work could find jobs if they really wanted them," "The Strategic Defense Initiative will end war forever," "Removing this ethnic group from our society will strengthen our national character and our economic base," or "Women are not interested in arms negotiations and issues of war and peace, only in the social activities of the wives of national leaders." In short, without the capacity to think and act critically, we would never move beyond those assumptions we assimilated uncritically in childhood. We would believe totally in the myths, folk wisdoms, and values we encountered in authority figures in our early lives. We would make no attempt to change social structures or to press for collective social action. What would be the point? If it was good enough for previous generations, it's good enough for us.

Our society is arguably in a state of greater flux—morally, technologically, and socially—than any other society in history. During times of personal and social stability, we can live as uncritical and satisfied consumers, on the assumption that what exists now will persist indefinitely. In the latter half of this century, however, when economic, technological, political, and social changes prompt crisis after crisis in our personal existence, thinking critically is a matter of sheer survival (Scriven, 1985). Unless we become critical thinkers during periods of crisis, we are condemned to view our lives as constantly changing, essentially irrational sequences of random happenings that are out of our control. We are like psychologically shipwrecked voyagers, desperately clinging to whatever piece of psychic flotsam we can find as we are tossed in the turbulent seas of personal and social change. We seek solace for these traumas in religious cults, political dogmas, the promises of fanatical, totalitarian leaders, and drug abuse.

As Fromm (1941) remarked, the prospect of freedom without reason is enough to drive us into psychic, physical, and political enclaves that promise to find our reason for us. Subsuming one's individuality in a religious cult, in political fanaticism, or by becoming an alcoholic are contemporary analgesics to dull the pain of apparently being blown around wildly by the winds of destiny. Individuals in this state of critical helplessness often rationalize their situation through a belief in the workings of a powerful but inaccessible fate. Unable to see their individual lives as cultural products, they become passive spectators of the passing political, economic, and ideological seasons. Unaware of how collective action can trigger social change, they develop attitudes of acceptance and resignation to whatever changes are visited upon them by external circumstances. Existence is seen by them as essentially chaotic, with no meaning or rationality.

The ability to be critically analytical concerning the assumptions underlying our own actions and those of others is organizationally and culturally beneficial as well as personally liberating. Participants in relationships who are able to recognize that their habitual expectations of each other's conduct are reflective of cultural conditioning can probably communicate more honestly and openly with one another (Rogers, 1984). A factory or business in which a critically informed work force is encouraged to examine the assumptions underlying policies and habitual practices, and to challenge these when they are inimical to communication or demeaning to particular groups, will likely be more productive and less subject to crippling stoppages (Schein, 1985). Critically reflective teachers are likely to foster classrooms in which challenge and excitement are found (Shor, 1980). Societies in which citizens scrutinize critically the actions, decisions, and justifications of political leaders will be ones in which the dangers of totalitarianism and demagoguery are substantially reduced (Glaser, 1985).

How We Acquire Assumptions

How do we acquire in childhood the assumptions that we
begin to examine critically in adulthood? Assumptions are the
seemingly self-evident rules about reality that we use to help
us seek explanations, make judgments, or decide on various actions. They are the unquestioned givens that, to us, have the
status of self-evident truths. People cannot reach adulthood
without bringing with them frameworks of understanding and
sets of assumptions that undergird their decisions, judgments,
and actions. These assumptions influence how we understand
cause-and-effect relationships (for example, seeing crime as the
result of poverty as opposed to as the result of laziness). They
inform our criteria regarding what is good behavior in others
(for example, showing concern for others' misfortunes, ignoring conventional mores, ruthlessly pursuing one's self-interest).
Assumptions help construct our understanding of what we judge
to be "human nature." They fundamentally influence how we
conceive of the duties and obligations that determine what is
seen as appropriate conduct in personal relationships. Finally,
they shape how we view the political world. They underlie how
we decide on the legitimate spheres of interference by governments in our lives (for example, taxation, conscription, permis-
sion or denial of our rights to abortion). They help us decide
what rights we think individual citizens have, and what obligations governments may legitimately expect from us.

Assumptions are central to what Polyani (1962) calls *implicit personal knowledge*. They are the personal givens that we
accept as self-evident. Yinger (1980, p. 16) describes how we
use these assumptions as the basis for implicit theories, "the
unexamined or unconscious theories that allow us to structure,
interpret, and make sense of our world. . . . Implicit theories
become the lens and filter for everyday experience, dictating
what one sees and how one interprets it." Making explicit what
is implicit in how we look at the world is a central task of critical
thinking. It is also the purpose of a new mode of social and
organizational research called *action science* (Argyris, Putnam,
and Smith, 1985), which studies the assumptions, implicit
theories, and tacit knowledge embedded in people's actions.

The most important decisions we make in our lives (who we marry, where we work, how we raise our children, what we expect from our elected representatives, how we treat our parents, what we consider the limits of friendship obligations) are made on the basis of these assumptions. Before understanding how we can analyze the assumptions informing our actions, we need to know how these assumptions are initially acquired. The sets of assumptions we possess about human nature (for example, that people are naturally violent or innately benevolent), or about the organization of social life (for example, that because people are naturally violent [benevolent] we must ensure that social institutions and laws keep this aggression in check [release the latent altruism possessed by us all]) comprise frameworks of understanding. Mezirow (1985a) describes the two kinds of assumptions comprising these frameworks of understanding as *psychological assumptions* and *cultural assumptions*. Psychological assumptions are inhibitory rules that are unconscious but that cause anxiety and guilt when we violate them. Examples of these would be ''Never confront people,'' ''Never perform less than perfectly,'' and ''Never express feelings.'' Cultural assumptions are embedded in the dominant cultural values of a society and are transmitted by social institutions. They inform our conduct in political, economic, occupational, and religious spheres. To Mezirow (1985a, p. 145), ''one learns to overcome these distorting cultural and psychological assumptions by bringing them into critical consciousness.'' How educators and other helpers might encourage this kind of critical thinking is a central concern of this book.

Human beings are not so many tabulae rasae—featureless psyches on which skilled mind-manipulators can draw whatever mental maps they please. In trying to find meaning in our lives and to make sense of the things that happen to us, we seek frameworks of understanding that we can impose on the bewildering chaos of our existence. We may find other people's frameworks foolish or repugnant, but we cannot deny that most people make sense of their worlds through some interpretative perspective. While I may disagree with someone who tells me that rock music is meaningless tripe and of no redeeming musical value, or that anyone disagreeing with the president must be a communist, I cannot claim that these views are irrational, in the sense of not being grounded in any framework of values, beliefs, or ways of looking at the world. In terms of the interpretative frameworks possessed by people who hold these beliefs, their views are entirely reasonable. In disagreeing with them, I am really calling into question the accuracy and authenticity of the frameworks of understanding and interpretation within which these views are formed.

The problem with much contemporary discourse at the privately personal level (in relationships or with family members) or the publicly political level (in media debates or parliamentary proceedings) is that affirmations frequently masquerade as arguments. In exchanges based on simple affirmation, no understanding of alternative viewpoints is possible. The case is stated, not discussed. Such exchanges are characterized by frequent use of premature ultimates—that is, statements uttered with such finality and conviction that the possibility of counterarguments is severely reduced. An example of a premature ultimate is "Building nuclear weapons is how we preserve democracy." Anyone trying to counter that argument runs the risk of being slandered as undemocratic or un-American. Another example is "Capital punishment is the only way to deter murderers." People calling such a declaration into question would be tainted as promurder. Contemporary debates over sex education in schools, the morality of abortion, and school prayer are full of premature ultimates—uncritical affirmations pretending to be reasoned arguments.

When premature ultimates are exchanged, those involved frequently believe their views to be so self-evidently truthful that articulating the assumptions underlying them is unnecessary. Along with this belief goes the conviction that opponents of one's views are operating from behind some irrational blockage. If only they could see the world as it really is, we say, they would surely agree with our ideas. I have had conversations with people who argued that poverty is caused by individual laziness; that anyone can find work in a recession if he or she really wants it; that British people are innately more cultured than Americans;

that rock music has produced a generation of sex and drug fiends; and that watching television sit-coms or listening to AM radio rots the brain to the extent that no discriminatory capacities are left for more demanding artistic forms. My initial reaction is to think that anyone expressing these ideas is fundamentally misguided. Yet people holding these views are obviously not innately capricious, unhinged, or totally irrational. Hence, when I disagree with someone offering these opinions it is important to realize that what I am contesting are the frameworks of understanding—the implicit assumptions regarding how the world works or how people behave—that underlie these beliefs.

Developing Authentic Frameworks of Understanding

If we want people to look more critically at ideas and behaviors that we feel are questionable, we must try to help them examine these objectively. It is not enough simply to accuse those who disagree with us of operating under false assumptions. For any effective communication to take place between people, there must be a readiness in those involved to try to understand each others' perspectives. Before I accuse someone who maintains that ''watching sit-coms rots the brain'' of operating under false assumptions, I must be prepared to enter that person's mental framework of understanding so that I can understand this idea from his or her viewpoint. I must try to appreciate the framework within which that person is forming beliefs about the world. Having done this, I must then lay bare my own assumptions on the matter. These two conditions hold true for discourse on a whole range of matters.

The conditions by which we can recognize whether or not people are engaged in full discourse are specified by Mezirow (1985b, p. 19) as follows: people have full information about the matter at hand, they can reason argumentatively, they can reflect critically about assumptions and premises, and they have sufficient self-knowledge to assure that their participation in discourse is free of self-deception. Participants in such discourse are also judged to be free of constraint or coercion, and they enjoy full equality and reciprocity in assuming the various roles involved in the interchange. Powell (1956) expresses this idea in another way, arguing that communication—"making common certain matters of knowledge, of purpose, of belief, of feeling, and of action"—is the aim of education and the mark of a civilized society. Anything opposing full communication (such as lying, prejudice, ignorance, anger, fear, and partiality) is, by definition, antieducational. Educators are charged with exposing false assumptions, with combating prejudice, and with fostering authentic discourse.

The problem arises, however, of how we define ideal, full discourse and how we recognize an authentic framework of understanding. Mezirow (1985b, p. 5) claims that an authentic framework (he uses the term *meaning perspective*) can be recognized by its being "(1) more informed by complete and accurate information; (2) more inclusive, discriminating and integrative of experience; (3) more free from the influence of internal or external forms of constraint or coercion; (4) more critically reflective—informed by a clearer understanding of the historical, cultural and biographical reasons for it having been acquired in the first place and of the functions it fulfills; and (5) more permeable—open to discourse with alternative perspectives on disputed validity claims." But how do we decide that some piece of information is more accurate and complete than another? How do we recognize superior discrimination? How do we distinguish between learners being unfairly coerced and learners being strongly encouraged to undertake tasks that are painful (such as being critically reflective) but that we feel, in good conscience, to be in their own best interest? How do we know when understanding is clear and when it is muddled? These issues in facilitating critical thinking are considered at points throughout this book.

Conclusion

Critical thinking is a capacity recognized as important not just by educators, helping professionals, academic psychologists, and philosophers, but by most adults themselves. They will not generally use the term *critical thinking* to describe what they have experienced, but when asked to talk about their most significant learning it is aspects of the process of critical thinking that are frequently cited. For the past few years, I have run workshops on understanding and facilitating adult learning; they have typically attracted as participants adult and continuing educators, school teachers, nurses, health educators, trainers and human resource developers, and social activists. At the beginning of each workshop, I ask participants to choose the most significant learning they have experienced in the recent past. I suggest that they think about learning as occurring within one of four broad categories: learning about oneself, learning that is job-related, learning about one's society, and recreational learning.

It is startling how frequently learning about oneself is chosen by participants as the most significant and memorable form of learning they have experienced. When asked to analyze this learning further, in terms of its being focused on skill acquisition, knowledge gain, behavior change, or insight realization, participants invariably emphasize the last category. The specific form of their insight realization usually concerns coming to recognize and question some typically accepted, common-sense behavior that has previously significantly influenced their actions. Interestingly enough, these insights concerning the inaccuracy of previously accepted assumptions are usually reported as having been unanticipated. They have been prompted by some unforeseen crisis, the aftermath of which has seen the people concerned reflecting on what has been learned about themselves and about the uncritically internalized assumptions by which they have been living.

These participants, as educators and helping professionals, might be said to be atypical of the larger general population in terms of their reflective orientation to life. Yet this is an oversimplification. In the expectations they voice at the outset of workshops, and in their evaluative comments, participants repeatedly stress that they have come in order to acquire specific and practical tips, methods, and techniques that they can take

back and use in their own practice settings; so they can hardly
be said to be attending with a uniquely reflective orientation.
They mirror very strongly the pragmatic tenor of American
culture in their determination to get something useable from
the workshops. If they are typical of at least a section of the wider
society, the capacity for critical thought and action may be much
less dormant than might be imagined. It is to examining how
this capacity might be awakened and sharpened that this book
is devoted.

4

How Critical Thinking
Sustains a Healthy Democracy

If one feature in our society appears to hold constant, it is the certainty of change. Mezirow (1983) writes that "the focal concern of adult learning, especially in our culture with its high intensity of change, is with reordering one's life when dislocations occur and inherited recipes for problem solving do not seem to work" (p. 1). In personal relationships, at the workplace, in the political realm, and in images of the world as portrayed on television, the last twenty years of this century are as far removed from the 1940s and 1950s as other centuries have been from those preceding them. Making sense of, and trying to feel some sense of control over, these changes is central to becoming critically thoughtful.

In personal relationships, our conceptions of rights, obligations, duties, and appropriate behaviors have undergone major alterations in the last three decades. The decline of extended-family obligations, the emergence of the women's movement, changes in the divorce laws, the increased availability of birth control methods, the increase in single-parent families, the slowly decreasing stigma of homosexual and lesbian lifestyles, and the declining influence of traditional religious values on sexual and marital conduct have all significantly changed the way relationships are viewed and lived.

51

At the workplace, changes in technology have altered fundamentally the organization of production. The growth of the service economy, the onset of the information age, the idea that computer literacy is an essential employment skill, the economic success associated with Japanese management styles (such as quality circles), the fact that increased occupational and geographical mobility is a condition of career· success, and the dependence of Western industrial nations on resources (such as oil) owned by societies previously considered under- or less-developed have all wrought enormous changes in the ways work is organized in industrial societies.

Politically, we have entered the era of mass representative democracy. For those citizens who are excluded from the power elites in government, industry, or the military, the expression of individual views or dissent is of little consequence unless done within the context of a political movement or pressure group. Decisions that fundamentally affect our lives are made by individuals who are professionally lobbied by well-financed political action committees. The need.to avoid offending powerful interest groups is a major consideration in the policy framing and decision making undertaken by these elites. Candidates stand a realistic chance of being elected to office only if they have substantial private wealth or if they are supported by wealthy groups. On matters basic to our individual survival—such as declaring war or building, deploying, and using nuclear weapons—decisions are made by a tiny minority on behalf of the majority. To parents, it is a frightening realization that the kind of educational system within which their children will be schooled and the health care facilities that will be available for their family members are beyond their control, unless they are economically able to afford some choice in these matters. To all citizens, whether or not we die in a nuclear holocaust appears to be something over which we have no control.

An additional source of complexity is caused by the fact that the mass media of communication—broadcasting and the press—are the means by which we gain much of our information on issues affecting our lives. These media, particularly television, are technically complex and seem distant from us as individuals. One consequence of this perception of distance is that "ordinary" citizens (that is, those who do not belong to a powerful interest group) come to see themselves as passive viewers of a drama enacted on a stage that is wholly inaccessible to them. The framing of policies and making of decisions that fundamentally affect us all sometimes appear to occur in a televisual realm of noninterference. We switch on our sets each day to learn of decisions that have substantial consequences for our individual lives: a government's declaring of war, cutting interest rates, reducing public spending, reforming educational provision, or changing the law. Yet the relaying of these decisions is accomplished through a medium that only emphasizes and deepens our sense of powerlessness.

Given the sense of distance induced by our learning of political decisions through televised briefings, it is little wonder that the number of people voting in national elections has declined in recent years. When we feel that decisions affecting us are made at a distance both technologically and politically far removed from us, our typical response is a feeling of powerlessness. We become cynical about the workings of the political process, claiming that "my vote doesn't really count." Or we resign ourselves to the fact that "it doesn't make any difference who wins; they're all the same anyway." Learning about the political world only through television effectively elevates policy discussion and decision making to a level of total noninterference where individual citizens are concerned. The actions of political leaders seem to be as arbitrary and inaccessible as the weather; the declaration of war becomes an arbitrary act as inaccessible to individual influence as a hurricane.

One fundamental purpose of encouraging adults to become critical thinkers is to help them feel a sense of personal connection to wider happenings. Kretovics (1985, p. 56) writes of the need to develop critical literacy in people so that they have "the necessary tools and skills to make sense of the social relations, material conditions, and cultural milieus in which they exist and their relationship to the wider society and dominant rationality." Such critical literacy includes forms of political and media literacy, not just the ability to read and write. Those involved in developing these kinds of literacy will be "providing students not merely with functional skills, but with the conceptual tools necessary to critique and engage society along with its inequalities and injustices" (p. 51).

When people view social changes or political decisions as somehow mystically removed from their own existence, they frequently turn inward, focusing exclusively on their private lives. If we feel that uncontrollable and reified forces are shaping the configuration of our individual lives, we may well retreat to the apparent security of the one sphere in which we feel some sense of control—our personal growth and relationships. Our attention and energies become focused on exploring inner space rather than outer workplace and political worlds. It is surely no accident that the staggering upsurge of interest in movements devoted entirely to personal growth has been concurrent with a decrease in community activism. The last twenty years have witnessed an increased absorption in self as against social involvement. Look at any noncredit proprietary adult school's offerings and you will be struck by the number of courses on personal growth. These might focus on anything from spiritual development through meditation to creating home interiors that reflect their owners' personal tastes. In New York City just such a school, the Learning Annex, features in its November 1985 catalogue courses on "How to Flirt," "How to Get Past the First Date," and "How to Strip for Your Man." Visit any bookstore and you will notice the numerous popular psychology books that purport to be manuals of self-development. Tune in to television talk shows and you cannot avoid seeing a parade of pop psychologists talking above love, relationships, and improving your appeal as a likely romantic partner.

The decade of the politically active 1960s is, with hindsight, coming to be seen as something of a temporary sociohistorical aberration. Activists of that time believed they were involved in a fundamental transformation of society. Although there is a high level of contemporary interest in that decade, it is in the form of a nostalgia craze. The 1960s are coming to be viewed as a quaint—but ultimately irrelevant—decade. By way of contrast, the conservative affluence of the 1950s, the

"Me" decade of the 1970s, and the swing to the right of the 1980s all share one fundamental similarity: to a majority of people living in these times, the prime purposes of life are perceived as being individual gratification and personal growth, unconnected to broader social purposes or forces. As a period, the late 1980s have far more in common with the 1950s than they do with the 1960s. The glorification of personal wealth of the Yuppie subculture is typical of the same unqualified faith in affluence as Macmillan's "you've never had it so good" ethic in Britain and the belief in Eisenhower's America that a split-level, two-car-garage house was the inalienable birthright of every American and the key to personal happiness.

The dark side of this moon of individual gratification and absorption in a privatized lifestyle is the growing sense of uneasiness, unnameable anxiety, and frustrated perplexity felt by those who subscribe wholly to this ethic. Above the Porsche, the microwave oven, and the compact disk player hovers the specter of the nuclear mushroom cloud. Nagging at the subconscious of aerobics enthusiasts is the awareness that a chemical leak or accident at a toxic waste plant will nullify in thirty seconds of inhalation years of dedicated body sculpture. Too explosive for upwardly mobile designers of computer software to acknowledge explicitly, but probably suspected nonetheless, is the realization that a high-tech innovation could effectively render several years of their work completely irrelevant. "The problem that has no name" is the phrase used by Betty Friedan (1963) in *The Feminine Mystique* to describe the sense of alienation and uneasiness felt by women who were experiencing profound discrepancies between the fulfillment they expected from playing the role of dutiful housewife, subservient spouse, and dedicated mother, and the stagnating and constricting reality of their lives. This same unnameable anxiety is felt by all those who dimly perceive that broad social forces could alter their conditions of personal existence unexpectedly, and irrevocably, without any opportunity for these same individuals to shape the form, or affect the extent, of these alterations.

The unexpected and often cataclysmic nature of technological advancement; the ever-present threat of nuclear annihilation; the seemingly fleeting nature of friendship in a time of frantic occupational and geographical mobility; the statistical likelihood of divorce that accompanies the decision to marry; the apparent impenetrableness of a television world in which the actions of characters unrecognizable in most adults' daily lives are invested with profound meaning and significance—all these trends and forces are indicative of the apparently chaotic and uncontrollable nature of existence.

Connecting Private Lives to Public Issues

We have seen that people frequently perceive themselves to be helpless in the face of overwhelming social forces. They regard their individual lives as relatively insignificant brush strokes when viewed against the broad canvas of social, economic, and technological changes. In particular, the connection between personal situations and wider social changes is often ignored. Local community conditions (a factory closing down, a farm foreclosure, rural depopulation) can sometimes be accepted as inevitable—"natural" events with as much logic to them as changes in the weather. Personal crises (divorce, cancer, a heart attack) can be viewed as purely private events in an enclosed world. The fact that increases in all three areas are linked to broader social and technological changes (increased occupational and geographical mobility, increased consumption of processed foods and animal fats, decreased consumption of dietary fiber) may be completely ignored.

When the world is perceived as fundamentally uncontrollable, and when major events in our lives are viewed as unpredictable and inexplicable, we feel powerless. Individuals trying to make themselves into critical thinkers or hoping to encourage this capacity in others are trying to replace this sense of powerlessness with the conviction that the world is *not* governed completely by accidental happenings beyond our understanding. Adults who are critical thinkers do not have to possess a fully evolved explanatory framework through which they can account for everything that happens in their lives. However, they do realize that personal traumas are not always to be viewed either as difficulties visited upon them by an angry supreme being or as merely one more indication of a wholly chaotic world. Critical thinkers try to place the events of their individual lives within the context of broader social forces. They do not underestimate the importance of unpredictability in life, but they are aware of the ways in which personal lives are partly social products. A child's experimenting with drugs is not immediately interpreted as evidence of the personal inadequacies of the parents. The monthly performance of a work team is not seen as being as inexplicable as the monthly sunshine level. The sudden focusing of news broadcasts on a theme barely mentioned in previous months (such as drugs or illiteracy) is not accepted without some reflection on what might have caused this.

Critical thinkers make explicit the connections between the personal and the political in their lives. They are aware that individual crises often reflect wider social changes. They know that what might initially be regarded as an idiosyncratic, wholly personal tragedy (divorce, dying of AIDS, unemployment, drug abuse) is frequently a problem shared by large numbers of people. One of the best expressions of this linkage of personal difficulties and broader social forces is that undertaken by C. Wright Mills (1959) in *The Sociological Imagination*. Mills explored the connections between what he termed *private troubles* (such as unemployment or divorce) and *public issues* (broad social and economic changes). Private troubles occur in the context of our individual lives and are seen as wholly idiosyncratic by those affected by them. There may be no awareness of a causal connection between a personal tragedy and broader socioeconomic trends or political changes. Hence, unemployment or divorce might be seen as wholly accidental happenings or as the result of personal inadequacies.

Private troubles are, however, social products. Mills writes that "inside a marriage a man and a woman may experience personal troubles, but when the divorce rate during the first four years of marriage is 250 out of every 1,000 attempts, this is an indication of a structural issue having to do with the institution of marriage and the family and other institutions that bear upon them" (p. 9). A critically reflective person is aware that individual biographies are partly social products and that values, beliefs, and behavioral norms are culturally produced. From this awareness springs an understanding that changes in individual lives are often inextricably linked to alterations in wider social structures. In *Mass Society and Liberal Education*, Mills (1954) declared that the task of educators is to help people understand how their individual biographies are constructed by broader social forces. Realizing this is a liberating experience, he asserted. When people see that private problems are reflective of some wider dislocation or contradiction in the social structure, they realize that collective action is sometimes necessary to deal with what they had thought to be individual problems. Instead of an individual feeling overwhelmed by mass society and immobilized by personal difficulties, he or she realizes that "what he thinks and feels to be personal troubles are very often not only that but problems shared by others and indeed not subject to solution by any one individual but only by modifications of the structure of the groups in which he lives and sometimes the structure of the entire society" (p. 14).

We can see in the spread of AIDS (Acquired Immune Deficiency Syndrome) how the most private of tragedies has become an activator of collective action, in the gay community in particular. Although the AIDS virus attacks heterosexuals (especially intravenous drug users), it has generally been associated with a homosexual lifestyle. Because of the condemnation of the values and actions of this subculture by the dominant culture, very little public money was initially made available for research in how to combat the virus. The connection between a friend or lover dying of AIDS, the absence of media attention devoted to the disease, and the lack of government funding for research, especially in the 1980s, has been made explicit through plays such as Larry Kramer's *The Normal Heart*. As I write, a debate is raging in the New York City school system over the teaching of sex education classes in which homosexual activity and the contracting of AIDS are discussed. Gay activists across the country are pressing for increased governmental funds to be made available for research on an antidote to the virus, and the media are beginning to cover demonstrations and marches held to highlight this issue. The gay community has realized that only by mobilizing for collective action will the political changes needed to relieve personal traumas be achieved.

Other writers have also explored this connection between private troubles and public issues. Keddie (1980) notes how helping professionals who view their clients as "disadvantaged" are often guilty of "a severing of the connections between the *political* nature of social problems and the individual who presents problems which, if they are severe enough or sufficiently troublesome to others, will be dealt with as individual problems by the social worker, the police, the remedial teacher" (p. 87). To Wexler (1983), academic social science "makes us content with the present, portraying it as natural and inevitable" (p. 2). As an alternative to this, Sullivan (1984) proposes a critical psychology that "would provide a critical interpretation of what is happening within people within the context of wider social structures" (p. x). He argues that if psychologists seek to understand individual biographies as being partly framed by social forces, they will seek ways to help clients change their lives in beneficial ways. Fay (1975) outlines the task of critical psychologists as being to help people "to understand themselves in their situation as the product of certain inherent contradictions in their social order, contradictions which they can remove by taking an appropriate course of action to change this social order" (p. 97). Critical sociology, in Hansen's (1976) view, helps people to recognize that "the biography of our own life cannot be understood until the many relationships it involves are understood, until the economic and social conditions in which we grew are fathomed" (p. 231).

The women's movement offers a good illustration of how perceiving the connection between personal troubles and social forces leads to social as well as individual change. In her study of women's collectives, Hart (1985) writes that "only through an intersubjective recognition of shared experience can previously simply private and idiosyncratic feelings be validated as subjective experiences of a general impersonal, objective context of repression" (p. 124). Mezirow (1977, 1981) views this activity of "relating one's discontent to similar experiences of others or to public issues—recognizing that one's problem is shared and not exclusively a private matter'' (1981, p. 7)—as an important stage in the perspective transformation experienced by women who re-enter college after a period raising families. Through their creation of support and consciousness-raising groups, women have become aware that what they had perceived as individual difficulties and purely personal traumas are, in fact, problematic situations experienced by many. Within women's groups the emphasis is on articulating one's own and others' experiences and envisioning a way of life different from that currently lived. Participants engage in ''creating their own knowledge'' (Spender, 1980), in ''speaking for themselves'' (Gayfer, 1980), and in ''re-visioning themselves'' (Callaway, 1981). Thompson's (1983) descriptions of women's learning groups emphasize the collaborative questioning of prevailing, predominantly male modes of knowledge, the generation of alternative perspectives and frameworks of interpretation, and the collective attempt to create new ways of thinking and living.

Some of these new ways of thinking and living are local, such as creating a neighborhood women's center or a refuge for battered wives. Others involve challenges to social structures such as educational institutions, or the occupational sector, where law has mandated against discrimination based on sex. Women have also been successful in challenging cultural mores regarding sexual stereotypes and expectations of innate capacities of women and men. They have initiated a heated public debate on what are acceptable forms of artistic representation of sexual eroticism, particularly where eroticism is linked to violence visited on helpless, submissive women. In the creation of legislation furthering equal opportunities at work and in education, and in the establishment of organizations such as Planned Parenthood of America, women have viewed structural changes within the wider society as inextricably connected to individual liberation.

Linking Critical Thinking to Collective Action

I have argued that a crucial component in developing critical thinking is assisting people to interpret their personal troubles in the context of wider social changes. There are, admittedly, many personal troubles that are more individualistic than others, such as unwanted pregnancy, sudden physical disability, and extreme forms of mental illness that have their origins in neurological and biochemical imbalances. Nonetheless, most personally problematic situations do have some social dimension to them. Locating the social context for such apparently private difficulties may be the first step in assisting people to effect change. When problems are seen as partly the result of broader social changes rather than as wholly the consequence of ingrained individual inadequacies, some possibility exists for taking action. It may be, of course, that sometimes the broad social forces that underlie changes in personal circumstances are apparently so massive as to freeze individuals into a stance of resigned inactivity. How can parents take action to reduce the possibility of their children dying in a nuclear war? How can a manufacturer going bankrupt prevent the rise in OPEC oil prices that has taken him so far into debt?

The answer is, of course, that individually we frequently *are* immobilized by the breadth and power of those social forces apparently ranged against us. A skilled helper will assist people to locate their individual change efforts within a context that is sufficiently familiar and meaningful to allow some prospect of results. The slogan "Think globally, act locally" is a useful guiding principle for this aspect of helping relationships. Concerned parents can form, or join, a local discussion group on nuclear disarmament, can decide whether or not to join a local nuclear freeze group, can contact national organizations concerned with peace education, can press for local schools to include peace education issues in their curricula, or can consider various civil defense measures. Alternatively, they can join survivalist cults, enlist in the military, or campaign for the election of spokespersons who are strong on deterrence as an international relations policy. Most of these actions are, of course, collective; that is, they involve combining with others to press for the changes that are desired. Indeed, change for collective social action is generally distinguished by two characteristics: it involves taking action in combination with other people, and it is aimed at improving some aspect of life for what those involved see as the better.

When our critical thinking leads us to become involved in helping people mobilize for collective social change, we may well be faced with difficult value choices regarding those social change directions we wish to encourage. In the example of nuclear policy just mentioned, the action initiatives open to individuals are diverse and sometimes contradictory. Some helpers will feel comfortable assisting in the development of a fledgling nuclear freeze campaign, while others may believe such a movement to be ill-conceived at best, unpatriotic at worst. The example illustrates, however, that helpers are not value-free, amoral automatons. They will sometimes feel ethically bound to refuse to support people's declared intentions. When helpers are faced with assisting in actions that they judge to be immoral, badly misconceived, or unnecessarily harmful, they have no option but to opt out.

Central to critical thinking is placing one's own situation in a broader context, so that aspects of one's problems are seen as connected to broader social forces. Helping people explore the often contradictory and ambiguous nexus where private troubles and public issues meet often entails making clear the connection to social action. As Carr and Kemmis (1983) point out, those encouraging critical thought in others seek "to transform the self-consciousness of individuals so as to make it possible for them to collectively determine the sort of life they wish to live and the sort of action they need to take in order to bring about the social conditions under which a way of life is possible" (p. 129). To community workers and social activists, becoming involved in collective action is natural and inevitable. To educators, therapists, counselors, and psychologists, this involvement might well be seen as much more ethically doubtful. They may be much more comfortable asking people to locate their individual problems in social contexts than with trying actively to change those contexts. They may prefer inviting people to consider alternative interpretations of their worlds to trying to realize some of those alternatives.

What cannot be avoided, however, is making clear the

importance of collective action to changing individual lives. Oppressed minorities (whether ethnic or sexual) and oppressed majorities (such as women, or black people in South Africa) will often be unable to effect any substantial change in their individual lives without collective action. The histories of the labor movement and of civil rights activism graphically demonstrate the connection between individual improvement and social change. In America and Britain, these movements have advanced the general condition of working-class men and women, and of ethnic minorities, though the deep, traditional structural inequalities of social class and ethnicity remain more or less intact. What change has been wrought has not always been through parliamentary debate and reform. There have been strikes, mass demonstrations (both peaceful and violent), and deliberate challenges to the law. In democratic societies, collective action for social change may be undertaken without the necessity for violent revolution, though civil disobedience sometimes may involve more limited conflict. In the stress laid by politicians and opinion leaders on the inviolable necessity of respecting the law of the land, it is sometimes forgotten that the United States was founded after a deliberate and sustained refusal to recognize the legitimacy of the law of the time (that of Britain). Compared to totalitarian dictatorships, however, America and Britain are fortunate in their democratic capacity to accommodate change without the need for violent revolution. It is not illegal to belong to labor unions, to hold demonstrations, or to campaign for alternative ideas and philosophies in these countries.

In other societies, however, drawing people's attention to visible inequities, and making them critically aware of their oppressed condition, may produce violent results. As C. Taylor (conversation with author, Nov. 21, 1986) points out, raising the consciousness of marginal and oppressed groups regarding their condition can be a profoundly destabilizing act. It carries the risk of harsh consequences as well as of life-changing victories. Ewert (1982) writes that "few would now deny that defining problems in structural terms is a political process that might result in putting bullets in disadvantaged people's guns, at least within an oppressive social system. The responsibility for unleashing a process that can potentially exceed controllable limits rests with the adult educator'' (p. 34). In a candid discussion of a community development project in Africa, he describes how an agent's participatory assessment of a village's needs led to consequences far beyond those anticipated:

> Linkages between oppressive social structures and local economic problems were established beyond reasonable doubt. The development agent, however, had intended to identify some problems that could be addressed through a community education program. He and his colleagues had then expected to teach farmers how to raise rabbits, improve chicken production, and plant soybeans. The community discussion instead focused on the need for revolution, a totally unanticipated political development in the context of extreme oppression.
>
> Reflection on this incident later led to one suggestion that the program could generate more lasting changes by distributing guns than by talking about agriculture and health. After initiating the process of examining needs and analyzing local problems, the community development team found themselves involved in something they could no longer control.
>
> Further discussion of the risks involved in such a course of action led people from the village to conclude that nothing could be gained, and that lives could be lost, by pursuing a political solution. They were later proven right when another village that had been involved in a similar community development program in a different region of the country was massacred by government troops. People there had decided to resist exploitation by political leaders (unjust taxes, military roadblocks, blatant theft by government officials, and so on) but virtually the entire village died in a machine gun attack on the village [pp. 33–34].

This is a dramatic vignette. Fortunately, when we try to become critical thinkers, and when we seek to develop this facility in others, we are not usually faced with the kind of life-threatening situation described by Ewert. There are, however, crucial ethical issues raised by attempts to change someone else's way of perceiving the world. While any number of writers encourage educators to advocate social change, very few address the risks involved in doing this. McKenzie (1978, pp. 68–70) is one of the few to observe that educators who seek to encourage critical thinking have an ethical duty to point out to those involved the risks accompanying actions springing from this new state of awareness.

Conclusion

Developing critical thinkers is a complex but vital activity. It entails facing up to ethical dilemmas whose resolution is only partial and ambiguous at best. Developing critical capacities in ourselves and others invites criticism from those who are ruffled by being asked awkward questions. It will frequently be in the interests of some dominant individuals and groups *not* to have people become critical thinkers. Critical questioning is the last thing those in positions of power who are autocratically seeking to retain the status quo wish to see. This is true in all dimensions: for political leaders who wish to preserve an inequitable distribution of power in favor of a dominant class; for employers or labor union leaders who gain ego-aggrandizement from controlling the destinies of employees and union members; for teachers who wish to inculcate in learners some preconceived ideas about how the world works; for parents, spouses, or lovers who are trying to maintain an unchallenged hierarchy of power in family and other intimate relationships.

Trying to help others become critical thinkers is almost bound sooner or later to open us up to accusations of bias. One of the first adult educators in America, Lyman Bryson (1936), believed that in helping adults "to acquire a more alert attitude toward their already accepted and verbalized beliefs, and toward all new things offered to them" (p. 65), educators would eventually become criticized by political leaders and opinion formers. Educators and others trying to help people become more critically aware are wise to be open and honest about their biases from the outset. No educational effort is entirely free from the underlying values and assumptions of the facilitator. No educational activity can be free of, or untainted by, value biases. It is best to acknowledge this fact, to state these values and assumptions clearly from the beginning. In Eble's (1983, p. 32) words, "There is no way teachers can avoid declaring values short of denying their existence as people." Indeed, recognizing and discussing the legitimacy of these biases are themselves among the most important educational endeavors we can undertake. As Meyers (1986) points out, the creative tension involved when teachers' personal, subjective ideas are subjected to objective analysis can prompt a great deal of critical thought. When learners are asked to apply methods of objective analysis to teachers' personal biases and subjective opinions, "the tension between differing perceptions and modes of thinking produces the disequilibrium so valuable in challenging their present values and thought structures and helping them develop new modes of thinking" (p. 93). Far better for helpers and educators to declare these values, assumptions, and biases from the beginning and to make a critical examination of their validity a central part of the educational and helping activity.

Evidence of adults exercising critical thought is one of the chief things we look for when assessing the democratic health of a society. Encouraging the kind of debunking skepticism involved in critical thinking often brings people into conflict with established norms, laws, and institutions. Official definitions of social order, dominant values, and normative behavior are imposed and maintained by those in positions of power and authority. To question the legitimacy of such official definitions (for example, "It is the duty of a populace to fight war whenever the government decrees this") can be interpreted by those in authority as an intrinsically subversive activity. In fact, the opposite is true. At the heart of democratic processes, particularly in representative democracies such as the United States, there must be a willingness and an ability on the part of citizens to subject their elected representatives, the policies they enact, and the justifications they provide for those policies to a continuous critical scrutiny. In complex industrial societies, where the onset of the computer age has made possible governmental surveillance to an unprecedented extent, the power of elected representatives and security agencies can be held in check only by an informed populace watching their actions carefully. A freedom of information act through which security and surveillance agency activities can be scrutinized and publicly challenged is an institutionalized form of critical thinking in a democracy. The lack of such an act in Britain at the present time is a source of wonderment and puzzlement to Scandinavians and Americans.

In sociopolitical terms, thinking critically entails the habit and ability of asking awkward questions. Questions such as "Why are nearly all faculty at my college white, and nearly all the service staff black or Hispanic?" Questions such as "How can a government condemn other countries' shipments of arms to a nation as wrong, when we're doing the same thing secretly?" Questions such as "Why is a group of people challenging the government in one country labeled 'freedom fighters' while a group doing the same thing in another country is labeled 'terrorists' by our government?" Being critically alert also means being able to make connections between personal circumstances (such as the closing of a local health facility, a farm foreclosure, or the appearance of more street people in a town) and broader political happenings (cutting health services budgets, removing farm subsidies, or adopting community mental health policies and consequently reducing residential care for the mentally ill). It means being able to question the accuracy of politicians' justifications for what is just (such as requiring citizens to fight for a war a government has declared) and what is necessary (such as using millions of dollars to build a new defense system). It means questioning the validity of any claims for universal truth (such as "Build this weapons system and the world will be safe from war forever").

For the continued health of a democracy, helping adults become critical thinkers should be a fundamental concern of educators, trainers, community workers, social activists, counselors, therapists, and others in the helping professions. Only if adults' powers of critical analysis and reflection are nurtured will a truly responsive democracy flourish. In this regard, *not* to encourage the development of critical capacities is inherently antidemocratic. Far from critical thinking being some kind of cognitive guerrilla terrorism destructive of democracy, it is only through such thinking that citizens can hold their elected representatives publicly accountable for their actions. Without citizens who are in the habit of asking awkward questions, governments will be more likely to feel justified in keeping secret actions that they would prefer not to be public. Critical thinking does not imply a negative pessimism or disrespect for democratic processes; it only implies a disrespect for those who ignore such processes. Put simply, the spirit of critical thinking can be summed up as the realization that "not only is the world not what it appears to be, but it could be different from what it is" (Berger and Kellner, 1981, p. 6). A readiness to ask why things are the way they are, a capacity to speculate imaginatively on alternative possibilities, an inbuilt skepticism of the pronouncements and actions of those who are judged to be in positions of political and economic power—these are fundamental ways in which the processes of critical thinking, analysis, and reflection in adults can be recognized.

✌ *Part 2* ✌

Practical Approaches for Developing Critical Thinkers

Part One outlined the central components of critical thinking and discussed its personal, occupational, and social significance. In Part Two the focus of attention shifts to examining various methods, techniques, and approaches that can be used to develop critical thinkers. Chapter Five offers general guidelines for encouraging critical thinking in others. Chapters Six and Seven focus on the two central activities involved in critical thinking: helping people analyze and challenge the assumptions under which they, and others, are thinking and acting, and exploring and imagining alternatives to their current ways of thinking and acting. In both these chapters a range of specific techniques are presented that readers can apply to their own situations.

69

5

Effective Strategies for Facilitating Critical Thinking

How do we know that people are being helped to think critically? If we were to happen upon a group in which this activity was happening, what would we see? How would we judge whether or not it was being done well? What advice would we offer to someone who was trying to think critically but was running into difficulties? What rules might we offer to help those involved in this process?

In any group in which critical thinking was being developed, several things would be happening. The two central activities in which group members would be engaged would be those of identifying and challenging assumptions, and exploring alternative ways of thinking and acting. Diversity and divergence would be accepted, even encouraged, so that in problem-solving groups there would be no attempts to bring matters to some form of artificial resolution. Flexibility of format and direction would be welcomed. Risk taking and spontaneity would be valued. Facilitators would model openness and critical analysis. There would be no presumption that perfection is the chief characteristic of successful facilitation. And there would be skepticism of final answers. As Meyers (1986, p. 47) puts it, ''In the reflective classroom, both teacher and students will appreciate the fact that some problems may remain forever a mystery.''

71

The functions performed when we try to help someone think critically are multifarious. They may all be evident in a single encounter, conceivably within an episode of very short duration. They are not sequential or hierarchical; the complexity of human interactions is much too dense for simple models or for the applications of standarized sequences. Many of the activities will be performed concurrently; one can motivate, for example, while affirming an individual's self-worth. The following rules of thumb are offered to guide the practice of those helpers and educators who seek to help people think critically.

Affirm Critical Thinkers' Self-Worth

When we encourage critical thinking, it is important that we assure people—through our actions and our words—that we respect and value them for their own selves. We should take pains to ensure that challenging questions are not posed in ways that threaten the fundamental integrity of individuals. Thinking critically is intimidating to people who are not used to doing it, and they may easily come to feel that helpers who try to coax or nudge them into questioning familiar assumptions are somehow attacking them. If this happens, these people will remove themselves from the activity. If leaving is not an option (for example, when attendance at a critical thinking course or workshop is mandated by someone in authority), they will mentally disengage from what is happening. There is no point in helpers' asking critically insightful questions and practicing a devastating critique of generally accepted assumptions, if people are insulted or intimidated in the process. The worst thing a helper can do is to suggest, by a verbal response or some kind of body language (smirk, sigh, quizzically raised eyebrow) that someone's comment, writing, or other form of contribution falls pitifully short of some desired critical standard. We can certainly ask searching questions about why people think and behave in the ways they do, and this involves challenging their familiar and comfortable assumptions. But we must always keep in mind that people's egos are frequently invested in being seen as capable, competent, or sophisticated, and that a helper suggesting to someone that perhaps he or she is operating under false assumptions threatens this self-concept. There is an uneasy tightrope to be walked in developing critical thinking in others; we must balance between respecting their integrity, so that they do not resist our efforts, and ensuring that sufficiently hard and challenging questions are asked to prompt them to scrutinize habitual assumptions. This balancing act can be rehearsed through role plays and simulations, but it can be effectively developed only through actual practice. In particular, it requires helpers to examine their own activities critically and to be ready to learn from their mistakes.

Listen Attentively to Critical Thinkers

The necessity of listening sensitively to clients and learners is probably the most commonly identified skill of helpers. The ability to enter the patient's deeper phenomenological world is placed by Mahrer (1983) at the heart of his experiential psychotherapy, and practically every text on counseling or psychotherapeutic practice includes a chapter on listening skills. Taking on others' perspectives, and coming to understand things from their viewpoints, is the essence of attentive listening. Listening is not a passive activity; it requires a great deal of concentrated intellectual effort to be able to listen attentively to someone whose thought processes or modes of expression are idiosyncratic and hard to follow. Listening to verbal comments is actually only one of the ways in which we attend to someone's critical thought processes. Nonverbal gestures, pauses, hesitations, silences, and corrections can all be indicative of motivations, currents of thought, or unrecognized conflicts not apparent in an individual's spoken words. Likewise, the postures of members of a learning group, the amount and kind of laughter evident, and the facial gestures apparent when certain individuals are speaking contain all kinds of information about the group dynamics that are coming into play.

When developing critical thinkers, it is important that we attend closely to all these verbal and nonverbal behaviors. We need to do this in order that we may make informed judgments about when to do what—about, for example, when to encourage conflicts to come out in the open within a group, or when to quiet an overly domineering member. We need to listen carefully to people so that we know how to frame critical questions in terms that they understand. As with all interviewing, there is no point in asking questions that we might feel are dazzlingly insightful if they will only serve to confuse or intimidate others. We need to frame questions and develop exercises that draw on people's past experiences, that refer to familiar scenarios, case studies, and typical situations, and that use easily understandable language and concepts. Listening attentively also helps us to recognize when apparently incidental comments or innocuous remarks conceal powerful implicit assumptions. We can build on these as they happen, to help people realize the significance of these remarks.

Show That You Support Critical Thinkers' Efforts

People who are beginning to think critically frequently need support. This may involve patiently listening to people's accounts of their ongoing trials and tribulations. It is essential to provide people with a healthy measure of support in all stages of their attempt to become critical thinkers. Calling assumptions and givens into question can be highly intimidating, and friends, colleagues, clients, and learners who feel that their self-worth is threatened by our encouraging them to do this will be blocked in their efforts to think critically. In the process of helping people become critical thinkers, it is as important to know when to provide unqualified support as it is to know when to challenge. Meyers (1986, p. 15) puts it as follows: "Teaching students new thinking processes involves gauging very sensitively the amount of disequilibrium that will do the most good. Too much can overload students and be dysfunctional, while too little can result in warm, wonderful classes where no learning takes place. . . . One of the keys to teaching critical thinking successfully is to simultaneously challenge students' old modes of thinking and provide structure and support for the development of new ones." Helpers must do their best to create materials and use methods that allow people to *risk* failure without feeling that in doing so they have actually failed.

Reflect and Mirror Critical Thinkers' Ideas and Actions

One of the most useful tasks we can perform as we seek to develop critical thinking in other people is to reflect back to them their attitudes, rationalizations, and habitual ways of thinking and acting. In doing this, we function as a mirror, allowing individuals to view their own motivations, actions, and justifications as if they were those of others. This can be a powerful experience. Daloz (1986, p. 234) describes this function as follows: "One of the more important aspects of the special mirror that mentors hold up to their students is its capacity to extend the students' self-awareness. To see oneself in new ways, from a range of different vantage points, is the chief way we distill what we are learning from the challenges and supports of our world." It is tremendously difficult to take on the role of an external observer of our own thoughts and actions simply by an act of will. No matter how strongly we resolve to try to see ourselves as others see us, we are inevitably caught in our own well-worn frameworks of analysis and perception. No matter how deliberately we attempt to view ourselves "objectively," we cannot escape our habitual patterns of reasoning. Trapped in our taken-for-granted sets of assumptions, we become unable to interpret our actions as motivated by anything other than pure, objective reason.

Teachers, counselors, trainers, colleagues, and friends can greatly assist other people to perform these mental gymnastics. By conveying to learners, clients, trainees, colleagues, and friends how their behaviors look to us, we can help them become aware of the assumptions under which they are operating. This mirroring activity is central in helping-activities as diverse as marital therapy, cross-cultural training, and industrial mediation. In all these settings, people can be helped to realize that their actions—both mental and behavioral—are affected by context, and that they are frequently connected to their personal histories. Realizing how one's behavior is perceived by others is a crucial first stage in being able to unravel the complexities of conflicts and destructive misunderstandings.

Motivate People to Think Critically

Motivating people to think critically is fundamental and crucial. Another person, whether this be a spouse, lover, friend, colleague, teacher, trainer, counselor, or therapist, can provide the encouragement and psychological motivation for us to act upon ideas that we have considered only tentatively. Considered in isolation, such ideas may remain at a half-submerged, partially realized level. They may be dismissed as "daydreaming"—essentially irrational diversions that are purely in the realm of fantasy. Desires for changes in the basis on which relationships exist, for alterations in one's work situation, or for political reform will be repressed as naive or useless speculation if there appears to be no chance for their realization. An important task of anyone seeking to foster critical thinking is to nurture a sense that this realization might be possible.

We must be wary, however, of motivating people to think critically to the point where we are encouraging expectations that cannot possibly be met. Anyone seeking to promote critical thinking in others should, in my view, also be bound by an ethical imperative to point out to learners and clients the potential risks involved in various change efforts that might result from this critical scrutiny. McKenzie (1978) views one of the central tasks of educators as that of inculcating an awareness of the risks accompanying the activity of criticizing and challenging established values and practices. Along with this, he argues, must go the deliberate attempt to develop in learners a certain kind of cleverness. This cleverness is evident in people's ability to judge shrewdly when the risk taking arising out of critical analysis is most likely to produce the desired effects, and when it is going to result in disastrous consequences for the individuals concerned.

Consider the following examples. Advocating drastic action in personal relationships (such as confronting one's partner with a "listen or I'm leaving" ultimatum) can sometimes be dramatically successful. At other times the bluff can be called, and the consequence is either the end of the relationship or the humiliation of the person giving the ultimatum. At work, challenging superiors, questioning company norms, and proposing change in work organization or reward systems may be praised as examples of dynamic management or exemplary worker participation. Those actions may also lead to the loss of one's job. In the political arena, challenging conventional ideas can prompt action leading to significant change. It can also lead to the loss of one's life.

When teachers, counselors, trainers, and other helpers motivate people to think critically, they must also alert them to the potential risks involved. Suggesting that there is a simple leap between a desire to change the world and the realization of that desire is to ignore the complexities of life and in particular to dismiss the importance of context. Individuals may, of course, choose to ignore the risks pointed out to them and decide to gamble their emotional comfort, job security, or physical safety in efforts to change their world. However, helpers are ethically bound to do their best to ensure that people realize the range of potential consequences (beneficial and harmful) of the actions they take as a result of critical thinking. If this is done as fully and painstakingly as possible by the helpers concerned, they possess a valuable psychological ballast in the event of later accusations that their ''help'' led only to negative consequences for those concerned.

A final comment on this point. Identifying the risks involved in critical thinking, and assisting people to realize that the most effective ways of realizing their ideas, desires, and dreams will vary according to context, may be seen by some as a sign of faintheartedness. Advising that risks be taken carefully, after due consideration of the potentially harmful consequences involved, may be interpreted as an unnecessarily cautious conservatism, stifling the forces of personal and collective change. I used to believe this myself and I may, I suppose, be getting unduly cautious as I approach forty. Nonetheless, it is my firm conviction that we should be shrewd concerning the best times for acting upon our desires for change, and able to make some informed calculations about when, and how, these aspirations can be realized most successfully.

At times, drastic action and sacrificial martyrdom may be the only (or the quickest) ways to effect change. In situations of extreme personal and political oppression, negotiating change with those holding power may not be a realistic option. How can one negotiate with those who believe that one's skin color, accent, or physical appearance necessitates genocide? For those who do not live in a situation of constant threat to life, however, the diversity of strategies for change and the complexity of settings involved necessitate some forethought about the risks and possible consequences involved. A certain shrewdness and flexibility in adapting change strategies to the demands of a situation are important skills when trying to achieve change.

Regularly Evaluate Progress

Thinking critically is a dynamic and ongoing process, so that the dividing lines between problem identification, diagnosis, exploration, action, and reflection are frequently difficult to discern. An important facet of helping people to think critically is to provide an opportunity for them to undertake periods of reflective evaluation or stock taking. During these periods, people can review where their critical analysis has taken them, they can make some judgments about the effectiveness of different actions in changing some aspects of their lives, and they can try to learn from whatever errors they have made. In providing formative evaluation sessions such as these, we can assist significantly people's attempts to understand their critical thinking processes. Patterns of behavior become clear, habitual responses are identified, and insights dawn regarding the nature of our assumptions and motivations.

One of the most difficult tasks helpers face is convincing people of the worth of this kind of reflective evaluation. In an understandable impatience to act upon newly realized insights, people may be consumed by their enthusiasm and rush blindly into whatever changes they are trying to effect. This enthusiasm is essential and should not be dissipated by unnecessarily dampening counsel. Nonetheless, the value of reflective evaluation should be emphasized from the outset. It is crucial that people avoid seeing such evaluation as an annoying distraction or irrelevancy when compared to the "real" business at hand—taking action. Stock taking and reflective evaluation are a central part of critically informed action.

Help Critical Thinkers Create Networks

Successful learning is frequently located in a social network of some kind, and learning how to think critically is no exception. As studies of successful self-directed learners make plain (Brookfield, 1980; Thiel, 1984), people who are exploring some area of new knowledge or skill frequently do so deliberately and self-consciously within a network of fellow learners. These networks serve to motivate their members, to provide a sense of support and belonging, to offer evaluative indexes (novices frequently chart their progress by comparing themselves to experts), and to comprise valuable information resources. Those who see themselves as wholly independent of learning networks are rare, and they often wish for more involvement in a group of fellow enthusiasts or learners (Tough, 1979).

When we develop critical thinkers, helping them form resource networks with others who are involved in this activity may make a crucial difference. Because identifying and challenging assumptions, and exploring alternatives, involve elements of threat and risk taking, the peer support provided by a group of others also trying to do this is a powerful psychological ballast to critical thinking efforts. Where such a network does not already exist, one of the most important tasks of those trying to facilitate critical thinking is to encourage its development. For those who begin to think critically because they are experiencing traumatic personal transitions or life crises, involvement in self-help support groups may be literally a life saver (Lieberman, Borman, and Associates, 1979). Alcoholics Anonymous, single-parent support groups (such as the "Gingerbread" network in Britain), groups for the recently widowed or divorced, rape relief groups, victims' groups, unemployment support

groups, and a whole range of groups for those who have undergone psychiatric treatment as resident patients and who are now
living in the community are examples of these kinds of networks.

Be Critical Teachers

A number of educators have described the development
of critical thinking in learners as *critical teaching*. Shor (1980)
defines critical teaching as assisting people to become aware of
their taken-for-granted ideas about the world. Drawing on
Freire's (1970a, 1970b) work, he describes how liberating classrooms become separate zones for changing consciousness in
which learners are able to break free from habitual patterns of
thought to view their worlds in new ways. Shor (1980) writes
that "by identifying, abstracting and problematizing the most
important themes of student experience, the teacher detaches
students from their reality and then re-presents the material for
their systematic scrutiny" (p. 100). Teachers function sometimes
as catalysts of discussion and inquiry, sometimes as contributory
group members. They perform such diverse roles as being advocates for missing perspectives, adversaries to propaganda,
recorders of sessions, mediators of divisive tendencies, and resource persons. They focus on contextual skill development, so
that cognitive skills are acquired in the exploration of genuine
student experiences.

Gamson and Associates (1984) describe the process of
educating students for critical awareness as *liberating education*.
Their reinterpretation of the concept of liberal education focuses
on fostering creativity, student self-direction, and an openness
to a diversity of interpretations of any particular topic, area of
knowledge, or theory. Young (1980) and Stice (1987) collect
together case studies of attempts to foster critical thinking in
classrooms, and the institutional and methodological problems
raised by this (Svinicki and Kraemer, 1980). Meyers (1986),
Daloz (1986), and Stice (1987) evolve new concepts of the teacher
in which the challenging of students' uncritically accepted
assumptions becomes a major aim of education.

There are many points of connection between critical
teaching and various forms of therapy, counseling, and social

work. The emphasis on becoming aware of taken-for-granted assumptions informing behavior, the focusing on people's perceptions of their own experiences, the encouraging of group scrutiny of relevant issues, and the presentation of alternative interpretations of reality are aspects of therapeutic and counseling roles that would be familiar to most teachers of critical thinking. Aronowitz and Giroux (1985), for example, describe the activities of transformative and critical educators who call into question the beliefs and assumptions underlying individual behavior and social norms. Through analyzing curricula, texts, and assessment techniques for the extent to which they reproduce dominant cultural values, teachers are able to demonstrate the culturally constructed nature of knowledge and so-called truth. This "deconstruction" of curricula, textbooks, and modes of evaluation so that students become skeptical of divinely ordained moral and behavioral "givens" is central to the task of critical helping.

The characteristics of critical teachers have been specified by Freire (1986) as competence, courage, risk taking, humility, and political clarity. Competence in communicating clearly with people and in managing group activities democratically is needed to ensure that people understand that alternative interpretations of the world are possible and that participants have a chance to explore these fully. Courage is needed to withstand the resistance to challenging assumptions that teachers who try to nudge learners away from their uncritically accepted ways of looking at the world are bound to encounter. Courage is also needed in those times when teachers face condemnation and criticism of their efforts by outsiders, and when they have to combat attempts to prevent them from engaging in this activity.

Risk taking is at the heart of all creative and exciting teaching, implying as it does that teachers as well as learners are fully engaged in the educational transaction. A willingness to risk experimentation in one's teaching is an important aspect of modeling change and promoting critical openness in learners. Humility is essential to teachers, lest they slip into the all-too-seductive (but appallingly arrogant) role of omniscient guru of critical thinking. Political clarity is a more controversial concept. What is politically self-evident to one person (for example, that human beings are patently unequal in their intellectual and physical attributes and should therefore be rewarded unequally) is heresy to another. To Freire, political clarity is the ability to break free from distorting perspectives imposed by oppressive groups so that we can see the inequitable and hierarchical relationships in society clearly and fully.

In his analysis of critical teaching, Meyers (1986) regards the chief component of this activity as building on learners' past experiences and existing mental structures to lead them from concrete operations to more abstract, reflective ways of thinking. He argues that "whenever teachers build bridges between concrete, everyday ideas and more abstract, academic concepts, they are fostering critical thinking" (p. 77). This involves "not so much communicating facts and information as teaching perspectives for analyzing and making sense of information" (p. 52). Critical teaching is helping learners to acquire new perceptual frameworks and structures of understanding. Meyers has several suggestions about how critical thinking can be fostered in formal classrooms. He suggests that teachers begin each class with a problem or controversy; that "creative silence"—periods of reflection during which learners and teachers can quietly ponder new perspectives—be encouraged; that traditional seating structures be replaced by small-group circles; that class sessions be two or three hours rather than fifty or sixty minutes; and that learners be given frequent opportunities to voice any of the anxieties, misgivings, and ambiguities they are feeling. What Meyers calls the *reflective classroom* is similar to the *connected classroom* identified by Belenky, Clinchy, Goldberger, and Tarule (1986, p. 221), in which the development of thinking is undertaken in small groups that accept that the process will be tentative, evolving, and uncertain.

Make People Aware of How They Learn Critical Thinking

Helping adults to understand their personal styles and patterns of learning is one of the most important, though least immediately tangible, ways in which people can be helped to become critical thinkers. The ability to reflect consciously on one's style of learning, and to become familiar with how this might be adapted or broadened to fit changed circumstances, is a crucial element in coming to know one's critical thinking habits. In recent years, there has been an upsurge of interest in the areas of mathetics, learning how to learn (Smith 1982, 1983), and metalearning. The concern of these three related areas is essentially the same. Theorists in all three fields feel that it is important for learners to become aware of various aspects of their personal learning styles—that is, "the characteristic and preferred way in which an adult engages in learning activities" (Knox, 1986, p. 20).

Certain questions can be asked of all learners involved in critical thinking activities. How do they develop and maintain the motivation for various learning adventures? To what extent are extrinsic motives (social contact, job advancement) and intrinsic motives (innate fascination with learning, being tantalized by problem solving) interrelated? How do they integrate the new ideas and insights generated by critical thinking into their existing analytical and interpretative frameworks? What general approaches do adults take toward exploring new areas of knowledge? Do they use trial-and-error methods, problem solving, or careful planning of short-, intermediate-, and long-term goals? Do they seem to be field-dependent (strongly dependent on cues and directions provided by others, needing social supports to maintain their motivation) or field-independent (designing their own individual learning plans, preferring to work without the company of others) in their learning activities? To what extent do previous experiences act as hindrances or stimuli to their development of critical thinking? In what ways do people feel most comfortable entering the new and potentially frightening intellectual terrain represented by critical thinking?

Finding answers to such questions is not merely an intellectually tantalizing exercise; it is also a means by which people can be helped to become aware of idiosyncratic tendencies, preferences, biases, habits, blockages, and aptitudes in their personal learning styles. Teachers, counselors, trainers, therapists, and others who help people to come to know their habitual learning styles are assisting them to exercise greater control in their learning. When we are aware of our typical learning styles, we can select from a number of strategies those that we know will be most effective. We can make more informed choices regarding mentors and teachers whose personal and pedagogic styles (for example, field-dependent or -independent) match our own. We can anticipate and adjust for the fright, pain, anxiety, or distress we know we will experience as we begin to think critically.

A number of sophisticated assessment tools and measurement scales exist for the use of educators who wish to investigate learning styles. Examples of these are the Myers-Briggs Type Indicator (Myers and Myers, 1980), the Kolb (1980) Adaptive Style Inventory, and the Self-Directed Learning Readiness Scale (Guglielmino, 1977). A simpler way to become aware of people's learning styles is to ask them to answer a number of very brief questions about a learning project they have undertaken. A learning project is any deliberate effort to acquire certain skills, knowledge, or insight (Tough, 1979). Projects can be as simple as learning how to operate a new appliance, or as complex as learning how to negotiate change within intimate relationships. If the concept of a learning project confuses people, simply ask them to think of what they know now (in other words, what insights or knowledge they have acquired) or what they can do now (in other words, what skills they have acquired) that they did not know or have six months ago.

Once people have a particular learning project in mind, we might ask how they set learning goals. Did they generate short-, medium-, and long-range goals, or did they follow their instincts and intuitions, deciding what was to be done next as they went along? We might ask what resources were used. Did they consult people (experts, friends, intimates, or other learners), or did they rely chiefly on nonhuman resources (books, cassettes, video tapes)? What learning strategies did they use? Did they follow a carefully planned sequence of progressively complex activities, did they use trial-and-error methods, or did they experiment with different approaches? We should also know something about how they charted their progress. Did they use objective measures to gauge success (such as a standardized chart, or comparison with experts), or was this measuring subjective (such as experiencing a developing feeling of self-confidence)? Finally, what about their experience of learning? What were the chief difficulties they encountered? What was most enjoyable about their learning activities?

Being aware of our learning styles means we can emphasize those areas in which we need to develop certain capacities; if we are extremely linear in our learning and stick rigidly to predefined goals and resources, we may benefit from trying out various lateral thinking prompts, or from deliberately placing ourselves in positions that require us to react quickly and spontaneously to unforeseen circumstances. If we deceive ourselves into thinking we are gestalt learners who need to wait until "the time is right," or for that fateful flash of inspiration to strike, we may benefit from practice in imposing a greater degree of structure on our apparently unpredictable, spontaneous learning style. Becoming aware of our learning styles, and learning how to adjust for weaknesses and emphasize strengths, is not a pedagogic exercise of interest only to academics. It is a fundamentally liberating way by which we can free ourselves of tendencies and inclinations that act to prevent us from becoming critical thinkers.

Model Critical Thinking

Observing role models to help us imagine, define, and practice the kinds of behaviors we would like to exhibit in our own lives is one of the most common means by which we learn. In terms of developing critical thinking, Meyers (1986, p. 47) observes that "by modeling reflective thought in lectures and discussion, teachers can do much to encourage this frame of mind in their students." People who are perceived as good role models by those who have fallen within their influence appear to exhibit certain features. In accounts of modeling within adult development (Levinson, 1978), psychotherapy (Rogers, 1980), adult education (Merriam, 1984; Daloz, 1986), and the business world (Roche, 1979), a cluster of typical characteristics of effecive modelers emerges. Although these people are sometimes described as mentors or facilitators, the qualities they are perceived as exhibiting are precisely those of effective modelers. Good modelers exhibit the following characteristics:

Clarity. Good modelers act in ways that are perceived clearly by observers. Put another way, if people were asked what made a certain person a good model, they would find it relatively easy to specify certain behaviors and personal qualities.

Consistency. Good modelers act in consistent ways. They do not change their behavior or responses to similar situations in ways that appear unjustified, irrational, or capricious. This is not to say that they do not act differently according to contextual factors; however, when they respond in markedly different ways to what observers perceive as essentially similar situations, they are ready and able to justify and explain the reasons for these different responses.

Openness. Good modelers are perceived as honest and as respecting the integrity of those with whom they deal. They are willing to account for their actions, to admit to frustrations and anxieties as well as to successes and pleasures, and to admit to dilemmas and ambiguities they are facing. This quality is essentially what Rogers (1980, p. 271) calls "realness" in facilitators. Daloz (1986, p. 220) writes of the need for the mentor "to reveal himself as human, not god" as a way of speeding the breakdown, in the minds of protégés, of the image of the mentor as an ideal authority. Beidler (1986, p. 78) believes that "being a model of intellectual and personal honesty will save you from the expectation that you need to know everything and will save students from shirking the responsibility of their own learning."

Good modelers are ready to talk publicly about why they act the way they do. Because they are perceived as genuinely open, their actions have an authenticity and integrity in the minds of observers. In describing the role of the modeler in action science experiments, Argyris, Putnam, and Smith (1985, pp. 331–332) write that a good model is "vulnerable in the optimal sense of the word, consistently communicating to participants, 'This is my view. I think it's right but I might be wrong, so let's take a look at it.'" Good modelers embrace risks by inviting criticism of their views. The need for role models of fallible and imperfect thinkers is identified by Belenky, Clinchy, Goldberger, and Tarule (1986, p. 217) as especially important for women in higher education.

Communicativeness. Good modelers are able to explain the reasons for their actions in terms that are understood clearly by observers. They are able to use illustrative examples, metaphors, and analogies in discussing what they hope to achieve by acting in certain ways. They are able to take a general activity such as "being open with clients/learners" and, when asked to explain how they accomplish this, break it down into its component elements (for example, encouraging criticism, responding fully to difficult questions, admitting to doubts and anxieties, altering decisions as a result of suggestions made by learners and clients). Argyris, Putnam, and Smith (1985) write of the necessity for people to make their reasoning public if they are to become critically reflective. Specifically, they advise "bringing one's views to the surface, while recognizing and trying to make explicit the inferential steps that led to them" (p. 297). They urge that participants reflect publicly on their reactions to other people's ideas and suggestions rather than keep these private.

Specificity. Good modelers exhibit external, specific behaviors that allow for interpretative imitation (not slavish replication) by observers. Observers can perceive particular actions, responses, and behaviors that they can try out, in appropriately adapted ways, in their own contexts. For example, people who model openness and honesty effectively are people who encourage critical scrutiny of their actions, who respond to questions about the reasons for their actions as fully and openly as they are able, and who are perceived as being willing to change their ways of behaving as a result of external criticism. Hence, if observers were asked why a teacher or therapist was a good role model of openness and honesty, they would be able to reply in ways such as, "Because she actively encourages criticism of her actions," "Because she does not 'duck' difficult questions about the reasons why she does what she does," or "Because she is willing to change her rules, requirements, and behaviors as a result of our suggestions."

Accessibility. Good modelers are seen as accessible by observers. They do not threaten or intimidate potential imitators by presenting visions of themselves as people whose abilities are so far beyond the reach of mere mortals that any attempts at imitation are doomed to failure. They are open to inquiries concerning their activities and are regarded by observers as moral equals, if not equals in terms of their possessing specific abilities.

Conclusion

This chapter has provided a number of general rules of thumb, techniques, and concepts for the practice of those involved in helping people to become critical thinkers. It is important to emphasize, however, that all these rules, models of critical teaching, and tools of learning analysis are contextually variable. None of them can be easily standardized, and they are all substantially affected by context. What is clear is that encouraging critical thinking is an activity as complex as the process of critical thinking itself. It requires teachers, trainers, counselors, and helpers who possess an unusual combination of qualities. They need to be self-confident in their ability to withstand criticism and disagreement and to be able to communicate that affirming people's sense of dignity and self-worth underlies all critical thinking efforts. They need to be skilled in a number of systematic instructional methods, but skeptical enough of the value of these to be able to abandon them when it seems appropriate. They need to have a general aim in mind, and a partly developed notion of how this is to be achieved, yet they also need to be open to changing both aim and methods according to participants' personalities, abilities, and past experiences. In short, they need a broad repertoire of pedagogic, modeling, and interpersonal skills.

❦ 6 ❧

Helping Others Examine the Assumptions Underlying Their Thoughts and Actions

Identifying and challenging the assumptions by which we live is central to thinking critically. It is also difficult and complex. Admitting that these assumptions might be distorted, wrong, or contextually relative is often profoundly threatening, for it implies that the fabric of our personal existence might rest upon faulty foundations. If our past lives have been lived on the basis of faulty assumptions, does that not mean that we have to jettison our current relationships, work, and political commitments in favor of some more authentic ways of living, whatever these might be? This possibility is perceived by most people when they are asked to examine the assumptions by which they have made major decisions in their personal lives. It is one reason why this critical thinking activity is frequently so strongly resisted. Another is the difficulty of performing the mental gymnastics entailed in identifying and challenging assumptions. Because of their ingrained, internalized nature they are almost *too* obvious. They are self-evident truths and, as such, we may not be able to see the forest of these assumptions for the trees of our common sense.

Identifying and considering critically the assumptions underlying our most comfortable ways of thinking and acting involve difficult and frequently unnerving activities. Becoming aware of assumptions that are so internalized that they are perceived as second nature or common sense is problematic precisely because of the familiarity of these ideas. Assumptions on, for example, what work we are naturally suited for, how the political world works, or why people behave the way they do in relationships are etched into our structures of understanding. They are pivotal elements in the perceptual filters that mediate our interpretations of reality. As Meyers (1986, p. 96) writes, "If our thought structures are the ways in which we organize our perceptions to make sense of the world, it seems natural that we would have a strong vested interest in maintaining those structures."

If becoming aware of these assumptions is difficult, challenging their validity is doubly disturbing, for in doing this we call into question beliefs and rules that have governed much of our lives. Wlodkowski (1985, p. 132) observes that "the essence of a challenge is risk and the possibility of failure. . . . To ask a learner to take a risk is to ask that person to make a deliberate personal encounter with the unknown." To challenge an assumption that until now has been accepted uncritically and unconditionally is to take a risk. Yet this very challenging of assumptions is at the heart of critical teaching. As Meyers (1986) points out, this can be a highly emotional and discomforting process; people are asked to look critically at cherished values and personal beliefs that are bound up with their self-concept. Teaching critical thinking is thus inherently disruptive and "involves intentionally creating an atmosphere of disequilibrium, so that students can change, rework, or reconstruct their thinking processes" (p. 14).

Challenge is central to helping people think critically. As Egan (1986) sees it, challenge is the last stage necessary before clients can develop alternative visions and scenarios. To Daloz (1986), a major function of good mentors is to challenge protégés: "The mentor may assign mysterious tasks, introduce contradictory ideas, question tacit assumptions, or even risk damage to the relationship by refusing to answer questions" (p. 213). Meyers (1986, p. 93) writes of "the disequilibrium so valuable in challenging [learners'] present values and thought structures and helping them develop new modes of thinking'' produced by teachers introducing alternative perceptions. Carkhuff and Berenson (1977, p. 198) believe that ''confrontation based upon deep levels of understanding results in a more full and immediate exchange between the parties involved.'' Challenge prompts self-scrutiny, consideration of alternatives, and the taking of action. It is not the same as abuse or denigration; it is not a license to insult someone or to behave in an unnecessarily autocratic fashion. Neither is it a convenient excuse for attacking another's self-esteem. The ability to challenge without intimidating, without threatening to the point at which someone will simply refuse to listen further, is one of the most difficult skills for helpers to develop.

Furthermore, the right to challenge someone must be earned. People will come to develop trust in the person challenging them only after observing that, over a reasonably long period, that person's behaviors match his or her words. It is no good, for example, for trainers or educators to declare that their courses will be collaborative and democratic and then proceed to set the curricular agenda for the course. I have attended seminars in which the leader spent the whole time lecturing to us about the value of discussion approaches, without any awareness of the irony of this theory-practice contradiction. As a facilitator of adult learning, it is inconsistent and destructive of trust for me to say I believe in self-directed learning and then to insist that learners follow my specific instructions. When helpers' actions contradict their declared beliefs and intentions, they have effectively forfeited their right to challenge.

Recognizing that personal givens and public truths are contextually variable assumptions (and that they might therefore be distorted or faulty) is hard to do on our own. If we are comfortable with our existence, it requires an almost Herculean act of will to start thinking critically about the assumptions governing our lives. We are imprisoned in our own histories and constrained by the inevitably narrow paradigms of thought and action we inhabit. Sometimes it appears as if the only way we can jerk ourselves out of these comfortably familiar paradigms is through our being confronted with tragedy or major unanticipated change. It may often take a major life crisis or trauma (divorce, unemployment, disability, war, fatal illness, bankruptcy) to prompt this critical scrutiny. Yet educators and helping professionals can often provide the stimulus and assistance necessary for clients and learners to identify and evaluate the validity of their assumptions *without* their having to experience major personal or occupational crises. Daloz (1986, p. 223) identifies as one of the crucial functions performed by helpers their ability to "toss little bits of disturbing information in their students' paths, little facts and observations, theories and interpretations—cow plops on the road to truth—that raise questions about their students' current world views and invite them to entertain alternatives, to close the dissonance, accommodate their structures, *think* afresh." To Daloz, an important aspect of being a good helper is knowing "when a good dose of confusion is exactly what a student may need" (p. 224), knowing when to introduce conflict into an otherwise placid or complacent learning group. He writes that "an appropriate dose of conflicting or counterintuitive information can raise questions about the student's givens" (p. 126).

In this chapter, I look at a number of techniques that can be used to help ourselves and others identify and challenge the assumptions by which we live. These techniques are critical questioning, critical incident exercises, criteria analysis, various forms of role play (including role reversal and critical debate), and crisis-decision simulations. Sometimes we can employ these techniques ourselves, as a way of discovering who we are. Sometimes helpers (some of whom will be friends or family members rather than recognized professionals) may use them to encourage us to engage in self-scrutiny. At other times, as with Schein's (1985) use of critical questioning and critical incident exercises to uncover organizational assumptions, combinations of these techniques can be used as formal procedures for probing institutional or societal givens.

Critical Questioning

Skilled critical questioning is one of the most effective means through which ingrained assumptions can be externalized.

It is a technique, long practiced in psychotherapy, in which clients are encouraged to become their own questioners and to develop habits of critical reflection independent of the therapist. Questioning can be used with individuals and with groups, and it has a long history of application in the qualitative (Van Maanen, 1983) and ethnographic (Dobbert, 1982) research traditions. As the central element in interviewing, techniques of questioning have been documented in many sources (Spradley, 1979; Patton, 1980; Guba and Lincoln, 1981; Taylor and Bogdan, 1984).

Critical questioning—that is, questioning designed to elicit the assumptions underlying our thoughts and actions—is a specific form of questioning. It is concerned not so much with eliciting information as with prompting reflective analysis. It requires a greater degree of sophistication, ingenuity, and training on the part of the questioner than is involved in, say, market research. Critical questioners must be able to frame insightful questions that are readily understood by subjects. They must be able to explore what are often highly personal matters in a sensitive way. They must be able to ask what might usually be considered highly intimidating questions in a nonthreatening manner. Very few people possess this mix of abilities naturally. To become a good critical questioner one needs a period of training in which basic skills are acquired, followed by a substantial period of experience during which these skills are honed and refined.

Some general guidelines should be borne in mind when helpers undertake critical questioning designed to elicit and explore fundamental assumptions.

Be Specific. Relate questions to particular events, situations, people, and actions. Do not ask general questions such as, "What do you think are the assumptions underlying your relationship?" "What is your philosophy as a helping professional?" or "What principles should lie behind the distribution of wealth in our society?" Such questions will be met with (at best) puzzlement or (at worst) distrust. One cannot expect people to provide quick and ready answers to such abstract questions, particularly if they are not used to thinking on a conceptual level. The vocabulary and apparent sophistication evident in such questions might be perceived as highly intimidating. The last thing one wishes to do at the start of an encounter designed to elicit people's assumptions is to threaten them with terminological unfamiliarity, or with the expectation that highly sophisticated conceptual thought is required. Subjects are likely to "freeze" or to provide habitual, conventional responses prompted by the need to say something—anything—to avoid being seen as foolish or uninformed.

Where critical questioning is concerned, it is better by far to concentrate on easily identifiable specific events. For example, if one is trying to elicit the assumptions underlying a relationship, one might ask the following: "Think back over the last month in your relationship and tell me about an event or situation that made you say to yourself, 'This relationship is really working as it should.'" Regarding the assumptions underlying a trainer's conception of good practice as a human resource developer, one might say, "Think back over the past few weeks. Was there an event or situation in which you felt you did a good job, when you felt a 'high' because of your success with a training activity? Tell me about it."

In answering these questions, subjects will typically describe particular happenings. In many cases the assumptions that are sought will come through clearly. If a person answers that a relationship was working well when one partner sacrificed personal concerns for the other's well-being, and gives an instance of this, that is a very revealing response. Equally revealing would be an answer in which the open acknowledgment and discussion of differences between the partners were identified as the best recent event in the relationship. If a trainer says that she experiences a feeling of deep satisfaction whenever she accomplishes exactly what her employer wishes, this says something significant about the assumptions underlying her conception of good practice. Similarly, a response identifying as professional success a client's refusal to follow the therapist's instructions, or a learner's departing from the established syllabus for a course, would say something significant about the assumptions of the practitioner involved.

There are other ways of asking questions designed to elicit assumptions about specific events or particular people. For example, one might ask people to describe the accomplishment they are most proud of in some particular sphere of action. Another approach is to ask people to choose a typical situation in which they are engaged (for example, teaching a class or counseling a client) and then describe to you how they would know whether they had done well. In relating successful accomplishments and achievements in which they take pride, people can be very revealing with regard to their general assumptions of what they conceive to be good practice in their field. For example, talking proudly of a recent class in which participants engaged in heated debate, and in which conflicting viewpoints were forcefully articulated, says a great deal about the assumptions underlying a teacher's ideas about the proper purposes and form of education.

Another useful approach is to ask people to imagine that they are required to judge the performance or abilities of someone who is to take over their role or function. One might say, "Imagine that you are leaving your job and have been appointed to the search committee to look for your replacement. What would you tell the other members of the committee were the most important qualities they should look for in your replacement?" In identifying the qualities needed for someone to be a successful mother, therapist, or educator, the person concerned will reveal much about the assumptions underlying her own thoughts and actions. For example, therapists stressing qualities of empathy, caring, sensitivity to feelings, and group-process skills as those necessary for someone to take over their roles are clearly revealed to be operating under a certain set of assumptions. On the other hand, those who stress skill in applying principles of conditioning and reinforcement, or the possession of a certain body of theoretical knowledge, are influenced by a very different set of ideas. Community activists who urge a search committee to look for someone with strong experience in organizing civil disobedience campaigns are operating under assumptions very different from those who urge that someone with good contacts in City Hall be appointed.

Work from the Particular to the General. This guideline follows naturally from the injunction to be specific in your questioning. In their provision of particular descriptions, explanations, and opinions, people will frequently address general themes, almost without meaning to do this. Grounding the exploration of a general theme within the context of a specific activity or occurrence helps people to feel that they are in familiar territory. People are generally much more comfortable with questions regarding the details of individual incidents than they are answering generalized, abstract questions. A skilled interviewer is able to realize when general themes are being addressed within the context of specific descriptions and will encourage discussion of the particular as a way of exploring the general.

Be Conversational. Many interviews are stymied by the interviewer giving the impression that a certain protocol or code of formality is required. Even the use of the term *interview* itself is somewhat intimidating, since it raises in people's minds specters of television interrogations such as those Robin Day (in Britain) or Mike Wallace (in the United States) might conduct. Keeping the exchange conversational, avoiding the use of academic jargon (such as *critical reflection*), and allowing one's own enthusiasms, anxieties, and experiences to be voiced are all ways in which an informal, nonthreatening tone can be established by the questioner. People are going to be very reluctant to talk about fundamental assumptions governing their lives to a person who appears to be following some standard, formal interview protocol. In particular, they will be unlikely to reveal themselves to someone who is unwilling to express something of his or her own personality in the encounter. A relaxed, conversational style, therefore, is essential if people are to feel comfortable talking about concerns that have great personal significance.

After several decades of talking to British manual workers, Zweig (1965, p. 265) concluded that good interviewers "make the interview an enjoyable social act, both for the interviewer and the respondent, a two-way traffic, so that the respondent feels not a 'victim' but a true partner, a true conversationalist." Good interviews are organic conversations in the sense that themes discussed in later parts of the interview develop out of, and are related back to, earlier elements of the conversation. The interview develops according to the internal logic of participants' exchanges and concerns rather than rigidly following some script of previously devised questions. It is inductive, because general themes related to the assumptions under analysis are identified in response to questions concerning specific events, situations, and people. The interview becomes an organic whole rather than a staccato interrogation session.

Critical Incident Exercises

Critical incident exercises have been used for over thirty years in the social sciences and education, ever since Flanagan's (1954) initial formulation of the technique. Briefly stated, the critical incident technique prompts respondents to identify an incident (*event* is a term preferred by some) that for some reason was of particular significance to them. The researcher provides a set of instructions on what kind of incident is to be identified, and respondents are then asked to write a one-, or at most two-, paragraph statement describing the incident. These statements are to be written as specifically as possible, with particular details provided as requested. The advantage of critical incident exercises in eliciting respondents' assumptions is that, as in critical questioning, the emphasis is on specific situations, events, and people. Instead of being asked to write about abstract concepts, respondents concentrate on describing particular happenings. These are, generally speaking, much easier to report on than are broad judgments or underlying assumptions. Some examples of how I have written and administered critical incident instructions to probe people's underlying assumptions are given below.

To Identify Workers' Concerns

Think back over the last six months and identify an incident at work that you remember as causing you the greatest discomfort, pressure, or difficulty. Write down, in no more than half a page, a brief description of the incident. Make sure you give the following details about the incident: (1) when and where it occurred, (2) who was involved (roles and job titles rather than personal identities may be given here), and (3) what it was about the incident that was so significant as to cause a problem.

Having collected the written responses to these instructions, a trainer or human resource developer would have a record of the concerns and feelings of workers regarding their anxieties and major difficulties. The advantage of this approach is that a collection of specific events is described. Whereas a general request that workers voice their problems might have led to vague rumblings of frustration, their critical incident paragraphs provide the trainer with exact descriptions of typical difficulties. Based on this collection of real-life descriptions, it becomes much easier to design meaningful training programs grounded in the actual experiences, needs, and concerns of participants.

An additional advantage of the critical incident technique is that the information can be obtained privately rather than by asking workers to define their problems in front of their colleagues. Direct questions, particularly if they require respondents to admit to difficulties, problems, and anxieties, are often difficult to answer publicly. Those people who have their egos invested in being perceived as effective workers are hardly likely to admit to experiences that demonstrate their inability to perform well in a particular situation. By providing anonymous written accounts of their typical difficulties, however, they are spared the danger of public embarrassment. By using a critical incident exercise in cases such as this, human resource developers are much more likely to obtain a collection of brief but revealing private records of the concerns of their workers.

To Discover Why Workers Persist in "Marginal" Occupations

Think back over the last four weeks in your work. Identify the event that gave you the greatest personal satisfaction, an event that made you feel you had done a good job. Write down, in no more than half a page, a brief description of the incident. Make sure you give the following details about the incident: (1) where and when it occurred, (2) who was involved (roles and job titles rather than personal identities may be given here), and (3) what particularly satisfying aspects of the incident gave you such pleasure.

The responses provided in paragraphs following the above instructions would help explain why workers in low-status, poorly paid marginal occupations (for example, nurses in the public sector, residential workers with the mentally handicapped) stay in their jobs when they could be earning more money elsewhere. Asking a general question about reasons for staying in the job would probably prompt generalizations focusing on "job satisfaction" or "following a vocation." The critical incident paragraphs will provide much more exact information on the particular kinds of fulfillment experienced by workers in these occupations.

Critical incident exercises can be used in two chief ways: at the outset of an encounter or at its end. At the outset, they are useful in suggesting fruitful areas for more focused exploration. The critical incident paragraphs provide us with hunches as to what are the most significant concerns and assumptions of respondents. Moreover, these concerns and assumptions are framed within directly observable happenings rather than in vague generalizations. At the end of an encounter, critical incident exercises can be administered as a form of validity check. The significant events described by clients or learners in their written accounts can be compared to their general feelings and opinions as voiced in an interview. If the critical incident responses and interview opinions are congruent, it is fairly certain that an accurate record of the subject's perceptions has been obtained. If the two data sources are divergent, this very discrepancy indicates fruitful avenues of inquiry that might be explored in further interviews.

To Understand Workers' Conceptions of Good Practice

Think back over the last six months in your work. Identify an event in which you thought a colleague behaved particularly badly or "unprofessionally." Write down, in no more than half a page, a brief description of the incident. Make sure you include the following details about the incident: (1) when and where it occurred, (2) who was involved (roles and job titles rather than personal identities may be given here), and (3) what struck you as so unprofessional about your colleague's actions.

The advantage of this approach is that subjects are really talking about themselves, without being consciously aware of this. When they criticize another's actions as unprofessional, they are saying something about their *own* conceptions of good practice. Yet they are not being asked directly to articulate the ideas or rationales that underlie their own conceptions of professionalism. This may well remove much of the pressure they would otherwise feel if asked to talk about their own professional lives. When I have tried this exercise with groups, participants regularly cite examples of unprofessional behavior that surprise them. In my own case, my greatest professional annoyance is when colleagues change the rules governing an encounter in midstream. Yet according to my own philosophy of education, I am supposed to endorse change and risk taking and to encourage flexibility. It is interesting to reflect that our choice of examples of unprofessional behavior in others really says something about our own ideas and priorities.

Criteria Analysis

Criteria are value-based judgments that we consult for our estimations of worth and merit. They are benchmark standards against which we estimate our successes and failures. Although sometimes masquerading as objective, criteria are inevitably subjective; they reflect the norms, values, and preferences of those devising them. They are also implicitly or explicitly prescriptive—that is, those subscribing to them generally believe that activities that meet their requirements are worthwhile endeavors. Criteria analysis is an excellent tool for organizational or group communication and team-building workshops in which the purpose is to make explicit the assumptions underlying people's actions within the group or organization. Once people externalize the range of assumptions informing the actions of different group members, they can begin to agree on those that should be commonly shared.

Criteria analysis, like critical questioning and critical incident exercises, focuses on specifics rather than generalities—in this case the specific criteria underlying judgments about particular activities or events. The technique of criteria analysis requires those involved to make explicit the standards and judgments they employ when determining that an activity is successful or good. Central to this technique is identifying indicators by which the satisfaction of these criteria can be recognized—observable behaviors, actions, or situations through which the satisfaction of criteria can be seen. Without providing indicators, it is all too easy to mouth platitudinous clichés that masquerade as criteria. For example, one might say that a good relationship is one characterized by mutual respect, or that a successful helping relationship is one in which clients or learners exercise increasing independence. These are warmly comforting sentiments to which most people would subscribe, but they tell us little about the specific activities, beliefs, and practices of the people involved. Asking for indicators, however, requires people to point to particular behaviors, actions, or instances. They cannot hide behind clichés. For example, participants might cite as indicators of mutual respect in a professional relationship their rotating unpleasant but necessary tasks and obligations, or they could point to their discussion and negotiation of key decisions. In helping relationships, increasing client or learner independence might be observed in a readiness to challenge "expert" advice, a willingness to depart from pre-established rules, or a decrease in requests for advice or consultations.

These indicators meet the twin necessary conditions of indicators: they are directly observable, and they are unambiguous. One might, of course, quarrel with their validity and challenge their accuracy. For example, participants in a relationship could appear to be negotiating a key decision in an open, respectful way, when to a skilled observer the subtleties and nuances of their interactions make it obvious that the decision has already been made in a manner reflecting an existing (though possibly unacknowledged) power imbalance. The accuracy of indicators is certainly open to dispute, and they may well become more specific and particular as we come to know more of the activity under review. The point is, however, that in offering indicators people are forced to place general and perhaps vague criteria in specific personal, professional, and societal contexts.

In my own work with educators, trainers, and counselors of adults, I have used the technique of criteria analysis to help these practitioners identify and analyze the validity of assumptions influencing their practice. This can be done verbally or in written form, depending on the context. The approach, however, is essentially the same; those undertaking this analysis are asked to respond to the following questions:

> Think back over your professional life and choose the most successful educational experience in which you were involved, either as teacher or learner. Why do you consider it successful? What features of the experience can you point to that were present at that time and that have *not* been present in other educational situations in which you have been involved?

> Imagine that you are a consultant employed to evaluate a program similar to the one in which you currently work. What features would you be looking for as evidence that the program you are evaluating is working well?

> Imagine that you have been successful in your application for an unlimited government grant to organize the best example of an educational program in your field of practice. What methods and curricula would you use to put this program in place, and how would you know that you had been successful in achieving your goal?

> Imagine that practitioners in your field have recently been accused of various kinds of malpractice or professional negligence. You have been given the task of heading a commission of inquiry to establish a code of conduct to govern their activities. What would be the three most important indicators you would choose as evidence that someone was performing professionally?

Imagine that you have been made head of the program in which you are currently working. Draft a one-paragraph mission statement that summarizes what you regard as the most important goals of the program. What evidence would you plan to look for to satisfy you that your mission statement was being implemented?

These differing approaches could be adapted to varying occupational and personal situations. Their overall intent, however, is the same—that is, to encourage people to be explicit about the values and assumptions underlying their judgments of good practice. The success of the technique depends on the extent to which people are able to specify the directly observable features and characteristics of the indicators they offer. Insisting on this means that it is much harder for them to mouth reassuring banalities and call them criteria.

Another criteria analysis exercise that I use builds on the principles of critical questioning already discussed. In a workshop, I pair participants and ask one member to be the interviewer and the other to be the interviewee. I give the interviewer the following instructions:

Your task is to find out what criteria your subject applies to determining whether or not she has done a good job—in other words, to find out how she decides that her efforts are worthwhile and that something valuable is happening. Do not be too direct or explicit in your questioning. For example, do not ask her straight out what criteria she applies. Try to be specific in your questions, so that your subject is asked about particular events, situations, and people.

Some possible questions you might use are the following: When was the last time you felt really good about a work experience in which you were involved? Tell me about it. Whom do you admire most among your colleagues? What is it about their activities that you find so admirable? What activities that your colleagues are involved in excite your imagination? Tell me about them.

As you ask these (and other) questions, be as informal, relaxed, and conversational as possible. Encourage your partner's spontaneous, unprompted comments and try to relate your questions and comments back to your partner's previous remarks.

Spend five minutes preparing yourself mentally for the interview, ten minutes conducting the interview, and five minutes explaining to your partner the purpose behind your questions. Then ask your partner to talk about (1) the experience of being a "subject" in an interview and (2) how he or she felt about your performance as an interviewer.

Role Play and Critical Debate

The role-playing technique is one that focuses on a central element in critical thinking—that is, the ability to take on the perspectives of others. In role play the intent is to help the clients or learners concerned explore the perceptual filters and structures of interpretation of another person. This is an extremely complicated and sophisticated activity and should be undertaken only with the full and adequate preparation of those involved. Its chief value for participants is in helping them integrate the cognitive and affective dimensions of their learning. Cognitively, one can read personal testimonies (journals, letters, and autobiographies) and gain some awareness of the attitudes and outlooks of the people one is studying. This exercise seems somehow static, however, when compared to that of experiencing (in however contrived or artificial a way) the emotions and feelings accompanying or integral to these attitudes.

For example, we can read with interest accounts describing the contradictions and ambiguities of trying to encourage self-direction in clients and learners who do not wish to depart from the dependent patterns of behavior sometimes encouraged and rewarded in therapeutic or teaching-learning relationships. Similarly, we can sympathize with those street-level bureaucrats who tell of the role conflicts and ethical dilemmas of trying to administer bureaucratically clean and correct rules in varying, distorted situations. However, our understanding of these contradictions, ambiguities, conflicts, and dilemmas, if it remains on a purely intellectual level, will necessarily be somewhat limited. It will be that much fuller and deeper if it contains an experiential component.

Role play brings to our consciousness some of the feelings and emotions involved in dealing with such contingencies. From role playing how people might react in typical situations, we are more likely to gain a fully rounded appreciation of the particular mix of thought processes, attitudes, perceptions, and emotions informing their actions. Role play is, therefore, invaluable as a prompt to perspective taking. It is also a useful training device that can help us prepare for emotionally charged or interpersonally complex situations we will be involved in at some later stage. It can get us used to having to make difficult choices in ambiguous circumstances. Although it can never prepare us fully for the experiential actuality of dealing with real anger or confusion, it can help us be less thrown when these necessities actually arise.

Since its origins in psychodrama (Moreno, 1946; Greenberg, 1974), role play has been used in numerous personal and professional contexts. Texts on helping relationships (Marshall, Kurtz, and Associates, 1982; Hutchins and Cole, 1986), teaching adults (Stock, 1971), experiential learning (Walter and Marks, 1981), and group processes (Corey, 1985; Jacques, 1984) usually include some discussion of the technique and a detailed description of its application. Several standard practices are evident. The various actors are briefed, verbally or in writing, on the situation in which they are expected to act out their role. They are given some information on the characteristic behaviors, attitudes, and history of the person they are playing. As a rule, they do not have access to the script directions of the other actors in the drama. The facilitator controls the action by casting the actors, indicating the beginning and end of the session, and leading the debriefing. During debriefing, participants discuss the role-playing experience, and any observers present offer their perceptions of what transpired. Video-taping the role play is particularly helpful for effective debriefing.

In terms of helping people identify and analyze their taken-for-granted assumptions, the variant of role play known commonly as *role reversal* is probably the most effective technique. Role reversal is commonly employed in negotiations seminars, industrial relations training, marital therapy, and cross-cultural training. The actors involved are briefed on roles with which they come into frequent contact but which they have never experienced themselves. During the debriefing sessions, they are asked to comment not only on their experience of the role they played themselves, but also on their perceptions of the behavior of those actors playing opposite them. This affords them a rare opportunity to see themselves as others see them. They can analyze the behavior of another person playing the role that *they* normally play in real life.

Role reversal is a dramatic technique. Its very drama, however, may obscure the central purpose of the exercise, which is to aid participants' reflections on the assumptions under which they and others normally operate. It is not uncommon for people to become so enamored of their part that they view the exercise as pure drama and as a chance to show off their acting technique. Role reversal should generally only be used when the leader is familiar with clients' or group members' personalities. If participants do not trust the leader, they will hold back from full participation in the exercise. Alternatively, they will be frozen by the anxiety induced by needing to give a good performance.

One variant of the role-reversal technique I have found useful in helping group members identify and analyze their assumptions is that of *critical debate*. Daloz (1986) suggests that asking people to take an unfamiliar perspective on an issue or to explain in a sympathetic manner a position with which they disagree is a useful aid to critical thinking. In my own adoption of critical debate, the facilitator frames a controversial motion about which group members are likely to have well-formed opinions and strongly divergent feelings. He or she then asks for group members to volunteer for teams that will speak for or against the motion. Not surprisingly, people tend to volunteer to join the team that most closely represents their own point of view. The facilitator then asks that group members reverse their chosen preference; in other words, all those who volunteered to speak *for* the motion are asked to be on the team speaking *against* the motion, and vice versa. If participants trust the facilitator sufficiently to agree to this switch with good grace, the exercise can be enormously beneficial.

The facilitator controls the debate in the following way. Each team is allowed a period of twenty to thirty minutes to prepare its arguments. One or two spokespersons are nominated to present the arguments the group has generated, and each team has ten to fifteen minutes to put forward its case. After each team has presented arguments, team members take five to ten minutes to discuss among themselves possible rebuttals of the other team's position. Each team is then allowed an additional five to ten minutes to present these rebuttals. At the end of the exercise, a debriefing period of twenty to thirty minutes is needed for participants to analyze the experience of acting out of character in arguing for beliefs, values, and ideas that they do not personally hold. During this time, they are asked to evaluate their success in arguing for viewpoints with which they are uncomfortable, and also to comment on their opponents' performance.

Crisis-Decision Simulations

A crisis-decision simulation is a technique in which people are asked to imagine themselves in a situation where they are forced to make a decision from among a number of uncomfortable choices. After making this decision, they are then required to justify and elaborate on the reasons for choosing this course of action above others. When people make difficult choices from among a number of unpalatable options, their assumptions (in particular, their basic moral values) will be at least partially revealed. Some sample exercises may make this clearer.

Imagine that you are in the aftermath of a nuclear explosion. In the company of eight other people, you are in a radiation-free, protected room that has space and air enough for ten. Three people who are stumbling around in the external environment discover the room, and all ask to be admitted. These are a doctor, a pregnant mother, and a teacher. Which of these three do you choose to admit?

This kind of exercise is often uncomfortable. It asks people to make the kinds of life-and-death choices that faced the character of Sophie in William Styron's *Sophie's Choice,* a mother in a World War II concentration camp who is asked to choose which of her two children will live and which will be sent to the gas chamber. With groups whose members are unfamiliar with each other, or who do not trust the leader, it may be more appropriate to use a less threatening example—perhaps something to do with their work, as in the following example.

Imagine that you are a continuing education program director. You have enough money in your budget to justify one extra course in this year's curriculum. You have course requests from three sources on your desk: (1) a request from your college president to mount a staff development seminar in computer literacy for faculty and staff, who have just been required to switch to microcomputers, (2) a request from a group of single parents who urge you to provide a course on claimants' rights so that they can obtain the welfare benefits to which they are legally entitled, and (3) a request from a local artists' society to run a weekend workshop on painting in oils, for which they are prepared to guarantee a large enrollment. Which course do you choose to offer?

When faced with such crisis-decision simulations, people will frequently begin to ask questions about the context of the crisis and to request information about the different options involved. They will want some knowledge of the possible consequences of each course of action and some details of the characters concerned. Such questions are natural and should not be avoided; indeed, they may be the occasion for some useful analysis in themselves. Asking people why they need a particular piece of information is frequently very revealing. In the first example, people will begin to ask if the pregnant woman has other children, if the doctor is a doctor of medicine or philosophy, and what subject expertise the teacher possesses. In the second example, people will ask if the single parents are divorced or have never married, if computer training courses are provided by the computer manufacturers, and if the artists have opportunities for study within their own organization. Having people make explicit the reasoning behind why certain pieces of information are required in order for them to make their decisions can be almost as valuable an activity as asking them to justify their eventual choices.

There are many other techniques that can be used to help people identify and begin challenging the assumptions influencing their thoughts and actions. Participation in T-groups and encounter groups can result in some startling instances of self-insight. The repertory grid technique (Kelly, 1955; Candy, 1981) probes how people develop concepts they use to order their world. Case studies can allow people to analyze situations similar to their own as if they were external observers. Games and simulation exercises can help people enter the mental frameworks of those they are requested to play in the game. Adaptations of Garfinkel's (1967) breaching technique, in which people are placed in situations in which their taken-for-granted assumptions are upset, can be useful. One example of this is Mezirow's (1981, p. 19) suggestion of placing learners used to traditional teacher-student relationships in situations where the educator refuses to give directions and acts simply as a resource person.

Conclusion

Investigating assumptions is difficult and dangerous. It needs skilled facilitators who can judge just how much ambiguity and anxiety people can accept before removing themselves from the experience. Such facilitators are not necessarily professionally trained therapists, counselors, social workers, or educators.

Friends, spouses, lovers, colleagues, and support group members can prompt us to become aware of our hidden assumptions and to analyze these critically. Sometimes they set out to do this directly. Frequently, however, they suggest the possibility to us by modeling the critically reflective behaviors that appear to have brought them to a state of self-understanding that we envy. Some additional examples of this modeling process are given in Chapters Five and Twelve. Now it is important to turn to the second component of critical thinking—imagining and exploring alternatives to our current ways of thinking and living—and to examine how we might assist others in this activity.

7

Techniques for Developing Alternative Ways of Thinking

At the entrance to Strawberry Fields, the garden in New York's Central Park dedicated to the memory of John Lennon, there is a circular mosaic framing the single word *imagine*. This word is one of the most powerful in the language. It refers to a capacity that is sometimes revered, sometimes reviled, but always present. It is hard to think of any civilization, society, or subculture in which creative imagination, in some form, is not apparent. Even the most traditional or rigidly authoritarian societies are characterized by creative imagination in some sphere, whether this be artistic, political, technological, or organizational. While the capacity for creative thought may be considered innate, there are visible variations in the extent to which different people exhibit it. Critics of institutional schooling, such as Reimer, Holt, and Illich, maintain that the capacity for creative thought is discouraged by schools that define pupils' success by their adherence to preset institutional norms and predefined patterns of reasoning and expression. Egan (1986) argues that schools punish the offering of divergent responses and that asking divergent questions is often construed as impertinence. Pupils quickly learn "that divergent thinking is not rewarded—at least not in school—and generalize from their experience to conclude that it is simply not a useful form of behavior" (p. 298). This perception is reinforced in adulthood when ''they witness large-scale social dissent and other forms of divergent thinking being ignored or even punished by society'' (p. 298).

The readiness to engage in imagining alternatives may not be apparent in many adults; indeed, there may often be a dogged determination to cling to ways of thinking and living that provide a comforting psychological and social familiarity. Taking a critical look at the assumptions by which we live is not an easy task, either cognitively or emotionally. It requires hard intellectual work for us to suspend our conventional beliefs and look for the taken-for-granted assumptions influencing our relationships, work behavior, and political conduct. It also takes considerable emotional strength and psychological courage to admit to ourselves that our familiar explanations and allegiances might need to be rethought and revised.

We are frequently caught within our own constructed and narrowly constraining paradigms—that is, the frameworks of understanding through which we make sense of the world. We define our needs from within these paradigms, and unless confronted with alternatives we may find it extremely hard to imagine these of our own volition. Educators and trainers who plan their programs based upon felt needs as defined by learners appear to be operating democratically. They may, however, be doing a disservice to these learners by implicitly condemning them to remaining within their existing paradigms of thought and action. Three examples may illustrate this argument: the felt need of a drug addict is for greater, cheaper, more regular, and purer supplies of the chosen drug; the felt need of the insecure lover is for greater and more uncritical amounts of approval from the partner; the felt need of the domineering parent is for continued assertion of authority over children who are trying to assert their independence.

In each of these situations it is possible to detect what might be called *real* needs. The addict needs to be weaned away from psychological and physical dependence on an artificial substance. The lover needs to develop a separate self-concept. The parent needs to recognize the child as a separate and growing being. We judge these needs to be real because if they are fulfilled the persons concerned will lead more satisfying lives according to our notion of what constitutes emotional and physical health. Unless we subscribe to an extreme form of existentialism in which all states of being, no matter how personally damaging, are accepted as being as valid as any others, we must recognize that we possess these value-based standards.

There will be many occasions when helpers feel impelled to prompt adults to consider alternatives to their present ways of thinking and living. Daloz (1986, p. 213) believes that the three functions of critical mentors are to support, to challenge, and to provide vision to their protégés. He writes that "in order to see how ideas different from ours exist in their own legitimate framework, it is necessary to leap out from our shell of absolute certainty and construct a whole new world based on some other person's ideas of 'reality,' other assumptions of 'truth'" (p. 228). Mentors can offer new cognitive maps, suggest new conceptual language, and serve as mirrors to help protégés see their actions from alternate viewpoints. Adults locked within constrained and unsatisfactory relationships, jobs, and political systems often cannot imagine other ways of conducting relationships, earning a living, or being a citizen. Helpers who are developing critical thinkers do not necessarily always have to accept adults' definitions of felt needs. They are concerned to help people imagine alternatives, question givens, and analyze underlying assumptions. These activities may be unsettling, painful, and anxiety-producing for all concerned, but we persist in them because we believe that out of such experiences come self-insight and more satisfactory lives. We regard those adults who exhibit contextual awareness, reflective skepticism, and imaginative speculation, and who can identify and analyze the assumptions by which they are living, as somehow more developed, mature, or adult.

People cannot be forced to imagine alternatives. While we might think it in the best interests of people to change their lives, this change must in some sense also be desired by the persons concerned. Trying to force adults to imagine alternative forms of work, relationships, or political involvements when there is absolutely no interest on their part in doing this is almost impossible. It is akin to trying to force an alcoholic to seek treatment for addiction when he or she refuses to admit to the addiction or to there being any problem to be solved. There must be, at the very least, an openness to considering alternatives once they are suggested. A skillful helper will build upon this nascent openness to help people engage in imaginative speculation. There are many individuals who, while not seeking to change their lives in any definite or deliberate manner, are nonetheless open to alternative forms of thinking and living. Sometimes this readiness will be because of feelings of perplexity, confusion, or frustration on their part. At other times there is an openness to this form of exploration because of an innate fascination with alternative ideas. People who are not in crisis are nevertheless often eager to experiment with new ideas, changes in behavior, and new structures. For some, the exact form of these experimentations will be clearly defined. For others, a skilled helper will be invaluable in suggesting options and clarifying choices.

Thinking Creatively

The characteristics of creative thinkers have been studied by a number of cognitive psychologists, and various terms have been developed to describe these people: *field-independent, lateral, holistic, divergent*, and *syllabus-free*. Field-independent thinkers are said to possess "a highly developed capacity for cognitive restructuring. They can impose their own structures on a field or, within a field, construct alternative structures" (Henderson, 1984, p. 34). Field-independent thinkers also "acquire concepts by a flash of insight after a number of trials" (p. 35), in a manner suggested by Gestalt psychologists. Lateral thinkers (De Bono, 1970; Brown, 1985) reject sequential, linear modes of reasoning and problem solving. Similarly, holistic learners (Pask, 1975) are those who "work on several ideas at once, advancing and testing 'multiple predicate' hypotheses" (Henderson, 1984, p. 39).

Divergent thinkers (Guildford, 1956) have an aptitude for generating alternative perspectives on problems rather than following predefined, standardized formats for problem solving. They do not presume that there is any one, standardized answer for a particular problem, preferring to view problems as having plural, contextual solutions. Syllabus-free thinkers (Hudson, 1966, 1968) are stifled by a formally structured curriculum, preferring to stray into apparently unrelated fields of interest. Botkin, Elmandjra, and Malitza (1979) propose the concepts of *innovative learning* and *anticipatory learning*, which are distinguished by "an orientation that prepares for possible contingencies and considers long-range future alternatives" (p. 12). Using forecasting techniques, simulations, scenarios, and models, anticipatory learning emphasizes learners and educators generating desirable futures and working toward these. Making enlightened choices from among multiple future possibilities is seen by Tyler (1983, p. 191) as the distinguishing characteristic of creative thinkers.

In an analysis of the "person of tomorrow," Rogers (1980) describes the qualities needed for individual survival as the twentieth century comes to a close. Among these qualities is an openness to new experiences, to new ways of seeing, to new ideas, and to unfamiliar concepts. People of tomorrow are *process* persons—that is, "they are keenly aware that the one certainty of life is change—that they are always in process, always changing. They welcome this risk-taking way of being and are vitally alive in the way they face change" (p. 351). They possess an antipathy to highly structured, inflexible, bureaucratic institutions and prefer to trust their own intuition and judgment for moral direction rather than relying on external authority. This penchant for nonconformity and reasonable risk taking is also identified by Egan (1986, pp. 296–297) as a distinguishing characteristic of creative thinkers. Other characteristics of such thinkers include optimism, confidence, acceptance of ambiguity and uncertainty, a wide range of interests, flexibility, tolerance of complexity, curiosity, persistence, and independence.

Some commonalities can be seen to emerge from these various conceptualizations of creative thinkers:

1. Creative thinkers reject standardized formats for problem solving.
2. They have interests in a wide range of related and divergent fields.

3. They can take multiple perspectives on a problem.
4. They view the world as relative and contextual rather than universal and absolute.
5. They frequently use trial-and-error methods in their experimentation with alternative approaches.
6. They have a future orientation; change is embraced optimistically as a valuable developmental possibility.
7. They have self-confidence and trust in their own judgment.

Developing these capacities is a major task of those helping adults to think critically. As Egan (1986, p. 298) points out, most of us have been socialized toward thinking convergently rather than divergently. We believe that there is always one answer to a problem, regardless of its complexity. Despite our repeated experiences in life, we persist in looking for the *one* answer, the quick fix, or the ultimate solution that will solve all our problems. Egan argues that helping professionals should encourage their clients to ask "impertinent questions" regarding quick fixes, a questioning typical of critical thinkers.

Asking impertinent questions often comes more easily when we are surrounded by others who are doing this. Argyris's (1976) experiment in fostering critical analysis of organizational assumptions among company presidents noted that "one of the first learnings was that the presidents could not invent the new meanings by themselves. They needed the feedback from others to learn, if the meanings they constructed were to be confirmed by others" (p. 221). The finding that they could not easily invent new and desired meanings frustrated and upset these executives, who prided themselves on their capacity to solve problems quickly. Meyers (1986) also notes the importance of group process to developing critical thinking among students in higher education. He quotes Smith's (1977) use of the Watson-Glaser Critical Thinking Appraisal and the Chickering Critical Thinking Behaviors Test to demonstrate how participation and peer interaction correlate positively with improved critical thinking scores.

Techniques for Imagining Alternatives

The success of techniques for imagining alternatives is assessed by the extent to which they help people break with existing patterns of thought and action. Most of these techniques focus on placing people in unfamiliar, sometimes stressful situations and encouraging them to reflect on their reactions to this unfamiliarity. Adams (1979) describes the process of sidestepping familiar perceptual, cultural, intellectual, and emotional blocks as *conceptual blockbusting*. This exploding of accepted patterns of problem posing, reasoning, and problem solving is central to a number of mental exercises, such as lateral thinking (De Bono, 1970) and synetics (Prince, 1970). Both of these focus on developing creative thought through metaphors, analogies, and adoption of unfamiliar perspectives in identifying problems and generating solutions. Role play and games and simulations, discussed in the previous chapter, can also be useful in this regard. The literature on T-groups (Bradford, Gibb, and Benne, 1964), sensitivity training (Lakin, 1972), encounter groups (Back, 1972), the laboratory method (Benne, Bradford, Gibb, and Lippitt, 1975), and model building (Lippitt, 1973) contains many suggestions for techniques that can assist groups in problem solving.

Several varying approaches to helping people imagine alternatives are considered in more detail in this chapter. These approaches are chosen for their accessibility. They do not require specialized training on the part of helpers, as would be required in the case of, for example, T-groups, encounter groups, or sensitivity groups. People engaged in facilitating these activities usually need a period of preparation to deal with the emotionally explosive aspects of group members' self-revelations that are likely to be involved. By way of contrast, the approaches and techniques discussed in the following paragraphs can be used by anyone seeking to imagine alternatives for themselves or to help others in this activity; they require of facilitators no special training or qualities, beyond a degree of sensitivity and a certain flexibility of interpretation and application. The techniques can be used in almost any group setting within educational institutions, workplaces, community action initiatives, or self-help activities.

Brainstorming

Brainstorming is an exercise in structured spontaneity, in that participants are actively encouraged, for a specified period of time, to think of as many varied, even outrageous, ideas as they can. Because of this emphasis on divergent thinking, the technique has, in Adams's (1979, p. 136) words, "been heavily spoofed and is sometimes identified with weirdness rather than thoughtfulness." The purpose of brainstorming is to reward originality of thought in an atmosphere in which habitual judgments are temporarily and deliberately suspended. The activity is generally structured around finding solutions to carefully defined problems. Groups are usually diverse and small (no more than twelve), and they engage in the activity for short periods (ten to fifteen minutes).

As formulated by brainstorming's "founder," Alex Osborn (1963), brainstorming sessions must follow four rules to be most productive: (1) no evaluation or criticism of ideas is permitted, to ensure that people are more concerned to generate, rather than defend, ideas; (2) participants are encouraged to suggest the most outrageous solutions they can conceive, on the assumption that these may often contain kernels of truth that can be extracted during the analysis session; (3) as many ideas as can be thought of are voiced, in the belief that out of quantity will come quality; and (4) participants attempt to build upon, integrate, and develop ideas that have already been voiced in the session.

During the period of analysis following the brainstorming activity, participants sort through the ideas and consider their appropriateness and feasibility. If more than one group is involved in the activity, a good idea is to ask groups to discuss ideas suggested by groups other than their own. This ensures that participants who suggested particularly fatuous ideas in the charged and enthusiastic atmosphere of the brainstorming session are not ridiculed or embarrassed in the colder, more considered climate of analysis. Because these are difficult activities, brainstorming groups need leaders who will firmly remind participants of transgressions of the rules, particularly the tendency to offer criticism of an idea at the time it is voiced.

Participants in brainstorming groups are engaged in a form of role play. They are trying to suspend their habitually critical, skeptical reactions to proposals (for example, "It's too complex," "It's too costly," "Others won't understand its purpose") and to think deliberately in divergent ways. The danger of participants' becoming enamored of the dramatic part of the activity (generating the ideas) and neglecting the analysis afflicts this technique in much the same way as sometimes happens with role play. On the whole, however, this is a useful technique to try with groups, since it has the one great advantage of rewarding various behaviors (generating wildly outrageous or excessive ideas) that are generally proscribed. It provides a safe environment for this activity and removes from participants the fear of punishment or ridicule that would normally inhibit these thought processes. Group members are able to engage in forms of imaginative speculation that they might normally avoid for fear of being perceived as deviant, insubstantial, or suspect in some other way.

Envisioning Alternative Futures

Fostering the capacity to speculate on alternatives for oneself and others is a common theme among educators and trainers of adults (Ilsley, 1984). Lindeman (1944, p. 116) believed that educators and trainers of adults were "heralds of the future" and that "adult education is always futuristic." For Freire (1970b, p. 72), the problem-posing method of education is distinguished by its "revolutionary futurity." To him, "the unfinished character of men and the transformational character of reality necessitate that education be an ongoing activity." Boshier (1980, 1986) has provided imaginative scenarios (or "future histories") of how a lifelong learning society can be created. The process of imaging (Boulding, 1976) or envisioning has been defined (Srivastva and Associates, 1983, p. 2) as "creating in one's mind an image of the desired future organizational state that can serve as a guide to interim strategies, decisions, and behavior." Bennis's (1983, p. 18) survey of chief executive officers and successful innovative corporate leaders identified as a common characteristic "the capacity to create and communicate a compelling vision of a desired state of affairs—to impart clarity to this vision (or paradigm, context, frame—all those words serve) and induce commitment to it."

Toffler (1970) and Naisbitt (1982) have popularized the idea of envisioning personal and collective futures, and a number of techniques have been developed for this purpose. In the Images of Potentiality workshops devised by Fox, Lippitt, and Schindler-Rainman (1976), participants imagine themselves one to five years in the future and then review from this future vantage point what has pleased them about the progress they have made on their imagined journey. To Ziegler, Healy, and Ellsworth (.1978), the deliberate and intentional coming together with others to invent and realize alternative futures is the most important way in which people can be helped to develop civic literacy. Kauffman (1976) reviews twenty-four exercises for teaching people to project their own situations into the future, including story completion, scenario writing, and community change. Although meant for use with children, many of these exercises can be easily adapted for use with adults.

Developing Preferred Scenarios

Helping clients to develop preferred scenarios is central to Egan's (1986) concept of what makes a skilled helper. A preferred scenario is a detailed, concrete description of a desired state. People are helped to construct such detailed scenarios by asking and answering a series of such questions as the following:

What would this problem look like if it were managed better?
What changes would take place in my present lifestyle?
What would I be doing differently with the people in my life?

What patterns of behavior would be in place that currently are not?

What patterns of behavior that are currently in place would be eliminated?

What would exist that does not exist now?

What would be happening that does not happen now?

What would I have that I do not have now?

What decisions would be made and executed?

What accomplishments would be in place that are not now?

Helpers do not merely pose these questions and allow people to struggle with them. They assist people to develop goals that are specific, realistic, and in keeping with their own values. Egan urges that goals be stated as outcomes or accomplishments and that people choose these from among a number of possible options they have developed. These goals are then converted into strategies that are "specific, realistic, substantially related to the desired outcome, owned by the client, in keeping with the client's values, and set in a reasonable time frame" (p. 329). People are helped to balance risks against the probability of success and to convert these strategies into sequenced action plans.

In constructing preferred scenarios, people may well be challenged by helpers or friends who provide a judicious mixture of support and challenge. Egan (1986, p. 274) writes that "in a way that respects clients' self-responsibility, friends can help clients make reasonable demands on themselves." Friends can also help us to maintain our motivation for change when we hit difficulties or become afflicted by periodic atrophy. This principle of social support is at the heart of most effective drug abuse programs. Once clients have been discharged from detoxification programs, they need the constant support of friends to help them resist the inevitable temptations of returning to their addicted lifestyle. The most common reason for recovered alcoholics or cocaine addicts resuming their habit is their inability to create a new social network of non-drug users.

When people are depressed by their current lives but hesitant to create new scenarios, Egan advises that helpers assist them to spell out in detail the consequences of remaining in their situations. The dismal images that surface might sufficiently distress those involved that they are impelled to consider how these consequences could be avoided. There will be occasions, however, when it is impossible to realize a preferred scenario. We may be stuck in unchallenging jobs because of the financial necessity to support children and partners dependent upon us. We may be unemployed in a town hit by chronic unemployment (as has happened in many mining and steel towns), unable to look for jobs in other locations because of irrevocable family commitments. We may be suffering from a terminal disease such as AIDS. In such cases helpers can do little on their own to effect any personal change. Their most valuable function will be to help people live as creatively as they can within such traumatic and difficult situations.

This realization of the limits to effecting change at the personal level is characteristic of much of the counseling literature. For example, Egan's techniques for encouraging clients to construct and realize preferred scenarios include the making of personal-decision balance sheets (in which clients take stock of the benefits and disadvantages of various courses of action) and the use of "prompt and fade" in projective speculation. In this latter approach the helper says, "Here are some possibilities. Do any of them make any sense to you?" or "Here are some of the things that people with this kind of problem have tried. How do they sound to you?" These approaches are suited to individual or small-group sessions in which an intensive exploration of the individual's situation takes place.

Futures Invention

The founder of the futures invention process believes that the task of educators of adults is "to aid and abet every controversy, every dispute, every conflict which adult learners are prepared to confront and learn about" (Ziegler, 1976, p. 283). This readiness to assist adults in questioning the validity of futures created for them by others is realized through their collective creation of alternative future scenarios. In the futures invention process, participants are encouraged to imagine first individual, then collective, futures they desire. Through a process of revealing, comparing, and negotiating visions of what participants most desire in their personal and social lives, a specific, concrete collective scenario is generated, or divergences in visions of the future are highlighted.

The futures invention process is most commonly conducted in residential workshops lasting from three to five nights, though participants may also choose to work in day-long seminars spread over a period of months. In her report on seven workshops focused on inventing the future of metropolitan Syracuse in New York State, Healy (1979, p. 193) describes how "a day's schedule usually involved nine to ten hours of difficult reflective and negotiating activity about participants' intentional claims on the futures under consideration." Although it is possible to engage in the process as an individual, the most common format is for participants to work in small groups, plenary groups, or policy teams.

Participants in futures invention workshops typically ask four questions: (1) Who am I? (2) What do I want to do? (3) How can I do it? and (4) What are the grounds for other persons to join with me in making these inventions? The following nine exercises comprise the stages in a typical futures invention workshop:

Goal Formulation. Participants write goals that represent desired changes to which they feel committed. These goals are concrete and specific, but at this early stage they are not limited by considerations of practicality. Ziegler, Healy, and Ellsworth (1978, p. 135) believe that "the *worst* mistake is to limit your imagination, to worry about how you are going to get there." The goal-formulation stage shares some similarities with the brainstorming process already described.

Indicator Invention. Indicators are concrete and specific signs by which participants would know that their goal had been achieved. As with criteria analysis (discussed in the previous chapter), the importance of indicators is that they focus participants' attention on particular aspects of their own lives and communities. By specifying indicators, people are less likely to descend into mouthing clichés about human growth or social development, which are comforting but have no concrete detail attached to them.

Consequence Forecasting. Participants attempt to foresee the beneficial and harmful consequences of achieving their goals. As with indicators, these consequences are specific and concrete and are expressed in terms of changes that will be wrought in individuals, neighborhoods, communities, factories, classrooms, businesses, or the environment.

Value-Shift Assessment. At this stage participants retreat into their individual imaginations and attempt to modify the goals, indicators, and consequences they have generated and foreseen so that they fit closely with their sense of their own selves. This purpose is similar to Egan's stress on ensuring that goals are in keeping with clients' essential values.

Scenario Construction. Participants select themselves into policy teams or other small-group forms so that they can work with others who share similar goals. Their task is to construct a collective future seen in commonly agreed goals, indicators, and consequences. This stage is often marked by disagreement, confusion, and conflict, and no clear consensus may emerge. In that case, group members may decide to regroup themselves into teams composed of more like-minded individuals, if they can find them. An important element at this stage is to set forth the assumptions—the common beliefs about shared givens— that underlie the scenario.

Writing of Individual Futures Histories. Participants imagine that their goals have been achieved and then try to construct the specific incidents and happenings that might have led up to these achievements. Plausibility, specificity, and identification of chronological sequence are the most important features of these future histories.

Writing of a Collective Futures History. Participants compare their individual futures histories and try to construct a collective futures history. Sometimes similarities do not emerge and the group has to take a step back to rewrite their individual histories. When a number of similarities are present, participants evaluate each others' histories and begin to construct a plausible common history.

Tactics and Strategy. Participants take the one incident from their imagined futures history that is closest to the real present they inhabit. They determine the resources (skills, experiences, knowledge) they possess and judge how best they might arrive at this point.

Collective Action. The final stage of futures invention is "bringing into existence and legitimating a new way of thinking, feeling, doing, in some concrete manner which constitutes the indicator, in the present, of more distant imagined and intended futures" (Ziegler, Healy, and Ellsworth, 1978, p. 146). This is the point of public commitment to collective action. Participants share their tactics with other members of their small groups and with other groups. Sometimes an entire large group agrees on a set of tactics. Sometimes specific subgroups or policy teams agree on their own futures, which diverge from the visions of other small groups. As Ziegler, Healy, and Ellsworth (1978, p. 147) acknowledge, "Sometimes there is no agreement at all, even though there may have been a great deal of learning."

Esthetic Triggers

Immersion in an esthetic experience or artistic enterprise, particularly when we are unused to such activities, can be a powerful stimulus to imagining alternatives. In particular, esthetic and artistic experiences can help us break through habitual, supposedly rational structures of reasoning. After being involved in an act of artistic creation, we view the world differently. At a very basic level, our sense of ourselves as active creators is enhanced, and we are more likely to view the world as malleable and open to our interventions. We are also more likely to acknowledge the importance of intuitive insight to our mental processes. Since artistic creation and appreciation both depend on and value intuitive and insightful capacities, we come to a clearer appreciation of their significance.

Many people spend the greater part of their lives trying to think in linear modes about decisions they have to make at work, in their personal relationships, and regarding their participation in political life. Typical of decision making in this linear-rational mode is the compiling of balance sheets of positive and negative aspects of certain courses of action. For example, when deciding whether or not to apply for, or accept, a new job, we may make one list of reasons why we should take the job and another list of reasons why we should stay where we are. When we are drawn into a new relationship, we probably engage in a similar process of evaluating the advantages and drawbacks of becoming involved with a new person, although this process probably takes place on a more intuitive level. Even the most indirect act of political participation—the making of electoral choice in a political election—will probably involve some balancing in our mind of the apparent merits of the respective candidates.

The chief assumption underlying these thought processes is that decisions can be made in some conscious, ordered fashion by weighing the relative merits of various relevant factors. To some researchers, the left side of the brain, which purportedly deals with this form of rational reasoning, is brought strongly into play when making these kinds of decisions. The belief is that people suppress the intuitive, emotional forces said to be located in the right side of the brain when they make such decisions, for fear of the distorting, irrational influences these right-brain forces might exert. The debate on brain hemispheric lateralization (the left-right brain controversy) is heated. Long (1983, p. 73) summarizes this debate as follows: "Researchers believe that the left hemisphere of the brain operates ˙on words and clearly defined symbols such as chemical and mathematical signs. It is described as being active, calculating, reasoning, and predominantly sequential and analytic in its functioning. The right hemisphere of the brain operates on pictures, is spatially oriented, perceives patterns as a whole, and operates in an intuitive, emotional, and receptive mode." Such preliminary conjectures regarding the physical location of certain cognitive functions are fascinating but as yet unproven. If these conjectures do turn out to be empirically based, they will revolutionize our understanding of learning styles and creativity. For the purposes of this discussion, however, it is enough to note that such a debate exists, and that esthetic triggers to imaginative speculation are often neglected because of their association with right-brain activities.

An enormous number of esthetic triggers to imaginative speculation are available. These encompass the whole range of written, aural, visual, and tactile artistic expression. Some of the most frequently used in prompting people to imagine alternatives are the following:

Poetry. Through poetic formats and conventions we allow ourselves to externalize our most private feelings. For some people, writing poetry provides a legitimacy for what would otherwise be dismissed as frivolous speculation or airy, meaningless mental wanderings. In a poem we can give voice to our wildest imaginings without fear of being criticized for our irrationalism. This is because we know that in the act of writing poetry one is usually *encouraged* to be "irrational" and creative (the two are frequently equated). Hence, writing a poem positively reinforces forms of imaginative speculation that we would be too embarrassed to admit to in other, more "rational" contexts.

Fantasy. Writing short episodes of fantasy can be enormously liberating. These fantasies may be exercises in straightforward projective speculation—for example, "How would you change your life if you won the million-dollar state lottery tomorrow?" or "If you were appointed the president or prime minister next week, how would you change the country?" or "What would you do to this school if you became its principal for the next academic year?" Other fantasies can be less focused; for example, as helpers we might ask people to imagine themselves to be Vietnamese peasants and write about their day, or to write on life as they imagine it to be after a nuclear war. Sometimes it is a highly provocative exercise to give people a single powerful word, such as *love, hate, pain, joy, fear,* or *paradise,* and ask them to put these feelings and states of being into words.

Drawing and Photography. People who are illiterate, or who feel uncomfortable writing even private fantasies, can be encouraged to depict their fantasies visually in paintings and drawings, or to use audio-visual approaches such as tape recordings, video sequences, sound-and-light shows, and tape-slide presentations. One does not need to be a sophisticated performance artist to depict love and hate in sound or pictures. Once a skilled helper has assured us that the exercise is not a test of our artistic or drafting capabilities, our imaginations are freed. An illustration of how drawing can be used to help people imagine alternatives can be seen in Freire's (1970a, 1970b) work with Brazilian peasants. These nonreaders are encouraged to draw pictorial representations of power relationships in their communities as a way of understanding that these relationships are humanly contrived and can therefore be changed by human actions. Arnold and Burke (1983) describe how drawing is used in Canadian workshops on Central America to help church people understand links between Canada and Guatemala. The Canadian GATT-Fly group (GATT-Fly, 1983) has used drawing as a way of helping people collectively construct a picture of their political and economic world, prior to discussing how this might be changed. Using a large sheet of paper and a few colored markers, group members are encouraged to draw simple pictures—rather like cartoons—that symbolize their situations and the pressures acting upon them. This technique has been used with people as diverse as members of fishing unions, farmers, native·people, immigrant workers, unemployed groups (all in Canada), sugar workers (Trinidad and Peru), peasant organizations (Nicaragua), and community organizers (the English-speaking Caribbean).

Barndt, Cristall, and Marino (1983) show how immigrant women in Canada have produced photostories to depict their experiences on entering Canadian society. Photostories are collections of photographs that, taken together, explore a particular theme. By juxtaposing images of women from billboard, magazine, and television advertisements with these immigrants' own pictorial stories of living and working in Canada, the immigrant learners can help women develop a critical understanding of how the mass media shape their images of themselves.

Songwriting. Community singing has long been used as a means of building some sense of group cohesion. The founder of the Danish folk high school, Nikolai Grundtvig, regarded songwriting as an important technique for building solidarity among adults. The folk song tradition in every society is a people's tradition in which "ordinary" citizens write songs about current events and shared concerns—songs that are simple to learn and perform. Sometimes more established performers create personal songs that become adopted as the rallying cries for popular movements. Songs such as "We Shall Overcome," "Give Peace a Chance," "This Land Is Your Land," "The Times They Are A-Changin'," and "Blowing in the Wind" all serve this function. These are in marked contrast to commercially produced songs that we consume but have no real part in creating. Arnold and Burke (1983) describe how community groups can write songs on themes that concern them by choosing popular songs (their examples include Johnny Cash's "I Walk the Line" and Woody Guthrie's "This Land Is Your Land") and writing new lyrics to these. Particularly effective are songs that address particular people, such as presidents, prime ministers, employers, and landlords. People can come to see themselves as creators of popular culture in this way, and if these songs are used at further occasions (conferences, demonstrations, rallies), their writers have a sense of being active creators.

Drama. Dramatizing commonly occurring, shared situations, and how these might be acted upon, is a powerful way of releasing imaginative speculation. In effect, these activities are extended improvisational role plays. Consider Lewis's (1986, p. 93) account of a graduate student's completion of a learning contract on the efficacy of mime as a vehicle for stimulating learning and promoting understanding: "In a ten minute vignette performed before forty of his classmates, the student and his friend portrayed the plight of the working poor in El Salvador. Subjugation and brutality, dominant themes in the mime, had great emotional and visual impact as demonstrated by the audience's body language and use of expletives." Through this performance, a topic that might otherwise have been investigated through traditional academic research (reading primary and secondary accounts of poverty or consulting officially compiled statistics) assumed an enhanced emotional significance to those involved.

Improvisational theater can be very effective in dramatizing common problems, concerns, and experiences. In improvisational theater the actors may often be volunteers from the group concerned. Actors ask audience members for suggestions of typical situations they face and for brief guidance on how they might respond to these. Shor (1980) describes a play-writing course for working-class adults at Staten Island College (New York City) that took improvisational theater one step backward to the script-writing stage. In their depictions of working-class heroes and flashily superficial superstars, his students created typifications of characters they recognized in their daily lives and then video-taped the resulting scripts. Shor reports that "the material and the acting were of uneven quality, but the impact on the class was extraordinary. They became awe-struck with themselves, when they viewed their completed tapes" (p. 257).

Exploratory theater is a technique for exploring work-related issues in which "the performers themselves, by virtue of their own employment and circumstances, occupy roles similar to those they are portraying. The scenarios are tied to real-life situations and characters the audience has known. Thus, audience participation is critical as both actors and participants draw interchangeably from their own experiences and those of their colleagues" (Lewis, 1986, p. 96). Participants in exploratory theater are all engaged in common work settings. The actors are volunteers from the audience who are willing to act out typical work situations. Because audience members and actors share a common work setting, they possess a common reservoir of work experiences. A moderator is appointed, who sets the stage for the improvisational drama, makes decisions about when the action should be interrupted or finally stopped, and leads interim and postperformance discussions.

Lewis suggests the following format for those engaging in exploratory theater:

1. Audience members identify a work-related issue or crisis and summarize this on a three-by-five-inch card.
2. Performers collect the cards and select one or two ideas as the basis for their improvisation.
3. The problem selected is dramatized by actors assuming identifiable roles in a specific scenario.

4. Actors stay in character during the presentation. Audience members can ask questions of the actors, who stay in character as they respond.
5. Action can be stopped at any point in the improvisation by the moderator, who watches the audience for particularly emotional reactions to the dramatization.
6. The performance ends at a "point of crisis" prior to any resolution.
7. When the dramatization ends, audience members share their reactions, feelings, and ideas.
8. In the postperformance discussion, run by the moderator, audience members discuss how they might transform the situation they have witnessed.

For audience members who wish to consider crucial concerns, but who might be embarrassed about admitting to experiencing difficulties at work, the exploratory theater technique offers a valuable cover of anonymity. Because the cards used by the actors are anonymous, particular problems cannot be attributed to specific individuals. If certain common themes are suggested by different groups, there may be a good case for developing a script that encapsulates these predominant themes and that could be taken to new audiences.

Conclusion

Using these esthetic triggers to help people imagine alternatives seems to contradict what is commonly considered to be an accepted principle in the psychology of learning: we need to ease learners into the study of unfamiliar material through a thorough grounding in material that is familiar to them. In contrast to that accepted principle, it is the very unfamiliarity of poetry, fantasy, drawing, photography, songwriting, and theater that is their most significant element for learners. By becoming involved in activities that we have traditionally avoided or never considered, we can have our powers of imagination released. Through immersing ourselves in the unknown, we may more easily be jolted out of the known. In our deciding or being asked to engage in a creative act with which we have no familiarity, or in opening ourselves to wholly new esthetic experiences, we may learn how to recognize and acknowledge the powers of imaginative speculation that lie within us.

Crucial to all the endeavors described above is some form of debriefing, analysis, and reflection. Although creating poems, fantasies, drawings, photostories, songs, and plays are significant acts in themselves, it is important that the creators be encouraged to reflect on the forces that inspired these activities. By recognizing how their powers of imagination have been engaged, people begin to realize that they possess creative, speculative capacities and that they can call on these for a variety of purposes. After imagining in fictional or dramatized form how their situations appear to others, and after hearing how others respond to these, people may find it easier to conceive of alternative ways of acting within these situations. If they have been able to imagine alternatives in poetry, fantasy, art, and drama, it will seem more possible to imagine alternatives in their own real lives. Once the capacity to imagine alternatives in esthetic domains has been realized, it is but a short step to considering how this activity might be replicated in relationships, work life, and politics. Practicing the skills of imaginative speculation is essential if we are to become critical thinkers.

❧ Part 3 ❧

Helping Adults Learn to Think Critically in Different Arenas of Life

Part Three focuses on four particular contexts of adult life in which critical thinking is crucial. The first of these is the workplace. Critical thinking among managers and executives has long been recognized as important, and Chapter Eight reviews the forms this takes and how it can be encouraged. This chapter also discusses the less commonly recognized process of critical thinking among shop-floor workers, particularly where these workers are involved in establishing worker cooperatives in the face of factory bankruptcies and closures. Chapter Nine explores the ways in which people learn about the political world and develop political involvements. Chapter Ten takes one medium through which adults learn about politics—television—and examines it in detail. How people can be helped to become critical television viewers who are alert to the biases inherent in television reporting is a central concern of this chapter. Adults' involvements in personal relationships are the focus of Chapter Eleven. Here, I examine how people can be helped to think critically about their involvement in love relationships, friendships, and parent-child relationships. Chapter Twelve identifies a number of general themes related to facilitating critical thinking. Some practical examples of how I try to develop critical thinking in my own work are given in the Epilogue.

133

8

Using the Workplace
as a Resource for Thinking
and Learning

The experience of work is multidimensional. Our work can be the cause of enormous frustration, excruciating boredom, and frightening alienation. It can induce feelings of loneliness, fear, resentment, envy, and a desire to profit from the misfortunes of others. It can also be the source of profound fulfillment and grant central meaning to our lives. Work can give rise to enduring friendships and marriages, or to lifelong enmities. For many, particularly those in single-industry towns (steel towns, mill towns, or university towns), work colleagues and friendship networks are inextricably intertwined. The nature of much blue-collar work has been documented in books such as Sennett and Cobb's (1972) *The Hidden Injuries of Class* and Rubin's (1976) *Worlds of Pain*, in which the routine degradation and mind-numbing nature of much working-class, blue-collar work (including housework) are detailed dramatically. Rubin puts it as follows: ''Only a tiny minority of us ever are involved in inventing our present, let alone our future. Ordinary men and women—which means almost all of us—struggle along with received truths as well as received ways of being and doing. For such people, at least one half of the waking hours of each day are spent in doing work that is dull, routine, deadening—in a

135

word, alienating and alienated labor'' (p. 160). Unemployed members of minorities are seen as being in the most disadvantaged work position. They have no reason for optimism, since their potential for advancement is often stopped at a crucial stage as a result of prejudice. The opportunities for developing any kind of critical thinking in such contexts seem, at first glance, to be bleak indeed.

White-collar work is usually portrayed somewhat differently. Gould (1980, p. 228) maintains that middle-class managers are more optimistic than hourly paid, blue-collar workers, because of the prospects for increased earning power, enhanced social status, and personal psychological development within their jobs. However, analyses of the experiences of white-collar work, such as Kanter's (1983) *Men and Women of the Corporation* and Lipsky's (1980) *Street-Level Bureaucracy*, show that middle-class work is not wholly fulfilling for those involved. Professional women face subtle, but nevertheless real and highly effective, sexist discrimination at the workplace. Public service professionals see themselves as caught inexorably and relentlessly in double binds; loyalties to clients or consumers are in opposition to organizational needs. When faced with this kind of role conflict, practitioners often deny that they have any scope for individual discretionary action. ''Street-level bureaucrats'' (such as teachers, social workers, social security officials, housing officers, and the police) commonly maintain that official policies and system norms and rules render them unable to make individual choices or discretionary decisions. As Lipsky puts it, ''Strict adherence to rules, and refusals to make exceptions when exceptions might be made, provide workers with defenses against the possibility that they might be able to act more as clients would wish. 'That's the way things are,' 'It's the law,' and similar rationalizations not only protect workers from client pressures, but also protect them from confronting their own shortcomings as participants in public service work'' (Lipsky, 1980, p. 149). A more compelling case for the need to develop critical thinking skills at the workplace would be hard to imagine.

Public service professionals who mediate between individuals and public service agencies often develop routines to process clients in standardized ways that become ends in themselves. Attempts by clients to deviate from these standardized procedures become interpreted as trouble emanating from "difficult" clients. Lipsky (1980) quotes studies of legal service lawyers and welfare workers who penalize those clients trying to circumvent or challenge established routines and procedures. Far from being concerned to help clients in as flexible a manner as possible, these professionals act in ways rigidly antithetical to critical thinking.

Basseches (1984), however, takes a more optimistic view. He maintains that "every work organization which defines itself as an autonomous unit confronts a vast variety of practical and cognitive challenges—opportunities for critical reflection—of the kind that would naturally stimulate adult development" (p. 338). In other words, in workplace settings where democratic participation and worker control are the norm, the conditions for critical thinking are favorable. In routinized production in which workers follow standardized patterns of productive behavior imposed from above, however, many workers quickly reach a state of equilibrium where they have mastered their jobs and confront no new developmental challenges. To Gould (1980), many industrial organizations are inimical to learning and personal development. He writes that "the workplace is not organized for human development and hence inevitably conflicts with the transformational process" (p. 225).

Sometimes the only reason for workers to challenge existing workplace norms is some kind of failure or major disaster at the workplace. In the aftermath of workplace disasters, a critical questioning of workplace practices and previously unexamined organizational norms is often initiated. As an example of this, Marsick (1987) quotes testimony to the presidential commission on the explosion shortly after launch of the American space shuttle *Challenger*. No one wished to voice his or her concerns about its safety, for fear of appearing troublesome or not being a "team player." Marsick argues that workers have been so conditioned not to raise questions that they may not know how to begin to think critically. They may also be highly suspicious of all organizational intentions. She warns against blithely assuming that management edicts announcing the need for participatory workplaces will induce a corresponding change in workers' behaviors and attitudes, without those in positions of authority modeling the desired change.

Friedlander (1983) also stresses the importance of workers' perceptions of anomalies, discrepancies, and crises as the occasions for prompting critical thinking. Perceptions of contesting ideas regarding fundamental work processes, or of discrepancies between official company norms and actual practice, can be the beginning of fundamental critical inquiry by workers as to how these differences and anomalies might be reconciled or explained. On such occasions, observing an anomaly prompts that form of critical inquiry known as *dialectical analysis;* we identify a contradiction and begin to explore how the differences between apparently opposed positions might be resolved, or how diverse ways of organizing the workplace might be integrated.

Critical Thinking at the Workplace

The association in many people's minds between critical thinking and the college classroom has meant that the significance of critical thinking to training and human resource development has, in general, not been appreciated. In fact, the critical thinking activities outlined in this book are valued in business and industry, even if they are not usually labeled as examples of critical thinking. The following seven management concepts, all familiar to trainers, human resource developers, and managers in business and industry, draw directly on the idea of critical thinking. *Strategic planning*—the attempt to project alternative future business scenarios and to plan responses to these— is one example of exploring and imagining alternatives. *Effective decision making*, in Johnston's (1986) words, "will require managers with an ability to ask questions and think critically and to recognize and deal with the unquantifiable" (p. 16). *Creative problem solving* has at its core the readiness to question critically the appropriateness of accepted wisdom and to free ourselves from the habitual ways of thinking and perceiving that govern our ways of organizing the workplace. *Situational leader-*

ship—the ability to change one's leadership style according to the demands of different contexts—requires a willingness to abandon fixed ways of dealing with particular situations. A recent report by the Business–Higher Education Forum (1983) observed that "sustained excellence in management will require, above all, adaptability to change" (p. 2). *Entrepreneurial risk taking* necessitates executives freeing themselves from conventional notions of what are accepted ways of operating a business. *Research and development activities*—in effect, company-sponsored attempts to institutionalize creative thought and action—can only be successful when those involved are encouraged to forget previously unquestioned organizational norms and ways of working. Finally, the activity of *organizational team building* begins with team members trying to gain a full and clear understanding of the assumptions informing each other's actions.

It is clear, then, that workplaces in which innovation, creativity, and flexibility are evident are workplaces in which critical thinkers are prized. Interestingly enough, it is just such characteristics that are identified by Peters and Waterman (1982) as indicative of excellence in their study of ten top American corporations. When organizational channels of communication are horizontal rather than vertical, as is advocated in what has come to be known as the Japanese style of management (Ouchi, 1981; Pascale and Athos, 1981), creativity of thought is more likely to surface. When criticism of prevailing workplace norms is encouraged in some form of collective forum, as is advocated by proponents of quality circles (Cohen-Rosenthal, 1982), leaps of imagination that take companies beyond currently accepted modes of production are more likely to take place. Critical thinking, then, can be seen as the central element in improving organizational performance.

The development of the Apple Macintosh computer, which the user operates by literally pointing on a screen to the machine function desired, is a good example of institutionalized critical thinking. During development of the computer, team members working on the Macintosh were housed in separate premises, relieved of all strictures regarding patterns of attendance; they worked as a democratic group, with no hierarchy

of authority or "typical" pattern of working. In effect, the team jettisoned entirely the previously accepted paradigm of computer use—that command functions should be contained on the same typewriter keyboard with the letters and numerals—and devised a mode of computer use that would appeal to all those nontypists who had not bought computers because of their apparent resemblance to typewriters.

Managers as Critical Thinkers

In a recent study of managerial learning (Lowy, Kelleher, and Finestone, 1986), a number of variables correlated with "high-learning" managers were recorded. High-learning managers worked in jobs characterized by variety, frequent contact with other people, and the opportunity to influence policy-level decision making. These jobs were stressful, ambiguous, and subject to frequent changes in the range of responsibilities. Managers enjoyed large amounts of freedom and ample support and resources. They were subject to high supervisory pressure and were motivated chiefly by the possibility of future influence on policy and by the prospect of promotion. They did not receive regular, clear feedback, and there was considerable ambiguity concerning the goals toward which they were working. In terms of personal characteristics, high-learning managers tended to define themselves as motivating and leading staff, they acknowledged the need to learn on the job, and they had an openness to information. They were required to seek out alternatives and to be constantly questioning ways in which existing practices might be improved.

This study confirms that the activities of critical thinking, such as recognizing and responding successfully to contextual complexity, ambiguity, and change, are central to learning at the workplace. These conditions are precisely those identified in Kanter's (1983) study of successful "progressive" companies—that is, those most innovative in quality of work experiments, job design, participatory management, affirmative action, and ability to adapt to changing circumstances. Kanter identified "integrative thinking" as the distinguishing commonality in these companies' successes—that is, "the willingness to move beyond received wisdom, to combine ideas from unconnected sources, to embrace change as an opportunity to test limits" (p. 27). These capacities are also, of course, those crucial to critical thought and action. In an analysis of critical thinking as applied to managerial actions, Neumann (1986) lists several instances in which critical thinking capacities are necessary: planning a strategic financial maneuver, redesigning a complex organizational structure, analyzing seemingly unrelated problems to discover causal commonalities, launching a daring marketing tactic, and balancing spontaneous, intuitive decisions with rational calculation of their consequences. Critical thinking in managerial life is recognized in attempts to solve real problems and take actions in a purposeful, logical way. The critical thinker "is aware of the malleability of perceived reality and dares, therefore, to initiate action that will reshape it" (p. 27).

This emphasis on the connectedness of critical thought and action parallels Weick's (1983) concept of *acting thinkingly* and the idea of *action learning* (Morgan and Ramirez, 1983). Acting thinkingly refers to the capacity exhibited by managers to perceive a situation, decide upon its salient features or problematic aspects, and take action without the benefit of rules or standardized procedures imposed from above. Action learning "aims to enhance the capacities of people in everyday situations to investigate, understand, and, if they wish, to change those situations in an ongoing fashion with a minimum of external help" (Morgan and Ramirez, 1983, p. 9). Those undertaking to prompt such learning are concerned with empowering people to "become critically conscious of their values, assumptions, actions, interdependencies, rights and prerogatives so that they can act in a substantially rational way as active partners in producing their reality" (p. 9). Marsick (1987) regards the concept of action learning as the most provocative and fruitful alternative to behaviorist models in understanding learning at the workplace.

In the study of high-learning managers by Lowy, Kelleher, and Finestone (1986), the lack of goal clarity, absence of regular feedback on performance, and ambiguity surrounding high-learning managers' functions and responsibilities contrasts markedly with behaviorist notions of successful learning. According to behaviorally oriented writers such as Mager (1968, 1975) and Mager and Beach (1972), some of the most important characteristics of successful learning are that learning goals are specified previously in precise behavioral terms, regular feedback on learners' progress is provided, and ambiguity is avoided as much as possible. Instructional processes are sequenced according to their complexity, so that learners are taken through a series of progressively difficult tasks.

Yet the reality of managerial learning at the workplace is evidently sufficiently complex and contextually specific as to call into question this behavioral approach to understanding learning. A behavioral approach may be well-suited to training people to perform previously specified tasks and acquire predetermined skills or bodies of knowledge. As Isenberg (1983) writes, however, "Accurate reasoning is possible only in a world where information is complete and certain, where criteria are unambiguous, and where cause and effect links are known. The conditions that allow accurate reasoning rarely exist in the world of the manager" (p. 241). Managers are more likely to develop and test plausible mental models of the uncertain situations they confront on a regular basis—for example, understanding a conflict between two vice-presidents, second-guessing a group president's agenda during an upcoming visit to one's division, or anticipating how competitors will respond to a new service or product. In all these cases, managers will essentially be thinking in contextual patterns. They will be taking action and adapting their decisions according to the demands of context. Morgan (1986) regards the development of this kind of contextual sensitivity as a major need for managers. He writes that "effective managers and professionals in all walks of life, whether they be business executives, public administrators, organizational consultants, politicians, or trade unionists, have to become skilled in the art of 'reading' the situations that they are attempting to organize or manage" (p. 11).

To Isenberg (1983), the strength of what he calls *plausible reasoning* is that "it suggests that managers need to abandon the search for certainty before taking action'' (p. 247). Put another way, they need to exhibit reflective skepticism. They must be cautious of any claims to total success or predictable certainty within their spheres of work. Instead of trying to decide actions on the basis of total accuracy, managers draw on their past experiences to speculate on possible solutions to problems. The manager calculates the risks involved in different courses of action and then decides, knowing that success is uncertain. Isenberg acknowledges that ''perhaps more than most experts, managers work within uncertain environments, knowable and known only in equivocal terms'' (p. 255). In such ambiguous, contextually variable settings, learning takes the form of critical inquiry and reflection rather than the acquisition of previously specified performance behaviors.

Weick's (1983) analysis of managerial thought in the context of action also emphasizes the interconnection between analysis and action. He argues that too much emphasis can be placed on reflection as an index of thinking, and that ''thinking is inseparably woven into and occurs simultaneously with action'' (p. 222). This is a useful caution. It would be a mistake to conceive of critical thinking in the workplace as recognized by leisurely speculation on one's own successes and failures. The development of critical insight comes about through analysis tied to action. Practitioners frequently do not have the opportunity for introspective episodes during which they can reflect on the usefulness of various responses to crises. Managerial actions can be taken more or less thinkingly—that is, ''they can be done with varying amounts of deliberateness, intention, attention, care, control, and pertinacity'' (p. 223). When someone is acting thinkingly, ''the action is coupled with some underlying meaning that explains and adds strength to the action'' (p. 223).

A good example of this is Burgoyne and Hodgson's (1983) study of informal managerial learning. Using a critical incident approach, these researchers asked managers to think aloud during critical work incidents, to recall their thoughts a short time after these incidents and describe why they acted as they did, and then to discuss subsequent developments and changed interpretations several weeks or months later. The most frequent form of learning was that associated with managers' changing their conceptions about particular situations and subsequently altering their actions in the future on the basis of these new interpretations and understandings. Only rarely was this learning consciously recognized as such; managers frequently reported that they altered their actions according to their new understandings, but that only after participating in interviews for the study did they realize that this was what was happening.

Critical Thinking in Workplace Democracy

One of the most immediately striking aspects of the voluminous literature on learning at the workplace is its almost exclusive bias toward managerial and executive learning. The literature on workplace learning discussed so far in this chapter, for example, concentrates almost totally on the activities of managers, executives, and other professionals. The learning styles and critical thinking activities of working-class, blue-collar employees are rarely mentioned in this literature. Yet shop-floor workers who participate in bidding for a company facing bankruptcy and establish a worker-owned cooperative would probably identify the learning involved as among the most significant in their lives. This form of working-class managerial and executive learning at the workplace is rarely studied in the organizational development literature. Blue-collar work is generally perceived as routinized and adaptive; workers are seen as responding to directions imposed from above regarding how and when to work, and the nature of the work tasks they will be performing. The presumption seems to be that critical reflection is the prerogative of managers, executives, and professionals. This might be because theirs are considered the only jobs in which such capacities are needed or in which opportunities for this kind of analysis exist. Or it might be because they are thought to be the only kinds of workers able to engage in such sophisticated cognitive operations as identifying and challenging assumptions or exploring alternatives.

Blue-collar life, despite the depressing portrayal of work tasks at the outset of this chapter, does offer opportunities for critical thinking, particularly where the introduction of workplace democracy is concerned. Those involved in creating and managing worker collectives, cooperatives, and self-management experiments need to undertake a great deal of critical thinking. In past years, the creation of labor unions was one of the greatest educational (as well as political) endeavors in which the American and British working classes were involved (Zinn, 1980; Thompson, 1968). Despite the accounts of union corruption regularly featured in the pages of the American press, labor unions still represent one of the most important forums for critical thinking for blue-collar workers. In these settings, paid officials, shop stewards, volunteer workers, and members learn to question the wisdom of accepting executive decisions simply because they emanate from the corporate head office. They become critically aware of just how easily the media can tar all union organizing activity with the same brush of corruption. And they learn to advance, support, and justify their positions in the face of sustained opposition.

Workplace democracy is a catch-all term used to refer to a number of different activities. In various texts (Bernstein, 1980; Kanter, 1983; Zwerdling, 1984; Woodworth, Meek, and Whyte, 1985; Simmons and Mares, 1985; Quarrey, Blasi, and Rosen, 1986; Greenberg, 1986), the following initiatives are subsumed under this heading: employee ownership, worker self-management, worker buy-outs, worker participation on labor-management committees, and quality-of-working-life experiments such as workers' redesigning their jobs, introducing flexible working hours and job-sharing schemes, forming autonomous work units in factories, establishing forums for grievance-airing, and creating horizontal rather than vertical systems of communication.

Despite the recent popularity of these ideas in American industry, concepts of worker control have been developed and implemented since the beginning of the Industrial Revolution. In the nineteenth century Louis Pio, Robert Owen, John Ruskin, and William Morris, among others, advocated or experimented with forms of worker ownership, profit sharing, and productive autonomy. In the years immediately following World War I, a system of factory councils was established in Turin, Italy,

under the influence of Antonio Gramsci. These factory councils were responsible for teaching workers the economic and administrative skills required for them to take effective control of
the production process. Recently, another Italian educator,
Ettore Gelpi (1979, 1985), has built on Gramsci's ideas to place
the acquisition of techniques of worker ownership and self-
management at the heart of worker-education schemes.

Perhaps the most popular form of experimentation with
workplace democracy in American industry over the last two
decades is the quality of working life (QWL) movement (Cohen-
Rosenthal, 1982; Simmons and Mares, 1985). This is not surprising, since it involves changes in organizational hierarchies
and patterns of communication, and even some degree of worker
participation in decision making, without affecting the ownership of factories. The organization of workplace production is
altered, but the economic basis remains unaffected. It is an adaptation of two styles of work organization: the Japanese style of
management (Pascale and Athos, 1981; Ouchi, 1981) and the
Scandinavian style of industrial democracy (Gardell, 1982), both
of which focus on collective decision making. The United Auto-
mobile Workers Union, the United Steelworkers of America,
and the Communications Workers of America have all negotiated QWL programs within their industries. With the popular
success of *In Search of Excellence* (Peters and Waterman, 1982),
the principles of the QWL movement are now well known to
trainers and managers throughout American industry.

In contrast to the QWL movement, the establishment of
worker cooperatives and collectives (usually after management
has declared imminent bankruptcy or decided to close down
plants) represents a fundamental economic, as well as procedural, change in the organization of the workplace. In the United
States, organizations such as the Industrial Cooperative Association (ICA), the Association for Workplace Democracy (AWD),
the National Center for Employee Ownership, the Twin Streams
Educational Center (Chapel Hill, North Carolina), and the
Highlander Research Center (Knoxville, Tennessee) have come
to function as clearinghouses, advice centers, and training centers
for employee ownership experiments. In Britain, the national

Co-operative Development Agency, the Co-operative Union, and the Industrial Common Ownership movement provide advice and support to the 1,000 or so cooperatives in the country (Stirling and Mellor, 1984). All these bodies advise workers on establishing cooperatives in response to plant closures, aid existing small businesses to convert to collective ownership, and assist in setting up new cooperatives.

The diversity of worker collectives and cooperatives can be seen in the following examples: the Workers' Owned Sewing Company (Windsor, North Carolina), the Dungannon Sewing Cooperative (Virginia), the Stevens Paper Mill (Westfield, Massachussetts), the Moose Creek Construction Company (Burlington, Vermont), the Space Buildershouse building cooperative (Carrboro, North Carolina), the Colonial Cooperative Press (Clinton, Massachussetts), the Family Homes Cooperative (Beckley, West Virginia), the Parkwood Manor O & O Supermarket (Philadelphia, Pennsylvania), the Weirton Steel Company (Weirton, Pennsylvania), Plywood Incorporated (Washington and Oregon), and Cooperative Central (Salinas Valley, California). In Britain, the "work-ins" of the 1970s (for example, those at the Upper Clyde shipbuilders yard and the Plessey factory) have been succeeded by worker-owned and -controlled businesses such as the British Triumph Bonneville motorcycle factory (Meriden), Scott Bader Commonwealth chemical products (Northamptonshire), and the *Scottish Daily News* (Glasgow).

Those involved in trying to establish worker cooperatives are engaging in some of the most significant learning in their lives. In particular, they are frequently required to exhibit the essential components of critical thinking. They need to recognize which of the norms governing workplace organization should remain from the precollective era, and which are inappropriate to a worker collective. They need to be ready and able to restructure administrative procedures around assumptions that are very different from those under which they formerly labored. They need to abandon the hierarchical patterns of communication they are familiar with and devise democratic ways to come to collective decisions. Accounts of experiments in worker democracy (Adams, 1982; Zwerdling, 1984) emphasize the integration of affective, cognitive, reflective, and psychomotor learning—an integration that is the daily reality of those involved. Reflection and action alternate, focusing chiefly on responding to immediate problems and concerns. Skills are developed, self-concepts change, knowledge is acquired, and insights into participants' internalized assumptions are realized in complex and shifting configurations. In the process, workers develop intimate relationships and group allegiances that may be unprecedented in their lives.

Participation in workplace democracy is not always an inspirational event. Zwerdling's (1984) account of experiments with autonomous work groups at the Rushton Mining Company (Pennsylvania) and three smaller cooperatives in South Bend (Indiana), Saratoga Springs (New York), and Herkimer (New York) describes how perceived discrepancies between ideals and actuality create cynicism and frustration among workers who have had their expectations of individual autonomy and creativity raised and then disappointed. In a study of the training of shop stewards for participation in four British companies, the ambivalence of shop stewards' attitudes to participation in management decision making was vividly documented. Within the context of years of management-worker conflict and class antagonism, participation was mistrusted as a management strategy for using "divide and rule" tactics to split the solidarity of the work force. The shop stewards in these training courses were convinced that management would resent and ignore any proposals they made. They were afraid of becoming distanced from their constituents, of being gradually socialized into the managerial class, and of finding the collective bargaining system diluted as a result of employee participation. Maintaining a presence in participation schemes was seen as useful "as long as representatives were cautious, adopted a vigorous 'oppositional' stance, argued the workers' case as strongly as possible, avoided duplicity and used the systems to get what could be had out of them" (Dowling, Goodman, Gotting, and Hyman, 1984, p. 26).

Basseches (1984) points out the folly that results when "workers who have had their cognitive structures shaped by years of work experience in, and socialization for, traditional hierarchical organizations and relationships (where they were asked to follow managers' orders) are then asked to participate in managing their own work'' (p. 361). Without adequate preparation for this assumption of control, these workers, not surprisingly, tend to fall back into traditional patterns of dependent or disobedient behavior. Much the same processes are observed when learners in formal educational institutions are asked to take control over their learning. As case studies of self-directed learning make clear (Brookfield, 1985), people require a period of initiation into the new mode of thinking and acting. The same need for people to be eased into critical thinking is noted in Argyris's (1976, 1982) accounts of how executives become double-loop learners.

For self-management experiments to succeed, Basseches proposes that workers need to develop concepts of themselves as competent and capable of initiative. They must be able to take on the perspectives of others, such as co-workers who perform different roles in the organization, and reconcile differences between these differing perspectives when making decisions. They also have to be able to balance macro-organizational needs with individual workers' needs (Basseches, 1984, pp. 361–364). Eiger (1985, pp. 141–143) sees the training of workers for democratic participation as a major adult educational need. Workers need to learn how to obtain, understand, and apply information traditionally reserved only for managers. Quality circle leaders and participants need some acquaintance with a broad range of skills, including those of critical thinking, group dynamics, and problem solving. Workers in plants in which new technologies are being considered need to be involved in the selection and introduction of these innovations. When workers are involved in strategic decisions at the highest policy levels, they must be able to understand and challenge corporate financial reports and management proposals.

In a comparative survey of workplace democracy experiments, Bernstein (1980) identifies six criteria that must be satisfied if attempts at workplace democracy are to survive. If any are absent, the democratization decays or a crisis occurs, forcing the establishment of the missing components. These components are:

1. Participation in decision making, not just profit sharing.
2. Frequent feedback of economic results to workers, in monetary as well as informational form.
3. Full sharing with shop-floor workers of management-level information and expertise.
4. Guaranteed individual rights, corresponding to basic political liberties.
5. An independent tribunal or court of appeal composed of fellow workers in case of disputes.
6. A particular set of attitudes and values described as a democratic, participatory consciousness.

We might add to this list the skills of critical thinking and action. When people who have previously thought of themselves as oppressed, or as followers rather than leaders, face the prospect of liberation and leadership through their involvement in shaping workplace environments, they face experiences that have far greater validity and meaning than any they could find within formal education. When workers become responsible for what were previously thought of as "management" decisions, they have to abandon their stereotypical notions of opposing camps within the factory or organization. When conflicting preferences are expressed over the organization of shop-floor production, then mediation, compromise, and inhabiting others' frames of reference are required. When the demands of the majority outweigh minority wishes (for example, on issues of smoking within work areas or the introduction of maternity leave), the chimera of a fully harmonious work environment is exploded.

In instances such as those described above, the functions of critical thinking come into play when workers acknowledge that their plans for immediate innovation—technological or organizational—are altered by the inexorable demands of market forces. When workers make explicit the visions they have of the future, and the reasons why they hold these to be self-evident, they are analyzing their assumptions. In recognizing the theory-practice discrepancy between their idealized visions of a fully humanized workplace and the need to stay in business lies an acknowledgment of the complexity and contextual nature of the world. When proposals for changes in communication systems are recognized as inadequate responses for dealing with underlying problems (such as rivalries and cliquishness left over from the nondemocratic era), reflective skepticism is observable. When cooperative councils make a determined attempt to jettison established ways of thinking about reward systems, marketing, or work organization, imaginative speculation is present.

Developing Theories in Use at the Workplace

In reviewing the analyses of managerial learning and workplace democracy, we have seen that one important prompt to critical thinking arises out of creatively exploring and resolving anomalies between theory and actuality—between what is supposed to happen and what appears to be taking place. But this is not the only form of significant critical thinking at the workplace. A great deal of many workers' time is involved in responding to unforeseen situations. We are faced with the necessity of varying our "standard" practices according to the situations we face. We question our habitual ways of working, we discard assumptions informing these when we find they do not work for us, and we try to generate alternatives to these. As we learn from these experiments, we develop a sense of what approaches work within what contexts, and we become skeptical of fixed, for-all-time solutions to our workplace problems—both central aspects of critical thinking.

For example, people whose work involves a great deal of interaction with others at the workplace (shop stewards, managers, personnel officers) learn how to vary their behaviors according to the contexts concerned and according to the personalities of those involved. They learn when to be directive, when to allow people to think aloud, when to challenge, when to support, when to listen, and when to reflect back what someone is saying. They can practice these abilities in simulations and role plays and begin to develop their powers of intuitive

judgment; the real honing and refinement, however, take place
in the course of their daily work. They are constantly testing
out hunches, intuitions, and guesses about what will work against
their own reality. When a strategy or technique goes well with
one group, in one workshop, or with one individual, they make
a mental note of the contextual conditions under which it worked
and store this until a similar situation emerges.

Most workers, then, are theorists, though they do not
dignify themselves by that term. But what they are doing bears
strong similarities to developing what Schön (1983) describes
as *theories in use*. Essentially, a theory in use is nothing more than
a collection of three kinds of ideas about effective work practices. These ideas are about (1) what approaches work well in
particular contexts, (2) some explanations as to *why* they work
well, and (3) a readiness to alter ways of working as dictated
by a recognizable change in circumstances. These theories are
developed in certain recognizable stages. Educators or helping
professionals, for example, observe their actions and those of
their colleagues to see what approaches work well with the learners and clients with whom they are concerned. They develop
hunches about how they might alter their practice and test these
out in different contexts. They become critically reflective concerning what approaches work best, in which situations, and
why these are successful.

In many professionals' work activities, creativity, playing hunches, intuition, and informed guesswork are central
features of what is considered appropriate practice. Such intuitively based activities employ theories in use (Argyris and Schön,
1974; Schön, 1983)—the privately developed, proven ways of
performing that are contextually specific, idiosyncratic, and
unmentioned in textbooks of professional practice. Theories in
use can be inferred from action. Argyris, Putnam, and Smith
(1985, p. 82) describe them as "cognitive maps by which people
design action."

Theories in use are differentiated sharply from *espoused
theories,* which are the publicly agreed upon norms and practices that comprise appropriate professional practice, the theories
that people claim to follow, even when their own actions con-

tradict this claim. In education, for example, one espoused theory is that learning should be problem-centered. Another is that education should help people become increasingly self-directed. A third holds that participatory methods are most suitable, because they help learners make connections between their own experiences and the ideas they are exploring, and because such methods increase learners' involvement with the learning activity. Although these are contradicted by most educators (including myself) every day of their professional lives, they still hold sway as prescriptions of what should be happening in classrooms.

Espoused theories tend to become reified, so that they are the unchallenged conventional wisdom of a professional body. Theories in use are kept private, since they frequently contradict many of the apparently revered tenets of espoused theories. Even when espoused theories do not work, there may be a reluctance on the part of many professionals to make public their critical analysis, since to do so is to appear to be either incompetent (unable to apply theories correctly to specific situations) or heretical. As Gould (1980) writes, "In some organizations employees are afraid of asking for a change because organizations view such requests as acts of disloyalty or as disruptions" (p. 227). In other words, publicly acknowledging that one is employing theories in use rather than espoused theories is professionally dangerous, since one is open to being regarded as an unprofessional and incompetent maverick.

Publicly acknowledging one's own intuitively based theories in use can also be personally traumatic. It is to admit to ourselves, as well as to others, that we are experiencing some cognitive dissonance between what we say we believe and what we privately suspect to be true. Argyris, Putnam, and Smith (1985) write of the ambivalence experienced in acknowledging theories in use. On the one hand, we wish to express these so that they can be tested further, refined, and sharpened. On the other hand, we want to cover them so that we can protect ourselves from the possible pain and vulnerability involved in admitting that we do not follow the precepts of our professional group. They describe how some participants in their workshops take protective stances: "They approach the learning process afraid to make mistakes for fear of appearing foolish or stupid; they shy away from experimentation and withdraw in the face of reflection; and they resent those who appear to be learning and blame them for their own experience of failure" (Argyris, Putnam, and Smith, 1985, p. 277). I know this fear well myself. It took me ten years of research and practice to admit to the severe theory-practice contradictions I experienced in facilitating self-directed learning (Brookfield, 1987a).

Developing theories in use is one of the most important ways critical thinking can be practiced at the workplace. It requires practitioners to reflect on the reasons why espoused theories are not working and to seek alternative forms of practice. Workers are thus engaged in identifying the assumptions underlying espoused theories and considering the fit between these assumptions and the reality of professional practice. When there is an evident discrepancy between these, workers develop new assumptions about what will work and then alter their practices accordingly. These alterations are generally done privately, so that there is no public challenge to the agreed-upon espoused theories. As these theories in use are proven to be effective through repeated testing against experience, workers become more confident about declaring publicly the hunches, intuitions, and guesses informing their practice. Their success will generally be noticed by fellow practitioners, and the assumptions underlying the theories in use will be made explicit. Over time there will be sufficient accretion of instances of successful theories in use that a paradigm shift will occur regarding how successful appropriate practice is conceived, and elements of the theories in use will assume the status of espoused theories.

As with many other aspects of critical thinking, theories in use are often developed after the practitioners concerned repeatedly encounter discrepancies between what should happen according to textbook injunctions and what appears to be happening in their professional realities. Argyris and Schön (1974) identify three common features of such theories: they are based on valid information gained from those involved in the professional activity, the professionals concerned are able to make free and informed choices over aspects of their practice, and the theories are constantly monitored and adjusted as they are implemented in real life. Theories in use tend to be micro-theories of action—that is, they are contextually specific ideas about what works in a particular institution, program, or group of people. Since institutional norms vary from organization to organization, it is difficult to generalize these microtheories to the macro level.

One process that is generally observable according to Schön (1983) is that of problem setting. This refers to "a pro-cess in which, interactively, we name the things to which we will attend and frame the context in which we will attend to them" (p. 40). Problem setting is not a technical competence; rather, it is an artistic exercise in which important situations are delineated, central concerns are expressed, and difficulties are identified. It is similar to Freire's (1973) concept of prob-lem posing. Both problem setting and problem posing antedate problem solving, and they differ from many problem-solving exercises in that the problems to be addressed are identified by participants rather than set by external authorities. They are grounded in employees' contextual awareness of the important aspects of workplace life.

Critical Thinking in Action

Developing theories in use, acknowledging the contex-tual complexity of work settings, and problem setting are all important elements in the process of critical thinking at the work-place. Schön (1983) calls this process *reflection in action* and ef-fectively demonstrates how critical reflection is tied to personal and workplace change. He points out that critical reflection is much more than a purely cognitive process of analysis and speculation. Instead, critical reflection in action is an artistic process. It is intuitive, improvisational, and creative. Practi-tioners make confident judgments regarding appropriate re-sponses to situations and problems for which no explicit ration-ale has been developed. In occupational life we are frequently faced with unexpected and unfamiliar situations to which we have to make some immediate response. In such situations our responses might be perceived as haphazard and irrational; in the calm after the storm, however, we are often able to see that our actions were grounded in our intuitive understanding of our field of practice and in our accumulated experience of dealing with other, related crises.

Periods of crisis, trauma, and unanticipated experimentation are frequently followed by musing and speculation. We wonder why we behaved instinctively the way we did, and what aspects of our actions were most appropriate or productive. In my first year of teaching in London, I would ride the commuter train back home at the end of each day pondering the differential successes I had had with various techniques in response to fights, disruptions, and general "acting up" of students during that day. I would think about the contextual variables that had been present when various strategies had been successful. For example, under what conditions would ignoring the behavior be successful? When and what kind of "acting up" should be humored? When was "cracking down" warranted, and under what conditions did it work? How much latitude could be expected, should be allowed, or should be encouraged? Schön (1983) calls this initial reflective period a process of constructing "a new theory of the unique case" (p. 68). Practitioners develop strategies, techniques, and habitual responses to deal with different kinds of situations, drawing chiefly on their acquired experience and intuitive understanding.

Because professional knowledge is "mismatched to the changing character of the situations of practice—the complexity, uncertainty, instability, uniqueness and value conflicts which are increasingly perceived as central to the worlds of professional practice" (Schön, 1983, p. 14)—we have to develop our own, contextually specific theories of effective professional practice. This requires a good deal of critical thinking. In my case, my previous undergraduate experience had provided me with a body of academic knowledge, but it had in no way prepared me to deal with the daily reality of classroom fights and disruptions. I had to call on my limited experience in dealing with conflict in groups to survive during that first year of teaching. In fact, my most useful responses were grounded in reflection on my own experiences (and I had had plenty) of acting up in *my* school days. Thinking about my motivations for behaving this way at school, and what deterrents, controls, and sanctions I had taken seriously at that time, was the most useful form of reflection in helping me deal with a daily series of crises for which I had no professional training.

The episodic speculation on one's responses to unfamiliar situations may be of extremely short duration in the midst of those situations. It may simply be a case of registering, in a period of five to ten seconds, that a particular technique or response was unusually effective. When a similar situation is faced again, the memory of that response jumps to the forefront of our minds (apparently without a period of prolonged reflection), and we try out the behavior again to see if it works. If it does, the initial registration or "logging" of its success in our memory is reaffirmed, and the behavior may well become a tried and trusted response to situations characterized by similar features. In other words, it becomes a theory in use.

Encouraging Critical Thinking at the Workplace

This chapter contains many specific illustrations and suggestions for helping workers recognize, develop, and share their own theories in use. Some more specific suggestions can be made, however, for how critical thinking might be developed at the workplace. The first of these concerns the fostering of what Argyris (1976, 1982) and Argyris and Schön (1974, 1978) define as *double-loop learning*, through which workers identify, question, and change the assumptions underlying workplace organization and patterns of interaction. Workers publicly challenge workplace assumptions and learn to change underlying values. Through confronting the basic assumptions behind prevailing organizational norms, values, myths, hierarchies, and expectations, workers help prevent stagnation and dysfunctional habits. They attempt to recognize when the organizational culture is injurious to productivity, morale, and communication.

Perhaps the clearest guidelines on how to assist people to become double-loop learners are contained in Argyris (1976, 1982). Argyris is particularly interested in the *nested paradoxes* evident in executives' reasoning. Nested paradoxes are forms of reasoning that lead to productive consequences in the short term and unproductive consequences in the long term. Each stage in the executive's reasoning process is identified, and the feelings accompanying its accomplishment are described. Executives are encouraged to write out scenarios of how they have solved work-related problems and then to analyze what they have written as if they were trying to help a friend. Skilled helpers then point out the contradictions between feelings and actions. Closely related to this is the *action science approach* (Argyris, Putnam, and Smith, 1985), in which group members analyze transcribed tapes of their previous interactions to help people understand the frames of reference within which they are behaving.

Argyris (1976) describes a series of learning seminars held over a period of four years in which the participants (mostly company presidents) became aware of, and began to challenge, the assumptions underlying their organizations' structures and operations. Participants were found to progress through four alternating phases: discovery, invention, production, and generalization. These phases were not necessarily sequential; realizations that occurred at later points in the process frequently caused participants to return to earlier points so that they could reconsider these with heightened insight.

In the discovery phase, case studies and tape recordings of participants' work behavior were analyzed to discover the theories in use employed by participants. The discovery phase focused the presidents' attention on discrepancies, inconsistencies, and unintended consequences evident in their real-life actions. In the invention phase, participants were encouraged to slow down their usual decision-making processes and to make explicit the stage-by-stage reasoning they used in trying to resolve those anomalies and ambiguities revealed in the discovery phase. Group members were encouraged to develop preferred scenarios in which the inconsistency was effectively dealt with.

In the production phase, the behaviors necessary to realize these preferred scenarios were produced in role-playing sessions. Finally, in the generalization phase, participants were asked to generalize wherever possible from successful behaviors and strategies for resolving discrepancies in particular settings to other contexts. This phase was the most time-consuming, and Argyris describes the process involved as "simmering" (p. 223). He freely admits that neither faculty nor participants were able to understand exactly what was happening during the simmering process. Techniques that were helpful to this process were the participants' listening to tape recordings of their sessions and talking to someone else (such as a spouse) about what had happened. Sometimes the memorandums that participants sent regularly to each other could be analyzed to trace the evolution of their critical thinking over a period of time.

The uncovering of assumptions underlying organizational cultures is an approach to developing critical thinking at the workplace that has been described by Schein (1985). The chief data-collection techniques used are adaptations of the critical incident and critical questioning techniques described more fully in Chapter Six. Schein proposes interviewing workers on their perceptions of critical incidents in the organization's history. Critical incidents are defined in this context as events that threatened organizational survival, that caused re-examination or reformulation of goals and ways of working, or that raised issues of employees' inclusion or exclusion from the organization's operations. Critical incidents might be developments for which the organization had no ready solution (such as the sudden oil shortage of 1973). They might be events that challenged existing norms and solutions (such as fraud or embezzlement). They might be events that provoked unusual tension (such as preventing unionization). The interviews are conducted with single individuals or with groups, the latter approach being especially suited to give those working within organizations a quicker insight into their own culture.

One particularly useful (and inexpensive) means by which critical thinking can be encouraged at the workplace is through managers, trainers, and human resource developers formalizing the informal modeling process that occurs naturally in all workplace settings. As described in Chapter Five, observing exemplary role models is one of the most effective ways through which people can learn how to think critically. Instead of urging employees to attend costly workshops on critical thinking, in which participants learn general, context-free critical skills, it might be more fruitful to release from their normal work duties those employees who are most adept at thinking critically, so that they can serve as informal critical thinking consultants to others in the workplace. Critical thinking is frequently a context-embedded skill; that is, it stands more chance of being used, and of affecting how people think and act in real life, if it is developed in the contexts in which it is going to be applied.

The advantage of this approach is that it avoids the danger that those attending workshops on critical thinking run by outside consultants will be unable to make any effective transfer of their newly learned skills to their actual workplace settings. When an exemplar of critical thinking within the organization is released to serve as a critical consultant, the possibility of transferring learning is markedly increased. The consultant understands the particular contexts within which employees are operating and appreciates the contextual constraints under which they function. The consultant is aware of the formal and informal organizational hierarchies operating to inhibit the development of critical thought and action. The consultant has direct experience of employees' most deeply felt concerns and anxieties, and knowledge of the penalties they fear might accrue from experiments in critical thinking. Knowing all this, the consultant can frame the activities involved in thinking critically in terms and contexts that other employees understand and appreciate. These can be practiced and applied in real work situations without employees fearing organizational penalties. Of all the techniques suggested and described in this chapter, it is the use of role modeling of critical thinking that holds the greatest promise for the development of this capacity in the workplace.

Conclusion

As we move toward the twenty-first century, the workplace is increasingly being recognized as a setting in which significant adult learning can occur (Marsick, 1987). The trends toward increased worker cooperation, participatory management, and a general democratization of the workplace appear inexorable. This chapter has shown that critical thinking is not solely the province of a white-collar, managerial class, but that it exists at the factory floor level whenever workers are encouraged by circumstance to re-design aspects of their workplace, or when they take it upon themselves to suggest alternative ways of organizing production. Fostering critical thinking at the workplace is something we should support not simply because of the benefits to be derived from higher productivity and greater worker satisfaction; rather, we should recognize the opportunity to exercise critical thought at the workplace as one of the chief ways in which we affirm our identities.

❦ 9 ❧

Analyzing Political Issues
and Commitments

Power is all-pervasive. It exists in personal relationships, in the
production and distribution of wealth, and in institutionalized
forms (such as military and police forces). As the International
League for Social Commitment in Adult Education (1987) states,
power relationships often work "through hidden cultural processes that make people believe that violence and poverty are
inevitable or even their own fault." A shorthand term used to
describe the development of critical awareness concerning issues
of power, control, and change is *political learning*. Political learning occurs when people become aware of the pervasiveness of
issues of power and control in all spheres of human interaction
and then work to alter the patterns and structures of human
interaction. It involves critical analysis, reflection, and action
in the world. It can take place in widely varying settings and
at different levels of involvement.

 Political learning is not necessarily about the stuff of
politics as formally defined—for example, the workings of the
Constitution, the separation of powers, the arguments surrounding proportional representation, procedures for passing bills
through Parliament. Rather, it is developing a critical awareness
of how hierarchies of power and status infuse all personal and
group relations. It is realizing that patterns of dominance and
submission become etched into the ground rules of relationships,

162

unless constant and determined attempts to prevent this are made by those involved. It is knowing that stereotyping, discriminating, propagandizing, and deceiving (both oneself and others) are endemic to relationships and interactions on personal, community, and national levels. It is working in concert with others to change organizational structures, unquestioned values, and habitual patterns of interaction. It is making explicit the connection between change in one's personal life and the need to press for often controversial and deep-seated structural changes in the institutions in which that life is embedded. And it is working collectively with others to bring about such changes.

Political learning happens experientially; indeed, in our personal relationships, in encounters with different cultures, and at a neighborhood level it is practically impossible not to undertake some kind of reflection upon the political aspects of our environment. Most probably, however, we do not conceptualize our activities as political learning. There are, of course, many people who experience political learning in a conscious and purposeful manner. They work for political party organizations. They are members of advocacy campaigns for consumer rights or environmental protection. They are union shop stewards or regional organizers. They work for single-issue causes such as the Equal Rights Amendment, the legalization or abolition of women's right to abortion, or positive discrimination for the handicapped. They are involved in ongoing struggles for the civil rights of ethnic and other minorities, or for a nuclear freeze and eventual nuclear disarmament. To them, political learning is a daily reality and is identified as such, though they may show a remarkable capacity for attending to issues of power and control in the formal institutional sphere while neglecting these in their personal relationships.

Political learning (becoming critically aware of issues of power and control in relationships, social structures, and economic arrangements, and learning how to work collectively for change) should be distinguished from learning about politics. The latter is a much more restricted and specific area of activity, in which are involved lobbyists, party workers, and activists who support a variety of groups and organizations. It includes such activities as becoming knowledgeable about formal political processes—for example, concerned voters learning about the complicated process of primary elections and party nominations that is necessary for the selection of presidential candidates; professional lobbyists learning how best to exercise influence on the passage of legislation affecting their cause; and groups of citizens studying the doctrine and consequences of the separation of powers. Learning about politics may be subsumed under political learning, but it is only one specific element in this general category.

Politics is a shorthand term for the processes by which decisions are made, wealth is distributed, services are regulated, justice is maintained, and minority interests are protected. At its heart, politics is concerned with issues of control and power— how control and power are gained, shared, abdicated, protected, abused, and delegated; how those without power can organize collectively to press for democratic change and a more equitable distribution of power. In this sense, personal relationships all have a political dimension to them. Usher (1981) comments that "political education is probably not about politics at all but about people and their development, by which I mean their personal development" (p. 53). In our relationships with our spouses, lovers, friends, colleagues, learners, and clients, we are frequently concerned to gain power over how decisions are made, how resources (finances or services) are allocated, and how their dependence upon us is formalized. How families come to decisions regarding the spending of money or the destination for vacations is a political process. It can be done democratically or autocratically. The same might be said about a couple's decisions on whose career comes first when one partner is offered an attractive position in another location, or which schools, religious groups, and youth organizations their children are to join.

As Mills (1959) recognized, political forces and public issues are usually evident in personal relationships. There is a glaring anomaly between a man's urging democratization of the workplace and his insisting that his wife function as a servant and domestic orderly. In the last years of his life, John Lennon frequently referred to his frustration at male political activists who would allocate women members of action groups to typing, child minding, and tea making. Those with a sensitivity to sexism and racism know how easy it is for members of dominant groups sincerely to preach collective participation, while their actions implicitly devalue the contributions of oppressed groups.

Political learning as described above is not restricted to those who watch "MacNeil-Lehrer News Hour," "Nightline," "Weekend World," or "Panorama." It is a daily reality for many adults as they reflect upon the societal forces, structures, and individuals who exercise power over their lives. Such power includes the power to decide whether people stay in work and are thereby able to feed, clothe, and shelter themselves and their families; the power to declare that people should consider themselves to be at war with another country; the power to alter the physical face of people's communities; and the power to frame, pass, and enforce laws that govern the behavior, expression of ideas, and artistic creations of citizens. Questioning the basis on which individuals, groups, and systems exercise these powers over one's life is the beginning of political learning. Political learning is evident whenever people notice, and begin to ponder, the discrepancies and inequities among groups in their societies. Making connections between personal crises and broader political happenings is at the heart of critical reflection on the political world. Imagining alternative ways in which power and wealth could be distributed, and structures organized, is a major prompt for collective political action. Asking awkward questions about the rightness of, and justification for, political decisions, actions, and structures is the focus of critical thinking about the political world.

Developing Political Commitments

Developing political involvements and commitments, however these might be defined, is of crucial importance in adult life. In adulthood we are brought face to face with the harsh realities of political living, particularly the consequences that policy decisions and legislative changes have for our individual lives. It is in adulthood, rather than in the earlier stages of life, that the experiential reservoir and cognitive sophistication needed for political thought and action are most likely to be present. It is in adulthood that the effects of governmental changes, policy initiatives, and legislative injunctions are personally experienced. People lose jobs, gain employment, move their residence, go to war, get divorced, or obtain an abortion as a result of political changes. These are familiar crises in adult life, and because such crises are not generally faced by children Wright (1980) argues that "an effective political literacy campaign is essentially an adult educational task" (p. 9). A major national report on adult education in Britain (H. M. Stationery Office, 1973) describes political education as "essentially a task for adult education . . . requiring as it does from its students a background of political experience, maturity of judgment and the serious motivation that comes from the challenges and responsibilities of adult life" (p. 12). The adult's accumulated life experiences allow for an appreciation of contextuality and complexity in understanding connections between personal troubles and public issues. Those life experiences also enable us to think critically about politics.

These judgments about adults' capacities to think critically about politics are based on an assumption regarding the nature of adulthood as distinct from childhood or adolescence. This assumption might be stated as follows: adults, by virtue of their greater range and depth of experiences in social living, are able to understand and reflect upon political issues, controversies, and concerns to a greater degree than are children and adolescents. This is, of course, only an assumption and is itself open to critical analysis. Some readers may be able to cite exceptions—politically sophisticated adolescents of their acquaintance who are clearly more developed in this respect than some adults. The student activism of the 1960s in North America and Western Europe, the role of the Red Guard in the 1968 Chinese Cultural Revolution, and the current wave of protest on American university campuses urging the divestment of university resources from companies with holdings in South Africa are all examples of informed political action undertaken by people generally thought to be in a transitional stage between adolescence and adulthood. In 1986 and 1987, students have been at the forefront of social-change movements in France (where major educational reforms were withdrawn after national student protests) and China (where students are calling for a democratization not just of the educational system but of the whole state).

Acknowledging that exceptions will always exist, it is still true that in adult life we come into contact much more directly with social services, public organizations, and the personal consequences of an unequal distribution of resources and life chances than we do in childhood. When we encounter these consequences in childhood and adolescence, we are less likely to perceive their cause as being embedded in the way our society is organized, structures are developed, and resources are distributed than we are in adult life. Although student protests may be familiar, the great mass of working young adults have not joined these movements. Even in adult life the connection linking individual biographies to social structures and economic forces is difficult to make for many people.

Notwithstanding this difficulty, opportunities do exist for developing critical thinkers who do not view political events as wholly outside their frames of reference. The connections between policy decisions, legislative change, and individual destinies can certainly be pointed out by helpers more clearly and dramatically in adulthood than in childhood. For example, the connection between a government maintaining high interest rates, and a wave of business bankruptcies, is clear to small-business owners and workers. The massive number of farm foreclosures currently taking place in the United States is perceived by farmers to be caused by governmental policy change—that is, the government's reversal from encouragement of mass production of certain crops in the 1970s to the current refusal to protect crop surpluses from cheaper foreign competition. The rise in unemployment in the British Isles is commonly blamed on the Conservative government's monetary policies of the last eight years. By cutting spending on public services, allowing foreign multinational corporations to have full access to British markets, and refusing to tamper with the operation of free-market forces, the government has caused millions of adults to be unemployed.

Nationally, a government's declaration of war and introduction of conscription do, of course, have a very dramatic impact on the lives of all its citizens. More locally, the closure of schools, hospitals, day-care centers, and residential homes for the elderly and the reduction of public services such as transportation and street cleaning are clearly linked by most of those affected to governmental actions. When a parent cannot go out to work because he or she has to stay home to look after a child who used to be placed in a day-care center recently closed due to budget cuts, the connection between personal circumstances and political forces is made very clear. When adult sons or daughters have to watch parents suffering because their arthritis, heart murmur, or cancer is not severe enough to place them in an "emergency" category, and to give them priority status over others on a waiting list for operations, the connection between this personal trauma and government decisions to freeze or reduce spending on health services is tragically evident. Less dramatic, but just as obvious, is the sense of loneliness and isolation felt by those in rural areas who have had their access to networks of friends and relatives severed by the closing of a railway line or bus service as a result of government spending cuts.

Readers can undoubtedly supply their own numerous examples of the ways in which their biographies have been affected by policy decisions and legislative changes. In my own life, the impending closure in 1980 (due to the public spending cuts imposed by the newly elected Conservative government) of an adult education center in which I was working caused me to accept an offer from the University of British Columbia in Vancouver, Canada, for a year's visiting professorship in adult education. What I imagined initially to be a year of temporary respite from fighting budget cuts in my department had far-reaching ramifications for my personal and professional life. Within the next twenty-four months, I experienced a divorce, sold my house,

saw my position at the adult education center eliminated, and
took two new jobs—one in England and one in the United States.
Had there been no threat of closure to my program in 1980,
it is questionable whether I would have initiated this odyssey
of personal change. In retrospect it is easy to ascribe to one's
actions a rationale that, in reality, was not present at the time.
In my case, however, I do believe that the change of government in 1979 (from a Labour government to Conservative) was
connected directly to the turbulence of the next two years of
my life. Private troubles and public issues were, for me, dramatically linked.

Concepts of Political Involvement

How adults might be helped to develop political involvements and commitments, and to think critically about political
issues, is the concern of many writers and activists, who advocate different approaches toward these activities. Various concepts are frequently mentioned in connection with this concern:
political education, political literacy, civic literacy, or citizenship education. The belief that is central to all of these concepts
is that politically informed citizens who can think critically about
political issues are ready to participate in decision making and
other political processes vital to the proper functioning of democracy. In other respects, however, there are subtle but important differences between them.

Political Education. Political education is most frequently
conceived as a process rather than a product or content area
(Usher, 1981). Tuckett (n.d.) defines it as "education about
how power works, how things get done, and how you control
the processes by which they get done" (p. 1). This educational
outcome is achieved through people working together to solve
problems, organize activities, achieve change, and create new
patterns of organization. Sometimes this is done in the context
of a course on, say, gender politics, in which collaborative approaches are used to encourage learners to regard their experiences as the formal course content. At other times these ends
might be achieved through educators working to assist com-

munity activist groups such as tenant rights organizations. Involving adult students in the management of adult education centers is another approach to making participation in adult education a democratic experience.

According to the UNESCO report *Learning to Be* (Faure and others, 1972), the essential characteristic of political education is that it is "linked to the just, efficient and democratic exercise of power" (p. 151). The report urges that this be achieved through people undergoing "an apprenticeship of active participation in the functioning of social structures and, where necessary, a personal commitment in the struggle to reform them" (p. 151). Political education, then, is most frequently conceived as assisting learners to gain experience of democratic processes through an involvement in some form of praxis in which collective decisions have to be reached and collective procedures and structures have to be created. These activities are, of necessity, frequently controversial. Whenever people begin to explore issues of power and control, and whenever they take action on these issues, resistance is bound to be encountered from groups who feel that their power or control is being challenged. There are considerable forces working against the development of critical thinking that might lead to political action. Establishments have a huge incentive to divert energy from critical reflection on political matters. Those representatives of the dominant culture who wish to retain values and structures that buttress their power have a vested interest in preventing people from asking awkward questions. They do not regard the questioning of conventional assumptions or givens as a good thing; rather, it is perceived as an intrinsically subversive activity.

Asking awkward questions about why power and wealth are distributed the way they are, or whose interests social hierarchies and institutional structures advance, is an example of critical thinking. Speculating imaginatively on alternative ways of distributing power, or on how hierarchies might be dismantled and structures changed, is also basic to being critically reflective. Educators and helping professionals who encourage people to ask these awkward questions about imbalances in power structures and wealth distribution are likely to be criticized by gatekeepers of the dominant culture. Helpers who try to promote political learning may risk (at best) public criticism or (at worst) loss of their livelihoods or, in some regimes, even their lives. It is no accident that some of the earliest victims of death squads in the aftermath of violent coups d'état are teachers, scholars, and writers who encourage people to ask critically awkward questions about the activities of those in power.

When learners are encouraged to explore their own biographies to understand how they have assimilated dominant cultural values, classrooms become democratic learning laboratories. When teachers behave with civic courage (Giroux, 1983) and act as if democracy were a living reality in their classrooms and society, they run the risk of offending institutional norms. Bryson (1936) warned teachers of adults that, if they encourage reflective skepticism in their students concerning simplistic solutions and doctrines offered by politicians, they will most likely face the dislike and ridicule of society and its leaders. When educators encourage learners to ask awkward questions about examination policies, criteria governing academic performance, and other institutional rules, they may gain reputations as mavericks and troublemakers. The knowledge that acquiring a reputation as someone who encourages people to ask awkward questions is likely to hamper chances of reappointment, promotion, and tenure is a powerful inhibitor to encouraging critical thinking in learners.

Once learners begin questioning the assumptions underlying conventional wisdom in academic subjects, they are likely to apply the same critical habits to analyzing their own lives and the political structures in which these lives are lived. It is logically and practically impossible to engage in *limited* empowerment of learners. One cannot encourage students to ask awkward questions only in areas that are compartmentalized as "safe." The habits of critical thinking are notoriously uncontrollable. If we acquire the habit of asking, "Why are things this way?" and "How could things be different?" in our academic involvements, sooner or later we are likely to ask these questions about the structures that elsewhere surround us. Hoggart (1983) acknowledges that "it would be possible but merely cosmetic to find a safer adjective'' (p. ii) than political. Jones (1986) writes that "the tension between adult education and government is, in its own small way, one of the necessary tensions of democracy" (p. 5), arguing that when a government finds the activities of adult educators to be uncongenial, this may be evidence that those educators are performing their proper function. Wright (1980) believes that "political education will always be controversial and perhaps especially so in an adult educational context in which adult citizens confront real issues" (p. 11).

Political Literacy. An alternative concept that has been used to describe the ability to think critically about political matters is that of political literacy. Defining and understanding this concept has, in recent years, been the concern of the British Programme for Political Education (comprising the Politics Association and the Hansard Society). The major report of this project (Crick and Porter, 1978) defines a politically literate person as one who knows "what the main political disputes are about; what beliefs the main contestants have of them; how they are likely to affect him; and he will have a predisposition to try to do something about it in a manner at once effective and respectful of the sincerity of others" (p. 33). Political literacy is a cluster of knowledge, skills, and attitudes that allow someone "to act, change his mind, appreciate other points of view, weigh evidence and arguments fairly and recognize the difference between truth and ideology" (p. 16). Politically literate citizens understand differing positions and arguments concerning issues, they are able to participate actively in political discussion, and they are concerned that certain democratic procedural values (fairness, respect for truth, tolerance) be exemplified in their political discussions and activities.

As part of a national report on Political Education for Adults in England and Wales conducted by the Advisory Council for Adult and Continuing Education (ACACE), Ridley (1983) argues against this concept of political literacy. He regards it as primarily concerned with cognitive skills, rather than action, and elitist in tone. He prefers to place the emphasis in political education for adults squarely on the acquisition of community-action and -participation skills rather than on understanding broad political issues of the day. Usher (1981) points out the danger of equating political literacy with seeing the validity of all points of view in understanding the complexities of political life. Effective political action, he believes, occurs when one is able "to recognize complexity but at the same time to pursue what one wants with single-mindedness" (p. 49). When we achieve too great an appreciation of complexity, it becomes difficult to generate the motivation to act simply toward a clear-cut end.

Civic Literacy. A third concept of critical thinking about politics is that of civic literacy. This has been elaborated by Ziegler, Healy, and Ellsworth (1978) and Healy (1979) as part of Ziegler's development of the futures invention technique. It is composed of three elements: understanding one's concrete situation, becoming clear about whether to accept or change that situation, and inventing and discovering ways to accomplish one's intentions. Mathews (1985) proposes the concept of civic intelligence to describe the kinds of critical thinking teachers should be encouraging in schools. The components of such intelligence are appreciating how others see situations, understanding how individual lives are connected to social structures, and a tolerance for disagreement. The skills of civic intelligence are said to be those of understanding other perspectives and distinguishing between facts and values.

Citizenship Education. More widely accepted than civic literacy, however, is the idea of citizenship education. This has been the subject of reports of the U.S. Department of Health, Education, and Welfare (Farquhar and Dawson, n.d.), personal treatises (Butts, 1980), radical critiques (Giroux, 1983), national symposia (Jones, 1985), reinterpretations in terms of the opportunities provided by mass communications (Barber, 1984), and a Canadian symposium (Brooke, 1983). These analyses generally recognize a fundamental tension inherent in the concept of citizenship education. On the one hand, it involves the inculcation of appropriately democratic values, becoming, in fact, "a process of socialization to the rules and values of a society" (Brooke, 1983, p. 11). On the other hand, it entails "a process of creating a critical consciousness regarding society and its values" (p. 11).

The most sustained analysis of how citizenship education might be interpreted in an adult education context is that undertaken by Lindeman (1961, 1945). As books on him (Stewart, 1987; Brookfield, 1987b) have acknowledged, he spent the decades of the 1920s, 1930s, and 1940s seeking consistently to place the development of democratic attitudes and habits at the forefront of organized adult education. To Lindeman, the purpose of life was the learning of democratic attitudes and actions. This learning took place throughout the lifespan, but it was most appropriate to adulthood. Only adults were fully aware of the complexities and contradictions of political living; a predisposition toward democratic habits could be inculcated in children, but it was in the adult years that a full appreciation and realization of democratic living could occur.

Democratic process, however, was not something Lindeman saw as coming naturally. It involved hard critical analysis, elements of self-denial, concern for others, the ability to take on the perspectives of opponents, and a willingness to live with majority decisions with which one felt uncomfortable. These attitudes had to be learned, and Lindeman felt that in encouraging democratic modes of thought and action, educators found their highest calling. To him, the fundamental purpose of any educational effort, and the criterion by which that effort could be judged successful, was the nurturing of the democratic spirit through democratic procedures. Learning democracy was not accomplished through sterile civics or citizenship courses. It could not be done just by reading the Constitution, or writing essays on the different functions of the legislative, executive, and judicial branches of government. Democracy was a *lived* process, and it invariably involved adults' attempts to change some aspect of their personal, occupational, and social worlds. Educators had to be ready and eager to involve themselves beyond the classroom with the activities of local community groups, tenant associations, community advocacy movements, environmental rights campaigns, efforts to create workplace democracy, and civil rights activities.

This involvement of educators did, of course, raise questions regarding the ethical responsibilities of educators. Through-

out his life, Lindeman grappled with the question of how far
educators should impose their preferences on others, how they
should deal with attitudes (such as racist or sexist denigrations
of ethnic minorities and women) that they found repugnant,
and at what point they should withdraw from learning groups
whose members had begun to take control over deciding their
own curricula and methods. He was adamant, however, that
"every social action group should at the same time be an adult
education group, and I go even so far as to believe that all successful adult education groups sooner or later become social
action groups" (Lindeman, 1945, p. 12).

Programs for Political Learning

The concepts and arguments discussed in the preceding
section all share one central concern: encouraging adults to
become critical thinkers about the political world. Given this,
it is reasonable to presume that educational provision toward
this end would be widespread. C. W. Mills (1954) certainly
believed this to be so, declaring that "to the extent that the adult
college is effective, it is going to be political; its students are
going to try to influence decisions of power" (p. 16). As Harris's
(1980) comparative survey of adult political education records,
however, those countries most concerned with organized political
education are newly independent, recently created, or adjusting
to the aftermath of traumatic social change such as war, economic depression, or revolution. In Western industrial societies,
there are few educational institutions that would declare the
development of adults' powers to think critically about politics
to be a central curricular aim. In Denmark and West Germany,
the folk high schools serve something of this function, as do the
Swedish study circles. In North America and Britain, however,
these kinds of activities are regarded as the province of community activist and advocacy groups, of political parties, of union
or business groups, or of nonprofit foundations such as the
Kettering Foundation or the Foreign Policy Association—in
other words, of a range of social and community agencies not
identified as "educational" by statute or custom.

   This reluctance of educators, trainers, and counselors of adults to become involved in organizing political education forums, classes, or workshops has been lamented by many. Jones (1986) declares that "adult political illiteracy is widespread" (p. 5) in Britain. Regarding the 1984 U.S. presidential election, Brightman (1984, p. 106) wrote that "this year's political campaigns have convinced me that the state of the art of bamboozlement has so far outpaced the discriminatory skills of the electorate that it creates a real and present danger to our democracy." Ellison (1984) notes that "curiously lacking from almost all Adult Basic Education programs is any meaningful consideration of our country's political systems and the means to effectively interact with them" (p. 109). Stewart (1981) observes that *politics* is a dirty word to educators and trainers of adults.

   In North American and British adult education, the need to develop learners' critical sophistication concerning political issues and processes, and to encourage their capacity for informed judgment, has frequently been stated. A great many writers ascribe to adult education some form of political function, either in terms of encouraging participation in democratically run learning groups as a training laboratory for democratic habits, or in terms of developing in adults the capacity to think critically about issues so that they make informed and responsible electoral choices. Hoggart (1983) writes of "that long and honourable tradition in British adult education which seeks to help individual citizens improve their knowledge of how their political system works and thus contribute more actively towards making a reality of the democratic assumptions and aspirations of that system" (p. ii).

   In the earlier part of this century, Albert Mansbridge, R. H. Tawney, Eduard Lindeman, and Lyman Bryson all wrote passionately of the need to use education to develop adults' capacities to think critically about politics. Lindeman (1945) believed that adult education was integral to the democratic struggle and necessary to counteract the influence of demagogues. He maintained that participation by adults in a network of neighborhood discussion groups examining issues of racial discrimination, the relative merits of free enterprise and socialist economic systems, the democratization of educational facilities, and the role of the United States in world affairs would ensure the future of democracy by raising critical awareness of democratic issues. Herring (1953) criticized the "galloping mediocrity" (p. 54) observable in adults' knowledge and understanding of political matters—a mediocrity that resulted partly from adult and continuing education programmers refusing to organize programs of political education. Crabtree (1963) argued that American adult education was invested with the imperative of making democracy function to the limits of its potential. Only when adult education was allied to some compelling political cause or movement was it fulfilling its historical mission. More recently, Knowles and Klevins (1982) have declared that "adult education is, or ought to be, a highly political and value laden activity. When individuals are involved in education they tend to expand: their awareness of self and environment, their range of wants and interests, their sense of justice, their need to participate in decision-making activities, their ability to think critically and reason rationally, their ability to create alternative courses of action, and, ultimately their power or control over the forces and factors which affect them—this is political action" (p. 16).

These exhortations all share a common theme. The purpose of education is to develop in adults a sense of control over their own lives and an awareness of the means by which they can create their individual and collective realities. People's abilities to realize their collective power, to imagine alternative realities, or to grapple with forces and factors impinging upon them are generalizable capacities. They go far beyond the exercise of voting in a particular election or the discussion of current political issues. Helping adults to realize that their value systems and behavioral codes are culturally and interpersonally received, not divinely ordained, is a political function. Once these internalized assumptions are externalized, it becomes possible to consider questioning and altering them. O'Sullivan (1980) expresses this as follows: "Students will come to appreciate the social location of their beliefs and values and come to some level of realisation of how their consciousness has been formed" (p. 321). Put more simply, adults come to think critically about politics.

Despite the general dearth of organized attempts to foster these capacities for critical analysis of the political world, there has been valuable work done by individuals in a number of different areas. The Participatory Research Project of the International Council for Adult Education has sponsored local initiatives in which issues of power and control were the operational focus. The year 1984 saw the establishment of the International League for Social Commitment in Adult Education. In 1986 a conference on critical pedagogy at the University of Massachusetts at Amherst had to turn away registrants. In universities, programs of peace education such as those at Bradford (England) and Teachers College (New York) have sought to explore how discussion of these issues might be integrated into the school curriculum.

Local peace education initiatives such as those described by Field (1983) and Taylor (1984), and "rights education" (Cohen, 1976) or "issues" courses (Brook and Garforth, 1986), show how adult and community education organizers can incorporate the critical discussion of political matters into the adult educational curriculum. Reports from the front illustrate the precariously volatile nature of such initiatives. In describing an issues course they organized, Brook and Garforth (1986) claim that "the ingredient which has, perhaps, made the programme so successful is its focus on controversy and its refusal to accept the received wisdom about bias" (p. 321). After mounting a course and exhibition entitled "Rich World–Poor World," which examined the interrelationship between world poverty, politics, economics, and militarism, the organizers (Gibbons and West, 1984) concluded that "many adult education students regard their activity as a retreat from the real world and object angrily to being confronted with controversial issues in an adult education centre" (p. 149). The discussion of political issues can only be accomplished, they believe, "in groups of people who know each other and have confidence in each other" (p. 149), notwithstanding the potential exclusion of alternative opinions posed by such homogeneity of membership.

Encouraging adults to think critically about politics occurs more frequently outside of formal educational institutions.

In the nonprofit area, the Public Agenda Foundation (Yankelovich, 1983) aims to stimulate debate on political issues (such
as the nuclear arms race, rising health-care costs, and technological unemployment) that have been aired on a superficial level
in the media. Central to the foundation's work is the distinction between mass opinion and public judgment. *Mass opinion*
is defined as "what the public thinks about an issue when it
first surfaces as a problem—however confused, uninformed, or
clouded with emotion that thinking may be" (Yankelovich, p.
3). *Public judgment* "is reached after people have reviewed the
options available to them in light of their own experiences,
values, and social and economic perspectives" (p. 3). The
Foreign Policy Association publishes annually a "Great Decisions" study handbook to be used by informal discussion groups
to explore foreign policy issues. The encouragement of living
room discussion of political matters was the chief purpose of
the Study Circle Consortium of New York State. This Ford
Foundation–supported project encouraged adults to develop personal positions on major political issues and to increase participation in the political process (Osborne, 1981). Attempts by broadcasting agencies to promote the formation of political discussion circles include the "What Rights Have You Got?" radio
discussion course of the British Broadcasting Corporation and
the Farm Forum movement and the "People Talking Back"
experiments of the Canadian Broadcasting Corporation.

The growth of communications technologies has caused
some educators to explore new forms of education for democratic
participation. The concepts of *anticipatory democracy* (Toffler,
1970), *participatory democracy* (Naisbitt, 1982; Zimmerman, 1986),
viable democracy (Margolis, 1979), and *strong democracy* (Barber,
1984) have been advanced. In these, the Athenian concept of
face-to-face democratic town meetings is supplanted by a network of computer-literate citizens who obtain government information, talk to each other, and express policy or electoral
preferences—all through a computer network. Margolis (1979)
proposes a computer-based network in which participants have
access to all computerized records of government agencies, to
major government documents, to information on current legis-

lative proposals, as well as to similar records from major manufacturing corporations, utilities, and banks. Such a proposal presupposes that all citizens possess personal computers and know how to use them, which is certainly far from the case at present. Several conditions for instituting Margolis's viable democracy would therefore need to be specified: that computer literacy would become a major educational task of schools; that personal computers would be made available as a right to people when they reach voting age; that a freedom of information act would guarantee individuals' rights of access to data banks in government agencies, nonprofit organizations, and corporations.

There is no doubt but that the onset of the computer age will bring with it innovations of crucial significance to democratic participation. Accessing government files by computer will make the business of information retrieval much more manageable for the community action group or private individual than is presently the case. There will be no need to visit national repositories of information to find out what these contain. By using a modem, anyone who has access to a telephone will be able to tap into this information on government and business main-frame computers. There is a tendency to see all technological developments as wholly negative to democratic processes. There is a *Brave New World* image of computer developments serving only as antidemocratic monitoring devices. Yet certain technological developments can assist political action groups to pursue democratic interests. Such groups can more easily keep in touch with each other; they can share information about their activities at short notice. It is now realistic to think in terms of national initiatives by advocacy and action groups that are geographically distant. Groups in Alaska and Arizona or in California and Connecticut can communicate, exchange information, and coordinate local action within a national initiative much more easily with the onset of computer technology. Barber's (1984) program for strong democracy outlines mechanisms (such as electronic balloting and a civic videotex service) by which "political talk" can be fostered through communications technologies.

It has also become much easier to collect and analyze masses of statistical data. The days of laborious mental calculation and rooms festooned with papers scrawled with calculations and figures are gone. For political groups who seek to document the economic or educational inequities in society through diverse sources of statistical data, the possibilities afforded by the computer for accessing and manipulating these data are most welcome. Computers can allow us to track developments and changes in governmental provision for social services. They can help us to analyze by social class, ethnic group, or geographical region who is receiving what. With access to a computer network, even the smallest and most isolated of activist groups can access information to lend plausibility to their efforts. They can also find out what others in groups across the country facing similar problems are doing about their situations. The crushing sense of isolation—of being the only group, neighborhood, or community facing a particular problem—that inhibits so many change efforts is much less likely if we can access a network of groups engaged in similar initiatives. For example, if we are trying to force an authority to tighten up policing of a toxic waste dump, we can find out what tactics other groups are using by accessing the relevant data base. We need not feel that we are acting alone or having to rely solely on our own wits to generate tactics to secure the changes we seek.

The kinds of technological changes discussed above cannot be ignored. Whether or not we welcome them, there is no turning back. The world of computer communications technology is with us, and in a decade our current hardware will no doubt seem hopelessly inadequate. Those involved in developing people's commitments, and with working for collective political change, will have to take account of these developments. Instead of criticizing them as yet one more step toward a wholly automated, controlled society, they should begin to work to find ways that computer technology might be made to work for their own cause. With the possibility of enhanced information exchange, increased speed of communication, and opportunities for national coordination of local group efforts afforded by computer technology, activists may find such technology to be an invaluable aid in their political change efforts.

Conclusion

Learning to think critically about the political world is a national imperative in any democratic society. In an era when the primary impetus for educational provision and curriculum development derives from the need to produce technically efficient workers, it is easy to relegate programs of political learning to a subordinate status. Yet as the Carnegie Foundation for the Advancement of Teaching report (Newman, 1985, p. 32) recently acknowledged, "the advancement of civic learning . . . must become higher education's most central goal." We live in a time when the divisions between the haves and have-nots— both within our own society, and on a global level between industrial nations and the Third World—are becoming increasingly evident. We live in a time when our elected representatives have in their hands the power to annihilate all of us—not through the prolonged process of declaring war, conscripting civilian armies, and ordering us into battle, but through a simple push of a button. We live in a time when political participation, both in terms of voting and in more sustained involvements in political organizations outside of single-issue advocacy, is waning markedly. We live in a time when it is all too easy to observe the passing by of the political world through a medium (television) that only serves to emphasize the distance between citizens and policy makers. We live in a society in which it is possible for organizations, both governmental and corporate, to collect masses of computerized statistical data about each one of us without our knowing that this is taking place.

Given these developments, the encouragement of people's capacity to think critically about politics must indeed be seen as a central educational endeavor. Even given the lamentable absence of programs of publicly sponsored political learning, all is not lost. Computers can be used to collect incriminating evidence about the governmental and corporate collectors themselves. Television can serve to heighten public awareness of an issue so dramatically that major political change results, as happened with the Vietnam War and Watergate. On a simpler level, the critical thinking techniques outlined in this book are very applicable to the analysis of political issues. How we might use these techniques to foster critical thinking about television's depictions of the political world is described in detail in the next chapter.

❧ 10 ❧

Developing Critical
Judgments About
Television Reporting

How does television shape our views of the world? How do we use television to make sense of happenings outside the immediate sphere of our lives? In particular, how do we use television to find out what is happening in the political world? Studies of how people watch TV news and current affairs programs (Morley, 1980; Graber, 1984; Robinson and Levy, 1986) reveal that television is not the stultifying force we believe it to be. In fact, it is not what television does to us that is important; it is what we do to television.

People commonly perceive television as an all-powerful, villainously omnipotent agent of socialization created for the sole purpose of lulling entire populations into uncritical stupefaction. This is the function of television as described in George Orwell's novel of totalitarian dictatorship, *1984*. People who subscribe to this argument believe that TV viewers are the passive dupes of cynically manipulative programmers. These programmers, so the argument goes, are deliberately transmitting an endless diet of bland sit-coms and mindless game shows, with the sole purpose of diverting viewers' minds from the inequities of capitalism, which they would otherwise see around them. Television programs are seen as palliatives—tranquilizers with

184

which we can ward off the pain of survival and more easily bear the poverty (spiritual and physical) of modern capitalism.

      This pessimistic determinism regarding the all-powerful effects of television presumes a remarkable vacuity on the part of human beings. Viewers are seen as wholly uncritical consumers, glued every minute of their nonworking time to behavior-shaping programs. As Nelson (1986, p. 59) puts it, this approach "sets up television as an abstract, monolithic collective consciousness which preys upon mystified individuals." Yet a twenty-year survey of research on the impact of television news on the knowledge of Americans about political events found that "certain news stories are understood remarkably well by the public, indicating that the public is neither as hopelessly ill-informed nor as incapable of learning as many believe" (Robinson and Levy, 1986, p. 15). Television viewers are not so many tabulae rasae—clean perceptual slates unsullied by the imprint of accumulated life experiences. In Kennedy's (1984, p. 1) words, they are "active and immersed in complex cultural situations where media influence joins other structures and forces in the whirling array of relationships which make up their 'living.'" Studies of how people actually watch television (Morley, 1980; Graber, 1984; Robinson and Levy, 1986) do emphasize the active role viewers take in interpreting TV images and narrative, agreeing with some viewpoints expressed, rejecting others, and ignoring many completely.

      Many viewers choose to ignore or actively oppose television's representations of the world. Fiske and Hartley (1978), Kellner (1979), Hall (1980), and White (1983) identify what they call *negotiated* and *oppositional decoding activities* in audiences, as well as *deferential* or *aspirational responses* (in which television's portrayal of existing social structures is accepted as accurate). In negotiated decoding, viewers accept the broad messages enshrined in TV programs (for example, that cutting public expenditure unleashes entrepreneurial activity) but contrast these with their own situations (for example, when budget cuts hit hospitals and schools in which family members are involved). Dominant values are broadly accepted but are interpreted within the viewer's idiosyncratic context. In oppositional decoding, on the other hand, viewers reject the assumptions and messages implicit in TV programs. Television images are interpreted from within a framework wholly different from the one intended. An example of a viewer doing oppositional decoding would be a nuclear freeze activist who interpreted every governmental mention of the need for deterrence as indicative of the military-industrial complex seeking to preserve its interests. Another example would be a labor union member who interpreted a news feature on the harmful effects of restrictive union practices as resulting from the pressures of company executives concerned to portray the union in a bad light.

What is interesting about negotiated and oppositional decoding strategies are the processes that contribute to viewers' active resistance to dominant stereotypes and values contained within TV images. White (1983, p. 281) emphasizes the need to study the "nexus of mediating conditions" in which viewers decode TV images and interpret them within their already developed frameworks of understanding. If television really is an all-powerful agent of socialization, how can we explain negotiated and oppositional decoding among viewers? In exploring this question, Kennedy (1984) argues that we should balance our view of television as an all-pervasive, controlling agent with the awareness "that we are after all active appropriators, selecting our own meanings out of all the myriad forces to which we are exposed, including television, in our particular historical and social contexts." This will redress the overly pessimistic imbalance caused by overestimating the power the media has over our lives.

Television and Political Socialization

In childhood, we are socialized into our respective political cultures in our families, schools, and neighborhoods. We develop party allegiances and learn appropriate political values and ideologies. Put simply, we learn (and are taught) to accept a cluster of explanations and interpretations of the political world, through which we filter news of current political events. These explanations and interpretations constitute a mediatory framework that is applied whenever we need to make sense of new issues or happenings. By the time of adulthood, we have evolved our own fairly entrenched attitudes and beliefs concerning political matters. The mediatory framework by which we explain and interpret new happenings is firmly in place. Barring cataclysmic revelations (such as those in the Watergate affair) and cataclysmic occurrences (such as becoming unemployed or being conscripted), these attitudes and beliefs are enduring. Politial allegiances become lifelong and attain the status of unquestioned givens in adulthood. We become Democrats, Republicans, liberals, conservatives, socialists, fascists, or communists, and we define ourselves politically in terms of these concepts.

In adulthood, television functions as a reinforcing agent of political socialization. It is not concerned with primary political socialization—that is, inculcating politically acceptable values, beliefs, explanations, and behaviors. Rather, it is an agent of secondary socialization, through which the acceptable ways of looking at the political world learned in childhood are confirmed and reinforced. Television inevitably reflects and mirrors the dominant values of the society in which it operates. Views of the world and interpretations of political events that would be considered radical, or at least strongly divergent from the values and attitudes of the dominant culture, receive much less expression than mainstream, consensual outlooks. For example, news broadcasts in the Soviet Union and the United States dealing with strategic arms limitation talks do not typically grant air time to politicians from the opposing country. Instead, the actions of each side are interpreted and presented to viewers from within the framework of the host culture's prevailing assumptions. Hence, each side regards the other as ruled by an expansionist ideology, bent on world domination and motivated by a cynical opportunism in any negotiations that take place.

Television also serves to operate in a more subtle, insidious manner to shape the way in which we come to understand and analyze political matters. It encourages viewers to interpret political issues, disputes, and events in a simplistic and unidimensional manner. Issues rooted in ideological or strategic differences are presented as personality conflicts. Complex policy questions are encapsulated in thirty- or forty-five-second summaries on the evening news. Most worrying, events within the political world are presented as if they were in a separate dimension, a twilight zone of unreality into which mere citizens cannot venture. A British report on adults' perceptions of the political world (Ridley, 1983) noted a widespread belief among citizens that the framing of public policy was an activity of such remoteness and noninterference as to be regarded much as they regarded the weather—governed by uncontrollable forces completely outside their spheres of influence.

Viewing a series of elevated images of political overlords on a television screen certainly obscures the connection between individuals' political powers and the actions of local and national political leaders. Watching leaders from the superpowers discuss the relative strength of their nuclear arsenals sandwiched between commercials for deodorants, or between shows such as "Wheel of Fortune" or "Entertainment Tonight," gives an air of unreality to political life. Learning about this life via a technology that cannot be comprehended by most encourages a sense of disconnectedness between the viewer and the events portrayed. It fosters a predisposition in citizen-viewers to be passive observers, tuning in nightly amid game shows, sit-coms, and soaps to discover how the world has been reshaped for them by their political superiors.

A number of studies (Glasgow University Media Group, 1982, 1985; Lang and Lang, 1984; Altheide, 1985) have explored how television frames adults' understanding and interpretation of political events, issues, and disputes. Empirical studies of local (Altheide, 1976) and national (Ranney, 1983) television news production have shown how the quality of "newsworthiness" is grounded in the logic of the televisual medium. That logic frames the context within which "relevant" or "important" issues are identified, it provides selected information on those issues, and it presents apparently objective reportage of events pertaining to those issues. Television helps to create the framework within which political discourse occurs, it provides information on which viewers and readers are expected to base their judgments concerning that discourse, and it offers a spread of opinion from which individual viewers select those ideas that seem most closely to correspond to their own views of reality.

What role should be played by those who wish to encourage people to become critical viewers of television? A useful metaphor in trying to answer this question is that of detoxification. In drug abuse treatment, the term *detoxification* means the process of ridding the body of poisonous and dependence-inducing substances so that people can live without the benefit of artificial stimuli. Educators, trainers, and other helpers trying to assist adults to become more critically aware television viewers can be said to be engaged in *ideological detoxification*—the process by which adults are weaned from dependence on, and adherence to, simplistic explanations of complex political realities. In this process adults are helped to realize that the versions of political realities presented on television are culture-specific, result from influence by vested interests, and reflect an ideological standpoint. The distorted, overly simplistic, and personalized treatments of political issues come to be seen for what they are—creations of a group of individuals working within a particular context rather than objective, neutral, and complete reports of political reality.

Through ideological detoxification, the perceptual poison and dependence-inducing habits of viewing and analysis are removed from individuals' minds. Viewers are encouraged to develop a healthy skepticism toward ideologically biased explanations of political events. Central to this process is encouraging viewers to consider interpretations of political matters other than those generally offered by pundits and commentators.

Media Literacy

Adults who possess some critical awareness of television's capacity for distortion in its supposedly objective reporting of events in the "real" world might be said to be media-literate. As a concept, media literacy is relatively new (Masterman, 1983; Robinson, 1986; Brookfield, 1986a). Put simply, media-literate adults appreciate the potential for selective distortion in televi-

sion's depictions of political life. They have developed decoding
filters and strategies whereby the content of news broadcasts,
current affairs programs, and coverage of the political world
can be assessed critically. They do not presume that television's
coverage of an event is necessarily an objective account of what
happened, and they are aware that implicit in apparently neutral
reporting are all kinds of judgments, biases, and examples of
selective editing.

Media-literate adults are not necessarily definitively knowledgeable about major policy issues of the day. To develop such
extensive knowledge would probably require them to resign from
their jobs, family responsibilities, and personal lives in favor
of full-time study of current affairs. However, they do have some
awareness of when political interactions are being interpreted
in terms of personality clashes, of when simplistic readings are
being given of complex questions, of when the presentation of
images is taking precedence over substantive discussion, and
of when the pursuit of apparent objectivity is masking the presentation of a consensual view from which are excluded deviant
or minority opinions. Put simply, media-literate adults are aware
that television versions of the world are a constructed reality
(Altheide, 1976; Tuchman, 1978). They see that television is
"a human construct, and that the job that it does is the result
of human choice, cultural decisions, and social pressures" (Fiske
and Hartley, 1978, p. 17). Through this demythologizing of the
medium, the awe induced by its technological trappings is replaced by an awareness of its socially created nature.

Recognizing Media Literacy. Media-literate adults are critically alert where the distorting power of television is concerned.
They display all or most of the following characteristics:

1. They are watchful for commentators' and news presenters'
    tendency to oversimplify policy disputes, ideological con-
    flicts, and interpretations of current events when such mono-
    causal explanations or unidimensional analyses are offered
    as objective reporting.

    Example: challenging the view that in arms reduction
    negotiations one side possesses total moral right and acts

solely according to strict ethical principles, while the other side is wholly immoral and conniving.

2. They examine political reporting for its acknowledgment of context, questioning "ultimate" explanations, "final" verdicts, or "universal" solutions.
   Example: questioning the view that industrial disputes can be understood as solely due to management ineptitude or union intransigence.

3. They are aware that a variety of ideological interpretations are possible on most issues and events; they realize that the same event could be reported in many different ways, according to the ideology (liberal, socialist, capitalist, communist, social democratic, conservative) of the presenters, networks, and dominant cultures involved.
   Example: realizing that the "freedom fighters" identified as responsible for a coup d'état by one government may be viewed as "terrorists" by another.

4. They possess the capacity to decode televisual messages, symbols, and narrative, so that the implicit assumptions and intended meanings encoded in these transmissions are identified and externalized for analysis.
   Example: recognizing that through a subtle juxtaposition of narrative and image, an apparently objective narrative report (of, for example, the numbers attending a demonstration) can convey highly emotive, provocative, and unacknowledged meanings (for example, when this narrative is accompanied by pictures of demonstrators charging police or spitting at counterprotestors).

5. They are alert to the likelihood (and actuality) of certain explanations of events taking precedence over other, more contentious minority interpretations.
   Example: recording the number of times certain explanations of an event are offered (for example, that declining school standards are caused by unprofessional, inadequate

teachers), to the exclusion of alternative explanations (for example, that the government has slashed the educational budget).

6.   They are aware of the possibility of repressive tolerance (Marcuse, 1965) in television programming—that is, a tolerance that allows minority, contentious, or unpopular views expression, but manages this expression so as to emasculate or neutralize its effect.
     Example: observing that programs containing views critical of government policy (on, say, affirmative action, arms control, or abortion) are aired only on public television and minority channels, and only at unsocial hours (early morning or late at night).

These ideal conditions are probably unattainable in one person, no matter how sophisticated a critical thinker he or she may be. Nonetheless, it is important that such conditions be specified. They will help us recognize when people are thinking critically about television and provide helpers in this area with some shared sense of the overall aim toward which they are working. It is unrealistic and self-defeating to insist that unless all these conditions are met, no useful work is being done. *Any* attempts to help adults develop filtering devices through which they might decode, demythologize, and sift the content of media messages are valuable. In a democratic society in which television is the single-most important source of information regarding the political world, the possession of some degree of media literacy by citizens is an unavoidable necessity for any kind of effective participation. It is one of the most important critical thinking activities we can encourage.

The Need for Media Literacy. In democratic terms, the need for a media-literate populace is irrefutable. Since World War II, American and British politics have become increasingly dominated by television. Candidates' televisual appeal is a major consideration in their electoral campaign strategies, and for those who lack such appeal (as did Margaret Thatcher when she first ran for prime minister in Britain), consultant firms are hired to work on the candidate to make him or her as televisually appealing as possible. Without a citizenry that can discern when media hyperbole is disguising a lack of attention to issues, or when congenial images are taking the place of policy statements and justifications, democracy is in danger. The habit of political debate and the ability to explore differing interpretations of issues and events will be much harder to acquire if the discussion of political matters on television is centered around the production of evocative images and associations. As Masterman (1983, p. 204) puts it, ''In every sphere of life, knowledge of the mediated and constructed nature of media messages will need to be part of the common stock of knowledge of everyone who is a citizen in a democratic society.''

If our thinking about what are to be considered important political matters, or about the suitability of different candidates for high office, is dependent on the manipulative wiles of media consultants, we have effectively ceded control over the democratic process to nonelected advertising agents. Candidates' images will become more important in electoral terms than their grasp of issues, their experience, their behavior under crisis, or their decision-making abilities. In her memoir of running for vice-president in the 1984 U.S. general election, Geraldine Ferraro frequently, and bitterly, recalls her frustration at the success of the Republican campaign in diverting attention to the personal popularity and media appeal of their ''great communicator,'' President Reagan. Her comparison of the televised debates to theater is particularly telling: ''You get to say so little, and what you do say is so well rehearsed that I'm not sure the public has any more idea of what the candidates really stand for than it did before the debate. And besides, that's not what a real debate is all about. A real debate involves a direct exchange between the opponents, a point-counterpoint. But the formats for these political debates are contrived—more like theater than an intellectual contest'' (Ferraro and Francke, 1985, p. 245).

The last thirty years have seen an increasing reliance on television as a means of securing political power, with a corresponding decrease in the importance of grass-roots canvassing—

candidates or their representatives speaking directly to voters. The portion of election and re-election budgets devoted to TV advertising has increased to the extent that it overshadows all other costs. As the 1988 U.S. presidential election approaches, for example, Gary Hart, one of the three Democratic presidential candidates in 1984, (now forced to withdraw by the same media attention that formerly fueled his candidacy) is still holding rallies to pay off his massive campaign debt incurred from use of TV commercials in the 1984 election.

The power of the TV image was realized for the first time in political history in the 1960 U.S. presidential election (Diamond and Bates, 1984). In John Kennedy's debates with Richard Nixon, a majority of the radio audience polled declared Nixon the winner. His grasp of substantive issues, his style of argument, and the intellectual powers he displayed were deemed more suitable for presidential office than were Kennedy's. The TV audience, however, thought exactly the opposite. Kennedy's relaxed visual demeanor contrasted with Nixon's apparent nervousness. On the basis of visual clues, a majority of TV viewers polled perceived Kennedy as likely to be a better leader. His youthfulness, his use of humor, and his ease before the cameras were contrasted with Nixon's perceived discomfort. The fact that Nixon was recovering from illness and had refused to wear stage makeup for the camera lights only enhanced this visual impression of unease and shiftiness.

The 1976 post-Watergate election provides another good example of how the presentation of simplistic televisual images engaged public attention more than did discussion of substantive policy issues. In the campaign run by Jimmy Carter, images of religious faith and family loyalty were evoked; the candidate was portrayed as essentially moral and truthful. This, so the commercials said, was a candidate who could be trusted—a powerful message in the immediate aftermath of Watergate. President Gerald Ford, on the other hand, was portrayed by media commentators as somewhat muddle-headed, an impression strengthened by a series of physical and verbal errors he committed during public appearances.

Although in the examples cited so far television worked in favor of Democratic candidates, the 1984 election showed that a televisually appealing Republican candidate could also turn the power of television to great advantage. The presidential election campaign of that year represented the apogee of TV advertising as a means by which people could be encouraged to vote for the various candidates. The Gary Hart–Walter Mondale contest for the Democratic presidential nomination was cast in terms of newness and youth (Hart) versus responsibility and experience (Mondale), with practically no mention of substantive policy differences between them. In the Reagan-Mondale presidential contest itself, the Republican campaign managers acknowledged their reliance on creating televisually pleasing images of leadership, prosperity, family contentment, and patriotism. James Lake, the press secretary for the Reagan campaign, declared that to be elected president a candidate had to project a vision of America on television and persuade enough people to subscribe to that vision (*New York Times,* September 23, 1984, p. 32). The first commercials for the Reagan campaign contributed toward this vision by projecting images of happy families, tranquil harbors, and sunlit suburban neighborhoods. These were followed later in the campaign by an eighteen-minute documentary-style commercial portraying the ecstatic welcome accorded President Reagan at the Republican national convention. The commercial included elements of his address to the convention and closed with the singing of "America the Beautiful." The *New York Times* described it as "overpoweringly warm, patriotic, romantic, nostalgic and confident" and reported that in the advertising world it was "widely considered the most luxurious, symphonic and technically proficient political commercial ever made" (September 14, 1984, p. A-18).

Although TV political commercials are forbidden in Britain, a similar reliance has been placed on media consultants to produce a televisually appealing party image, particularly by the Conservative party and the Social Democratic–Liberal Alliance. In the 1979 and 1984 general elections, the Conservative party hired an advertising agency (Saachi and Saachi) to coach Margaret Thatcher on her TV style. They suggested that she modulate her voice to a lower octave and that she speak more slowly and calmly in order to avoid appearing strident and hectoring.

Televised Conservative party political broadcasts employed actors to portray "ordinary" voters. The Conservative campaign relied heavily on creating photogenic events at which Thatcher would be featured and which would be shown on the lunchtime or evening news. The color of draperies and backdrop for press conferences given by Thatcher and her team was altered according to the impression (confidence, strength, or optimism) that was desired—a technique very similar to the extremely careful staging of President Reagan's campaign address, in which he was always photographed from beneath (to emphasize towering leadership), surrounded by bold colors (to emphasize strength), and pictured next to a giant U.S flag.

The techniques discussed are used, to greater or lesser degrees, by all political parties that can afford them, irrespective of ideology. In Britain and America, the chief opposition parties (the Labour and Democratic parties, respectively) placed a much greater emphasis than in past years on creating televisually appealing campaigns in the 1987 general election. Because the political and ethical correctness of the policies and ideologies of the political parties involved are now of secondary importance, media literacy requires that we recognize the ways in which politicians and media consultants use the medium of television to substitute the creation of comforting and appealing images embodying such qualities as firmness, compassion, strength, or prosperity for the discussion of basic policy and ideological differences.

An example of how politicians deliberately use TV news broadcasts, as well as commercials, to further their political interests is provided by David Gergen, White House Director of Communications until 1984. After leaving this post he gave an interview to the *Village Voice* (September 18, 1984, p. 10), in which he declared that the task of the communications bureau at the White House was to wrest control of the agenda of news and public policy issues from the press. Each day during the presidential campaign, the Communications staff would decide on an "issue of the day." That issue would be reported to every member of the White House staff, who would then speak to it at briefings and emphasize it in reply to questions asked by reporters on other topics. In this way the agenda of what were to become campaign issues was effectively set by nonelected media advisers. By presenting a united face on different issues of the day and refusing to speak to issues other than these, the White House staff forced reporters to focus on issues that they (the staff) wished to promote.

Encoding, Decoding, and Deconstructing Television

Central to the development of media literacy is the ability to understand how TV programs have been put together—how images are selected, how certain viewpoints are emphasized (and therefore implicitly approved) while others are excluded, and how judgments regarding what are important news events or political issues are revealed in the apportioning of time in broadcasts. The process of taking programs apart to reveal the assumptions and judgments implicit in news selection and explanation is called *deconstruction*. Deconstructing programs is defined by Masterman (1983, p. 207) as "breaking through their surface to reveal the techniques through which the medium produces its meaning." With judicious, professional editing, TV programs often appear in a seamless, natural flow. When we deconstruct a program, we are separating its parts into identifiable elements rather than viewing it as a neutral and objective whole.

Becoming media-literate involves more than simply deconstructing programs so as to be aware of how they were put together. Producers not only select which messages, images, symbols, and viewpoints constitute news events, they also frame the way in which we discuss these events, particularly the kinds of interpretations and judgments we habitually make about them. When we begin to notice how certain perspectives are repeatedly emphasized in the reporting of news items, how certain spokespersons are regularly used, or how certain visually provocative images are linked to narrative news commentary, we are involved in decoding programs. Decoding is a sophisticated activity in which we analyze broadcasts for the ways in which certain dominant values, interpretations, and meanings are implicit in the juxtaposition of images and narrative in programs. Williamson (1978) has shown very effectively how the values and meanings implicit in commercials can be decoded by critical viewers.

A central outcome of decoding television is that viewers realize that various interpretations of events alternative to those intended by program producers might be made; using these alternative interpretative frameworks, they can grant to images and narrative meanings very different from those intended by a program's producers. Once people begin to speculate on how and why certain interpretations, views, and messages are emphasized on television, they are going to wonder why other perspectives are excluded. They are going to wonder how apparently neutral events might have been reported from another perspective. They will begin questioning why certain explanations and interpretations are emphasized over others. They will be led "to a consideration of those voices *not* heard in the media, and to those which *are* heard, but which form part of a 'secondary' discourse which it is the privilege and function of the medium's dominant discourse to place and evaluate for us" (Masterman, 1983, p. 210). Examples of secondary discourse would be TV news treatment of strikers' claims, terrorists' campaigns, and pronouncements and activities of foreign governments perceived as hostile. In these instances, TV news reporting typically frames how we are to interpret events and ideas from the viewpoint of the dominant culture's values.

Hall (1980) describes the production of images and narratives that contain within them deliberately emphasized meanings as *encoding*. An example of encoding would be the reporting of a nurses' or teachers' strike as a threat to public health and welfare, and hence as a fundamentally antisocial act. The intent would be to confirm in viewers' minds certain assumptions about how public workers ought to behave, without ever making this value orientation explicit. Through the ways questions were asked of strikers, through employers being allowed to voice their opinions without critical questioning, and through juxtaposition of narrative reporting the strike with provocative images of pickets fighting police, patients being excluded from the hospital, or pupils being turned away from the classroom, it would be relatively easy to produce a news item that appeared to be neutral reporting but that in fact contained within it a highly partisan interpretation of the events concerned. Phrases that pass unnoticed within such news broadcasts, such as "Today workers again rejected the pleas of management," contain a number of hidden, implicit assumptions: that workers are persistently unreasonable (the use of *again*), that workers are somehow strident (the use of *reject*), and that management is quietly conciliatory (the use of *pleas*) but helpless in the face of workers' mindless resistance.

Decoding this encoding involves recognizing how messages, images, and narrative are invested with the preferred readings intended by a program's producers. We come to realize how judicious editing and selection, together with the framing of questions and offering of editorial comment, result in news events and reporting being invested with meanings intended by the program's producers. Morino (1985) gives an example of decoding an advocacy commercial—that is, one that is an attempt by the public relations office of a corporation to sell an attitude toward that corporation. In the commercial, a visual image of wolves in an idyllic woodland setting is accompanied by a narrative in which wolves' ability to stop short of fighting by using a complex system of snarls, howls, and grimaces is compared to governments' ability to preserve world peace through the deterrence afforded by each possessing a strong arms base. The relationship between peace and technology is stated to be positive, with technology guaranteeing the freedom to live. Morino (1985, p. 13) observes how "the menacing aspect of the arms race is put into a natural process, thereby turning a social process into a 'natural' one."

There are, of course, strong arguments to be put for the use of force and the need to use arms to defend societies that are felt by their inhabitants to be more just, democratic, humane, or religiously pure than other regimes. Indeed, within the peace movement one of the most frequent debates concerns those times when resistance through force is morally justified. In Morino's example, however, the possibility of such debates is excluded, since deterrence is portrayed as a natural evolutionary process.

Questions concerning the moral and ethical correctness of using force against other nations are, in effect, rendered illogical and unnecessary; for what is there to question if deterrence is natural and therefore inevitable? In decoding this commercial, then, viewers could raise several questions regarding alternative perspectives on this issue. They might ask about the dangers of a technical malfunction or accident triggering a nuclear war, whether the concept of a limited nuclear war is viable, and whether the use of force carries greater moral weight at some times than others. The answers to these questions are ambiguous and complex at best. In terms of critical thinking, however, the important point is that they are raised. Further suggestions on how commercials might be decoded by viewers are given by Williamson (1978).

Decoding Exercises

Several decoding exercises can be used to help viewers become critically reflective about the media. These are all simple, involving technology no more complicated than a standard video cassette recorder (VCR).

Analyzing Interviewer Actions. This exercise concentrates on examining the actions of TV newscasters as interviewers, discussion chairpersons, and anchorpersons. As most viewers can observe, TV interviews do not allow those being interviewed to address the camera in a direct, full-face connection with the audience. Interviewees and discussion participants are shown addressing each other, or the interviewer, but not the audience directly. When someone attempts to speak directly to the audience through the camera, the director cuts away from him or her to a shot of the interviewer or other participants. The message, by implication, is clear enough. Interviewers are mediators in command of the encounter, and they have the authority to veto expressions of opinion considered too upsetting, outrageous, or radical.

With the use of a VCR, viewers can analyze TV interviews to study how mediators control the direction of questioning, how they silence some contributors and encourage others, and how much time they spend on camera. They can observe the extent to which free and spontaneous discussion, unfettered by the mediator's agenda, occurs. One example of this kind of analysis is Handron's (1985) study of six "Donahue" shows dealing with current social and political issues. Her analysis examines how Donahue functions as the focal point and conduit of questioning in the show. He serves both as gate-keeper and prompter, sanctioning which approaches will be explored further while ensuring that a diversity of opinions is expressed.

Analyzing Interview Settings and Styles. Viewers can be taught to examine the settings of TV interviews with different parties involved in some controversial dispute. An example of this is the Glasgow University Media Group's study of how British TV news programs interviewed the participants in industrial disputes during the 1970s. They concluded (Glasgow University Media Group, 1976, p. 26): "All those things which enhance a speaker's status and authority are denied to the mass of working people. This means that the quiet of studios, the plain backing, the full use of names and status are often absent. The people who transcribed our material here pointed out to us that the only time they had difficulty making out what was said was in interviews with working people. Not because of 'accent' but because they were often shot in group situations, outside, and thus any individual response was difficult to hear. The danger here is that news coverage is often offering up what amounts to stereotypical images of working people."

If interviews with managers take place in quiet, well-lit boardrooms with only one company spokesperson, while interviews with strikers take place on a noisy factory floor or on picket lines with extraneous noise and activity, the viewpoint of one side implicitly receives preferential treatment. It is important to recognize that the technical setting for an interview is an important element of how much credibility the articulation of a certain viewpoint implicitly receives.

Viewers can learn to become aware of the setting and style of interviews and the way in which interviewees are treated. Are the questions put to representatives of both sides similar in tone, or is one side confronted mostly by critical questioning while

the other is permitted to use news interviews as opportunities
for airing their views? Do the questions themselves contain implicit assumptions? For example, asking a union leader, "Aren't
your members only bringing pain on themselves and others by
this action?" is heavily encoded with the message that strikes
are antisocial acts with no beneficial consequences to anyone.
Asking a management representative, "What harm is this strike
doing to the company?" or "What are the prospects for future
firings as a result of this strike?" may sound like neutral requests for information, yet both questions are encoded with the
same message.

   Analyzing the Juxtaposition of Narrative and Imagery. This exercise, designed to help viewers realize how powerful effects can
be created by linking apparently neutral and objective reporting of events to highly provocative visual images, breaks the
text of a TV program into its separate elements of narrative
commentary and visual image. In reporting of strikes, for example, commentary recounting the makeup of picket lines
might be accompanied by close-up shots of pickets shaking their
fists at people entering the factory gates, or of pickets forming
a tunnel through which nonstrikers have to pass. Inevitably,
the effect created is of violent and unreasonable strikers intimidating hard-working, loyal, and responsible employees. The
same logic frequently informs reporting of demonstrations. A
narrative commentary on the numbers involved, location, and
purpose of a demonstration can read dispassionately. But when
this commentary is superimposed on images of demonstrators
charging police cordons, chanting, displaying clenched fists, and
brawling with counterdemonstrators, a clear message is given:
demonstrators are essentially antisocial individuals apt to use
violent and aggressive behavior to campaign for their particular
cause. The demonstrators' cause, by implication, is also brought
into disrepute.

   It is paranoid, however, to presume that producers, directors, and reporters are all involved in some form of conspiracy
to discredit strikers and demonstrators. The kinds of juxtaposi-
tions of narrative and visual image described above are reflective
of the logic of the medium. In the minds of producers, directors,

and network executives, there is a consensus that "good" television has dramatic impact. Interviews with a union organizer who patiently outlines employees' grievances or an activist who analyzes the history of a political movement such as the nuclear freeze campaign are regarded as examples of worthy, but dull, television. The assumption is that conflict, strife, and confrontation are more visually provocative than "talking heads" (static interviews of individuals in a studio setting). "Good" television is held to be TV that imprints powerful images on viewers' minds. That televisual images can have a powerful effect on a mass audience is evident from the response to broadcasts from reporters who visited Ethiopia during the 1984 famine. The public reaction to the images of visibly shaken reporters speaking next to children on the edge of death from starvation was remarkable. Thousands of people called in to donate money directly to the TV networks showing these reports. Had viewers learned about the famine through the "talking head" of a newscaster on the evening news (even if the narrative had been accompanied by still photographs of the famine projected on a studio backdrop), it is hard to imagine public reaction being anything like as massive or instantaneous.

Constructing TV Programs. The most direct and powerful method to help people decode and deconstruct broadcasts is to involve them in making their own programs. If people have the experience of putting together news reports, short documentaries, or dramatizations of current events, they will have to face the same editorial and production decisions that occur on the much broader level of network TV. They will be selecting participants, constructing interview questions, apportioning time to interviewer and interviewee, and editing responses. A vivid treatment of the personal and collective power that can be released when adults are encouraged to use the technology of television to produce programs reflective of their own experiences is given in Heaney's (1983) account of the Rockford Interactive Media Project. In the Illinois community of Rockford, people learned to use video tape recorders "to create materials that would enhance critical reflection on day-to-day life and, at the same time, foster learning and understanding among others outside the community, especially government officials and persons with power'' (p. 41). Heaney writes that ''people with newly found voices are like lions let loose'' (p. 43) and that these video tapes became ''the voice of an otherwise silent community'' (p. 42).

Jarvis (1985) describes an exercise devised by the British Open University, a national education university for adults. In the residential summer session that students in the social sciences foundation course attend, participants are divided into small groups and provided with a number of photographs of a strike. The different groups are assigned to television stations in Britain, the Soviet Union, and the United States and asked to choose photographs to use in constructing a news broadcast on the strike from the perspective of the country concerned. Through a judicious selection of photographs, accompanied by ideologically appropriate narrative commentary, participants are able to report the same event in vastly different ways. The same photographs are frequently chosen to accompany narratives that are ideologically opposed in their interpretation of the causes of, and responsibility for, the strike. Because participants have constructed news reports in which values, assumptions, and ideologies are deliberately encoded, it becomes easier for them to decode real TV programs for their implicit biases and hidden assumptions.

In his work in Liverpool (England) and Belfast (Northern Ireland), Lovett (1975) argues that the advent of affordable video equipment and the increased access to cable television channels offer exciting opportunities for those working with working-class communities as community developers, educators, and *animateurs*. He describes working with local residents to help them produce radio programs on social and community issues, and to encourage the formation of local listening and viewing media study groups. Through programs in which people use their life histories, songs, personal reminiscences, and dramatized versions of significant events to recount and explore their experiences, the production of an oral and visual (rather than wholly literate) popular culture can be encouraged.

Content Analysis

Content analysis of works of literature, newspapers, advertisements, and magazines has been conducted by educators in a number of different settings for several years. The technological developments that have made VCRs affordable for educational institutions and individuals mean that this technique can now be applied to TV programs. It is quite possible, for example, to imagine a group dividing up among themselves the responsibility for monitoring a week's news broadcasts on the major networks, in order to examine the amount of time different networks allocated to the same news story. Or a group could focus on a particular issue (for example, a strike or an accusation of governmental abuse of power), with different members recording how much prominence various networks, newscasts, and current affairs programs gave to the views of the different parties involved in the issue. It would also be relatively simple to chart how news stories rose to prominence during various days or weeks, and then how they receded as other items were given attention. Members of a content analysis group could compare the news bulletins on different networks during the breakfast show, at lunchtime, and on the evening news, to study changes in tone and content reflecting how any one story was treated in one day.

Some of the most sophisticated developments in the application of content analysis to television have been made by the Glasgow University Media Group (1976, 1980, 1982, 1985). Over the past decade, the group has conducted content analyses of how British TV news broadcasts have reported industrial disputes, political activities (such as the contest for the deputy leadership of the Labour party), the establishment of the women's peace encampment at Greenham Common, the disarmament campaign, and the war with Argentina over the Falkland Islands. The findings of this ten-year content analysis research project are, according to the group, clear and consistent. The researchers conclude that "the kinds of information and explanation that appear in the news essentially flow from the dominant view.

Alternative facts and explanations, where they appear at all, appear in fragmentary and sometimes contradictory form" (1982, p. 116). Exercises as simple as counting the numbers of interviews granted to the different protagonists in a dispute indicates "whose views were deemed to be legitimate and authoritative voices in terms of the dominant view. Once inserted into the logic and flow of coverage they constitute what amounts to an 'official view'" (1982, p. 120). Hence, "information is both controlled and routinely organized to fit within a set of assumptions about how the world works and how it ought to work. The media relay the ideology appropriate to a population which is relatively quiescent, and actually promote that quiescence by limiting access to alternatives" (1982, p. 143).

The group cites a great deal of evidence to support these conclusions. With regard to strikes, for example, news bulletins regularly give the times, places, and numbers involved in strikes, but not the causes. Consistent use of the term *dispute* (as in "the teachers' dispute," "the sanitary workers' dispute," "the civil servants' dispute," and so on) implies that labor is the prime source of conflict in industry. Trouble is seen as emanating predominantly from workers, with only rarely a suggestion that management or government might have precipitated a dispute through, for example, firing workers without notice, imposing longer work hours without consultation, or reducing wages. The impression is created that strikes are random and meaningless disruptions to an otherwise ordered and peaceful society. In questioning the different parties involved in strikes, the group notes that "questions put to management tend either to be an open invitation to give their views or to lead directly to these. As a result such interviews are fairly harmonious: the 'devil's advocate' and the 'difficult' questions are reserved largely for shop stewards" (1982, p. 37).

The net effect of such coverage of strikes, according to the group, is to portray strikers solely as troublemakers. The causes of strikes, rarely reported openly, are suggested by the number of news stories concentrating on disruptive or work-shy employees, communist infiltration into unions, and unrealistically exorbitant wage claims. Production is normal, so it is implied, unless disrupted by an unreasonable work force. The group maintains that alternative explanations of disputes that focus on, for example, management intransigence or incompetence, wage manipulation, or the running down of various sectors of an industry are much less frequently offered. The researchers also maintain that there are very few news stories that deal with white-collar crime, such as tax avoidance, fraud, abuse of expense accounts, or the distribution of large dividends to shareholders while workers are being laid off.

The group's activities offer many examples of how content analysis techniques can be used to develop media literacy. People can count the number of interviews granted to the various parties in a dispute. They can record the number of times a certain explanation for an event is given. They can document the language and phraseology used most frequently to describe events or people. They can study the different kinds of questions put to the parties in a dispute. They can record the number of appearances made by ''establishment'' figures, such as government spokespersons or corporate chief executive officers, and compare these to the number made by demonstrators or strikers. They can scrutinize broadcasts for the range of alternative interpretations of events that are offered for viewers' consideration.

Autobiographical Analysis

As a technique, autobiographical analysis focuses on the individual's personal experiences of, and reactions to, television. People are asked to identify moments in their own lives when the picture of reality offered on the TV screen was contradicted by their real-life experiences. The intent is to focus on anomalies, discrepancies, and dissonances between life as it is actually lived and life as it is portrayed on television. When this exercise is conducted in a group setting, the group members realize that what were perceived as purely private anomalies are actually experienced by other people. Their personal discrepancies become legitimated through others' similar accounts.

The discrepancies chosen most frequently have to do with portrayals of family life rather than political events. Television depictions of family life as either debauched trauma (soap operas such as "Dynasty," "Flamingo Road") or idyllic harmony ("The Waltons," "The Cosby Show," "Family Ties") are criticized for their evident unreality. Adults today contrast the gentle banter and affectionate interchanges characteristic of such shows as "Ossie and Harriet," "Father Knows Best," or "Leave It to Beaver" with their own remembrances of much less affectionate marital and parent-child interactions; or they describe their puzzlement at the portrayal of small-town life as replete with the smoldering sexuality evident in "Peyton Place."

Sometimes people do choose examples of racism or class discrimination when identifying TV moments during which they felt themselves to be distanced from dominant cultural values. They contrast their perception of societal acceptance of all races and classes as portrayed in a family TV show with the reactions in their own families when they brought home friends from different ethnic groups or social classes. The recollection of parental disapproval of such action is contrasted with the broad acceptance of class, cultural, and ethnic diversity portrayed on television.

Once people begin noticing discrepancies between their own experiences of family life and television's portrayal, and once the perception of these discrepancies is reinforced by the confirmation of others, the way is open to applying these skills of critical analysis to other aspects of TV coverage, particularly the political. Once we begin to question the accuracy of depictions of family life on television, it is but a short step to begin questioning the accuracy of television's depictions of political events. We begin to wonder whether all possible interpretations of events have been given, and what biases, assumptions, and meanings are encoded in the way the political world is portrayed.

Conclusion

Adults can learn to become critically aware of television's potential for distortion. They can become skeptical of the validity of television images as accurate depictions of real life. Helping adults to become critical decoders of television is a central element in developing media literacy. The forms for encouraging media literacy discussed in this chapter are only selections from the wide variety of approaches, tools, methods, and techniques available. There is already much valuable work taking place to develop media literacy at a preadult stage. For example, in Masterman's (1980) analysis of teaching about television, he describes how school students can be introduced to the concept of genre (television comedy, pop music shows), how they can recognize ritual behavior at sports events, how they can analyze news broadcasts, and how they might produce their own video interviews. However, the concern with focusing on understanding the political and social world is perhaps particularly suited to those educators and helpers who wish to work with adults.

In adulthood, political events assume a much greater significance and prominence than they do in childhood. In childhood, political crises (wars, changes of government, policy reversals, legislative changes, budget cuts) certainly affect our individual lives. Most children and adolescents, however, do not make the connection between public issues (such as governmental policy changes) and their individual troubles. Although many adults also avoid doing this, I would argue that the sophistication and awareness needed to make this connection are found much more frequently in adults than in children and adolescents. Simply being forced to lead economically independent lives away from the immediate protection of the family unit brings us harshly up against the realities of social living. This is why developing media literacy in the political sphere is so important for those working with adults. In adult life, our past experiences, acquired knowledge, and more developed political understanding mean that we are more open to exploring television's portrayal of political life.

What of helpers' own interactions with the media? As well as working to develop media literacy among clients and learners, educators, trainers, counselors, and other helping professionals can press the broadcasting agencies to include minority viewpoints and a range of alternative interpretations of political life in their programs. In the desire to present an apparently impartial, objective view of news, it is all too easy for current affairs and news producers, directors, writers, and presenters to shy away from any detailed elaboration of an unpopular minority viewpoint. Such viewpoints can become informally blacklisted as too extreme or contentious. In Britain, the Glasgow University Media Group (1982) has offered instructions to readers of its works: "What to do, where to join, how to complain" (p. 160). Postman's (1986) critique of American prime-time television contains numerous recommendations on how educators might encourage critical skepticism of the media in schools. Barber (1984) provides guidelines on how television town meetings and plebiscites might be managed.

Helping adults become aware of television's ability to distort the world must be counted as a crucial educational and social task by almost any measure adopted. As well as assisting adults to create their own programs reflective of their passions, concerns, and experiences, critical helpers must work to help adults become active decoders of what they come to recognize as highly selective televisual images of the world. Adults should be encouraged to talk back to the·TV screen and to meet with others to discuss their contrasting interpretations of television messages and symbols. It is surely not too far-fetched to imagine a time in the near future when every adult and continuing education program in the country will create the opportunity—either through formal courses or through informal meetings and discussion groups—for interested people to come together to explore, compare, and contrast their perceptions of, and reactions to, television's depiction of political events, family life, and the world of work. In whatever mode and format they choose to work, educators and other helpers should regard the development of media literacy as one of the most important and influential ways in which they can develop critical thinkers.

❧ 11 ❧

Encouraging Active Learning Through Personal Relationships

Intimate relationships represent one of the most crucial, yet least studied, settings for critical thinking. In relationships we practice critical thinking a great deal, yet we rarely recognize or name it as such. Given that relationships are dynamic entities, distinguished by constant change, shifts in focus, and periods of reframing and renegotiating, critical analysis is often demanded. We are frequently required to be aware of the assumptions governing our relationships—especially when they no longer hold true—and to consider alternatives to how we have been living in relationships up to that point. Relationships pass through major or minor crises as participants in them face, interpret, and try to manage their own developmental transitions, some of which have occasioned these crises. The struggle to be aware of how each participant perceives what is happening in the relationship, and how this perception might be explored objectively by the other, is one that is central to clear communication. Only when communication is established between partners do an informed understanding of each other's point of view and the negotiation of changes in a relationship become possible. Perceiving clearly the assumptions and perceptual frameworks shaping our behaviors and those of our partner is central to critical thinking.

One reason why critical thinking has not been as seriously considered as it should be in the study of relationships is that we tend to think of it as a purely cognitive capacity that takes place only in college classrooms. As long as critical thinking as a process is seen to be confined to a number of intellectual operations, such as analyzing, discriminating, integrating, and synthesizing, its relevance to the emotionally charged area of intimate relationships will be hard to discern. Yet critical thinking is not some ascetic cognitive ritual observable only in the artificially created environment of the undergraduate seminar. It is an activity that is frequently embedded in contexts that are of great personal significance to most people: our work, our relationships, politics, and the media.

The psychic arena comprising family life, friendships, and marriages is the focus of many people's being, giving deep meaning to their lives. We may present partial representations of ourselves in our work life or in our community involvements. In intimate relationships, however, we reveal our most private identities. We allow the core of our being—that by which we define ourselves—to emerge. I know that the learning I have undertaken that I regard as the most profound and crucial is not related to my occupational identity or to my participation in formal courses of instruction. If I knew that universal extinction was due tomorrow, and I were asked to identify the learning that had been most important to me, I would probably think of the insights and understandings I had realized in the intimate relationships in which I have been involved. These insights and understandings have developed out of a process of critical reflection and analysis.

Examples of these processes of critical thinking in my life are not hard to identify. For example, a central activity has been my recognizing the assumptions informing my own behavior and the expectations I had for what was considered to be "proper" conduct within relationships. I have learned that there is no single road to permanent peace and stability in living intimately with others, and that the concepts of permanent peace and stability are themselves chimerical. What I felt I could legitimately expect of others in relationships has changed according to the historical and cultural contexts in which I have lived. It has also become apparent to me that there are multiple configurations within relationships, and various conflicting criteria one can apply to determining the success of an intimate relationship.

My most significant personal learning has had to do with how to develop relationships with people who are important to me. I have tried to learn how to begin fighting my own self-centeredness, vanity, laziness, and arrogance. I have tried to learn how to accept change in relationships as inevitable and natural, and to make a virtue of necessity by embracing such change as a creative force. I have tried to learn to be more open about my feelings (both affectionate and hostile), and to communicate these effectively to my intimates. I have tried to accept that no one person (whether spouse, lover, parent, child, or friend) can be the total center of my universe, and that I cannot expect another person to meet all my emotional, intellectual, and physical needs.

I have tried to learn a set of very complicated skills needed for intimate relationships—how to listen, how to comfort, how to air doubts and criticisms while preserving another's self-respect, how to compromise, negotiate, and communicate as fully and clearly as possible. I have tried to learn how to enter others' frames of reference, so that I can see situations in which my actions play a part from their points of view. I have had to work hard to understand other people's arguments, justifications, and beliefs from within the framework of their own perceptions. All these efforts have involved critical thinking. In particular, processes of critical thinking have been central to my (only partially successful) attempts to negotiate a balance between the conflicting needs, desires, and impulses of myself and others in these relationships.

These learning activities have been alternately difficult, rewarding, painful, joyful, frustrating, and satisfying. None of them has been fully achieved, and there is no doubt that I will be engaged in this kind of critical probing throughout my lifetime. At times I feel I have achieved some limited success in understanding the complex configurations of relationships in which I am a participant. At other times I feel as though I am driven by the same vanities and obsessions as I was at eighteen years of age. Indeed, one of the most significant critical realizations for me has been that one never achieves a point of emotional stasis, when all aspects of one's psychological zodiac are in a state of permanent harmony. Because of the ever-shifting configurations of intimate relationships, we are involved in a continual process of critical scrutiny—reflection, action, further analysis, new action, further reflection, and so on. We never reach a point of "final" or "full" personal development. Indeed, thinking that we have is one of the danger signals to look out for within relationships.

Several writers conceive of the ebbs and flows within personal relationships as a *dialectical dynamic* (Cronen, Pearce, and Tomm, 1985). According to this view, intimate relationships are like constantly changing kaleidoscopes in which partners seek constantly to reconcile and integrate their different interests and inclinations. To Basseches (1984), a participant in a dialectical relationship assumes that "my traits are not fixed and that the relationships I enter will shape who I become as much as they are shaped by who I am and who my partner is" (p. 26). Gould (1980) writes of the dialectic of growth and intimacy comprising the "transformational and developmental envy dynamics that make up the rhythm of joys and disturbances within an intimate relationship" (p. 233). As we watch our lovers, parents, children, and friends change, we too find our lives affected as we try to understand, oppose, or accommodate the changes in those we love.

Despite its apparent importance, very few psychologists, and even fewer educators, have paid much attention to the phenomenon of critical thinking within relationships. Anthologies by Gergen and Davis (1985), Duck and Perlman (1985), Perlman and Duck (1986), Rogers (1984), and Smelser and Erikson (1980) examine this area, and one of Carl Rogers's most enduring pieces is on "Significant Learning: In Therapy and Education" (1961). Considering the crucial importance of relationships in people's lives, however, the attention granted to learning within them has been minimal. The need for intimacy may be recognized (Merriam, 1983b), but its analysis from the perspective of critical thinking has been neglected. There are many popular treatments of relationships written from a simplified psychotherapeutic viewpoint, and many academic sociopsychological analyses that reduce human interactions to algebraic equations. But books such as Fromm's *The Art of Loving* (1956) and Storr's *The Integration of the Personality* (1965), both of which are intelligently and accessibly written, are rare.

I suspect that my feelings about the most important learning I have undertaken are not atypical; many people would probably select the insights they have gained about themselves through critically analyzing their involvements in intimate relationships as some of the most profound realizations they have experienced. Forming and living within relationships are, arguably, the most important of all our adult learning efforts, and the ones to which we ascribe perhaps the greatest significance. It is impossible to imagine adults traversing their lives without becoming entangled, unwittingly or by design, in an endless series of intimate relationships. Assisting people to be able to think critically within these relationships must be one of the most important functions helping professionals and educators can perform.

Significant Personal Learning

In analyzing the learning that occurs when people are critically probing the underlying assumptions and alternative ways of living within their intimate relationships, we need a term to distinguish the processes under review from other forms of learning commonly considered. I propose the term *significant personal learning*, an adaptation of Rogers's (1961) *significant learning*. Significant personal learning is coming to a state of that critical awareness within personal relationships which is distinguished by the following four characteristics:

1. It is self-consciously perceived as profoundly important by the learners themselves. For example, in studies of personal change (Mezirow, 1977; Musgrove, 1977), the learners inter-

viewed are quite explicit in recognizing the critical transformations and learning taking place as being of crucial significance in reshaping their lives.

2. It is frequently triggered by a major life crisis of some kind.
The kinds of self-reflection and appraisal characteristic of
significant personal learning are not usually initiated by
those who feel comfortable in their current relationships.
Adults are not likely to engage in such potentially painful
self-scrutiny without a powerful stimulus.

3. It entails a redefinition of some aspect of the self. For example, in Musgrove's (1977) study of adults in positions
of voluntary and involuntary marginality, his subjects were
reported to have stored their "real" selves until a crisis or
changed set of circumstances allowed these to emerge. The
artists, religious converts, and homosexuals interviewed had
voluntarily assumed positions of marginality because of
some sense of dissatisfaction with their previous identities.
They came to redefine themselves in terms of newly assumed
identities, some of which had previously been flirted with,
some of which were wholly new.

4. During this process, those involved call into question some
of the assumptions underlying the way they conduct personal relationships. They become more critically alert concerning the criteria governing "acceptable" conduct, the
appropriate roles and behaviors of participants in relationships, the false stereotypes that inhibit communication, and
the expectations that participants in intimate relationships
place upon each other.

Intimate Relationships as Contexts for Critical Thinking

Parent-Child Relationships. One of the most difficult tasks
we face when attempting to become critical thinkers within our
relationships is learning how to cultivate a genuine detachment
from our own emotions and self-interests. Only if we are able
objectively to understand another's criticisms, reservations, and
doubts can we begin to assess our own actions critically. This
is particularly the case with regard to parent-child relationships,
which are some of the most potent and traumatic in which we

are involved. To Gould (1978, 1984), the chief developmental task of adulthood is learning how to detach ourselves from the parental expectations we have uncritically internalized concerning what should be our proper beliefs and actions. In turn, we then have to learn how to assist our own children to negotiate their detachment from the expectations we have placed upon them. This process of creative detachment is frequently disturbing and painful for all concerned. If this can be accomplished with a degree of sensitivity on the part of parents, however, a tremendous potential for personal development exists.

For adult children, the realization that their parents are regarding them as equals instead of dependents, and that they are granting their desires, beliefs, and actions an unconditional credibility, is a liberating experience. For parents, being aware of how they try to shape children in their self-image (unwittingly as well as deliberately) is being unusually insightful. Being able to accept one's children's experimentation with values and actions, particularly if these conflict with one's own beliefs, is difficult. To accept that flirtations with apparently outrageous behaviors are part of children's quests for independence, that those behaviors probably make perfect sense to them, or that they are normal in the context of their own peer groups is to display exceptional wisdom. The most difficult aspect of this process is probably when children are involved with activities (such as excessive drug use) that parents feel objectively to be harmful or immoral. For parents to convince children that advice and warnings are grounded in objective concern, and not possessive parental paranoia, is complex and problematic.

For the chronologically adult child in a parent-child relationship, the most difficult transition to negotiate is that of establishing detachment while retaining bonds of trust, affection, and commitment with the parent. For the parent, the problem is how to create the conditions in which such a transition can occur. Parents need to assure children that separation from parents will not induce a withdrawal of parental affection. For the child, the problem is risking parental censure while trying to establish detachment. Underlying the fear of parental censure is the concern (perhaps not even acknowledged) over the potential loss of parental love.

Marital and Love Relationships. Partners in intimate love relationships generally acknowledge a greater sense of apparent control over the form and direction of those relationships than do people in parent-child relationships. In the act of choosing partners in this kind of intimate relationship, we exercise a degree of freedom that is missing from parent-child relationships. Knowing that we can change partners, however, places certain unique strains on a love relationship. When we decide to enter a love relationship, we typically possess an idealized vision of how that relationship will develop. This vision may be private, or we may share it intermittently with our partners. When the vision is so finely honed and specific that any diversion from it is seen as an aberration, it becomes a force inimical to, rather than nurturing of, a trusting relationship. Change and exploration are integral to most relationships; but when this change is interpreted as potentially destructive to this detailed vision, the disappointed partners inevitably begin to question the wisdom of their involvement.

At this point two options exist. The partners can begin to accuse each other of presenting false selves at the start of the relationship, typically charging each other with some kind of deliberate deception from the outset. Accusations such as "You're not the same as you used to be," "I never knew you were really like this," "Now we're seeing the *real* you," and "You've changed" are common. Alternatively, the partners can recognize the folly of adhering rigidly to previously idealized images about how the relationship should be and begin to consider how their idealized visions might be scaled down, integrated with the realities of their own lives, or abandoned. It is at this point that critical thinking begins. When partners choose the second option of recognizing the danger of keeping this idealized vision of the relationship private, real negotiation can take place between them. They begin to realize that there are no guarantees of permanent success in the relationship, however that success might be defined. They are willing to consider scenarios of how the relationship might develop that diverge markedly from those imagined in detail at the outset. They examine carefully the uncritically accepted expectations and assumptions informing the relationship.

Engaging in this kind of critical analysis is one of the most traumatic aspects of intimate relationships. Gould (1984, p. 40) argues that "one person's developmental imperative can be the cause of both necessary and unnecessary problems in a relationship. Development and continuing a relationship are often at odds." When personal development is sacrificed at the altar of the continuance of the relationship, this does not mean that the developmental urge is killed. To Gould, "it is only suffocated or sidetracked and is converted into either a high-tension center or a dead spot in the person's psyche, continuing to provide the impetus to grow" (p. 40). One of the most difficult things in a relationship is to recognize this developmental imperative as inevitable rather than as wholly threatening to the stability of the relationship.

In her analysis of changing ideologies of love, Swindler (1980) notes the emergence of a "love as a heroic struggle" myth. This myth perpetuates the belief that "a love relationship that does not require painful change no longer performs its function. The value of love, and its challenge, is that it must stimulate and absorb perpetual change" (p. 129). The power of this myth derives from its partial truth. A readiness to consider alternatives and a willingness to negotiate regarding partners' conflicting desires and aspirations are essential. Slipping into the "love as heroic struggle" myth does, however, entail certain dangers. It means that relationships might be deemed wanting, or considered to be somehow incomplete or less than fully developed, unless traumatic and painful struggle are continually present. For most people, conducting a never-ending scrutiny of each other is liable to be so stressful as to lead to the very dissolution of the relationship that both partners are doing their best to maintain. While it is important to be open to change, most people need periods of calm stability between periods of intense negotiation regarding change.

Friendships. For many people in societies characterized by high divorce rates, geographical mobility, and occupational change, friendships are the relationships within which their most intimate connections are made. Friendships do suffer from the same kinds of strains involved in other intimate relationships, but they exhibit one important difference. Participants in friendships typically do not hold tightly specified, idealized visions of the future of the relationship. This removes a major cause of potential conflict. Friendships are more relaxed relationships and frequently become havens for those seeking temporary refuge from the intensity of parent-child or marital-love conflicts. Within friendships, however, feelings of jealousy may arise when one of the friends becomes involved with a person, group, interest, or activity not shared by the other. Friendships can become as possessive as the other forms of intimate relationship. "Best" friends can be seen as significant as spouses, lovers, or parents. When best friends form bonds with other people or groups, we may feel betrayed. When they explore activities and ideas we do not share, we can feel neglected. For those who think of their best friends as their most intimate companions, these can be difficult moments in relationships. Indeed, such people may be unable ever to become reconciled to what they interpret as rejection.

Logistically and legally, losing friends is far less complicated than, say, losing spouses. Emotionally, however, the effects may be just as significant. The consequences of withdrawing friendship can be as distressing as any parent-child rift, divorce, or end of a love affair. The dissolution of friendships in which we feel that our "real" selves have been revealed (in contrast to the artificial public faces we usually reveal in settings such as the workplace) can be psychologically devastating.

The bonds of friendship are especially strong among people who feel themselves to be suffering from collective oppression. Among resistance fighters, in women's consciousness-raising groups, in political action groups, in gay rights advocacy groups, and in support groups for drug users, single parents, or the recently bereaved, the friendships and commitments that develop are intense in the extreme. Musgrove's (1977) study of marginal individuals documents this intensity. When these friendships founder, the effect is devastating. The psychological arena in which our "real" identities have been revealed has suddenly been removed. Faced with this, the "betrayed" friends might exact a swift psychological or physical retribution.

Expressing and managing jealousy in friendships require a great deal of sensitivity informed by critical insight. The processes involved are essentially the same as in parent-child and marital or love relationships. The friend who is accused of betrayal or neglect has to be sensitive enough not to react with such anger that the friendship is damaged further. The friend who feels betrayed has to try to view his or her feelings in as objective a way as possible. When trying to understand the psychological wellsprings of these feelings, this person is likely to be required to face some discomforting truths about the assumptions underlying the perceptions of betrayal. Recognizing and trying to understand these require a considerable degree of psychological courage and critical sophistication.

Recognizing Critical Thinking in Intimate Relationships

The central components of critical thinking are clearly evident in learning within relationships. The process of identifying and challenging the assumptions underlying our actions and ideas is a fundamental necessity if we are to make sense of our own, and others', behavior. How can we hope to communicate clearly and explore the differences in our intimate relationships if we are unaware of the assumptions driving our actions? We can believe that we are acting from the best of motives in criticizing, belittling, or punishing a partner when in fact our actions spring from assumptions about the rightness of our behavior, and the wrongness of another's, that may be quite inaccurate. Understanding the basic givens informing our partners' beliefs about what might legitimately be expected of us in intimate relationships is the first step toward discussing rationally the rightness of these. We may disagree about these assumptions; we may differ on what we believe are fair, just, or compassionate behaviors. But to be clear what these assumptions are is the first step toward negotiating some equilibrium with which we can be comfortable.

It is important to note that on many occasions a process of prolonged scrutiny and probing of the assumptions undergirding our relationships results in a reaffirmation of these assumptions.

It may well be that in airing issues, raising doubts, and offering criticisms, the partners in a relationship will come to a more complete understanding of each other's viewpoints and decide that they are satisfied to continue with their present arrangements. Any changes they make may be small in terms of externally observable behaviors. The point is that participants in such relationships have an informed commitment to their ideas and actions. They are aware of the assumptions they hold. They have examined them critically and concluded, after careful scrutiny, that they are justified and appropriate.

Arising out of the identification and challenging of previously unrecognized assumptions comes a degree of contextual awareness. This is evident when we realize that what we believe to be the "natural" order of things in a relationship often reflects social or subcultural prescriptions. Parents who realize that what they believe to be objective advice on the best career choices for their children actually represent a projection of their own unfulfilled ambitions are contextually aware. Lovers who realize that their ideas on what they consider to be acceptable and appropriate sexual behaviors are derived from external sources (parental behaviors, media images, erotic literature) as much as from their own internal drives and desires are alert to the importance of contextual factors.

Imaginative speculation—the capacity to imagine and explore ways of thinking and living alternative to those we currently accept—is an aspect of critical thinking that can be seen in intimate relationships. Marital partners and lovers who renegotiate central features of their relationships (for example, in regard to the distribution of household tasks, child rearing, and wage earning) are speculating imaginatively. Spouses who decide to develop and sustain peer networks, even though their subcultural mores dictate that marriage commitments place friendship relations in a subservient position, are speculating imaginatively. Parents who deliberately and consciously try to avoid replicating the kinds of domineering parent-child interactions they experienced in their own childhoods are speculating imaginatively.

Once people are aware of valid alternatives to what were

previously thought to be morally acceptable and inherently correct ways of living within relationships, they inevitably begin to question those beliefs, norms, and advice regarding intimate relationships that purport to carry universal truth and authority. Practicing this kind of reflective skepticism is traumatic but liberating. Wives who reject the submissive role models of wifely behavior laid down by parents, religion, or subculture are reflectively skeptical. Husbands who refuse to conform to notions of ''manliness'' (domination, authority, and even physical abuse) derived from peer groups, parents, or the mass media are reflectively skeptical. Gay and lesbian partners who do not view their liaisons as immoral, deviant, or indicative of serious emotional flaws in their personalities are reflectively skeptical.

One of the most difficult tasks of critical analysis occurring within intimate relationships has to do with being able to take on the perspectives of others—that is, to reinterpret our actions in the light of our partner's views of these. The possibilities for self-deception in relationships are immense. When partners are able to place before each other evidence about how they have been acting in self-serving rather than altruistic ways, each is forced to reflect on the possibilities for self-deceit. This process is, however, extremely difficult and complex to manage. It requires sensitivity on the part of the person offering critical interpretations, to ensure that these criticisms are not offered in a hostile way. If they are made in an injurious manner, this may well induce such a counterreaction that their possible accuracy will never be seriously countenanced. The partner receiving criticism also needs to be able to make giant interpretative leaps. In taking on the other's perspective, he or she can see how apparently altruistic behaviors might be interpreted less charitably than was previously supposed.

When critical thinking does happen in intimate relationships, the learning that ensues exhibits the four conditions of significant personal learning identified earlier. It is certainly usually regarded as important by the people involved. It is usually triggered by some kind of crisis, often when one partner reaches such a point of frustration that the criticisms have to be voiced no matter what the consequences might be. It frequently results in changes in the self-concepts of those involved: we come to view our actions and justifications much more skeptically than was previously the case and realize that we may be engaging in self-deception regarding the self-serving nature of apparently altruistic behaviors. Finally, it certainly entails an increase in the adult's critical capacities and inclinations, though these are primarily of a *self*-critical nature rather than occurring within the context of broader social or political action.

Encouraging Critical Thinking in Relationships

As is evident from this chapter, the need to encourage people to think critically about their participation in intimate relationships is crucial. From one point of view, developing critical capacities in this domain of life is especially hard, principally because of the emotional significance with which we invest our relationships. From another point of view, however, it may be easier to develop critical thinking skills in this arena, precisely because of the ready and immediate involvements people have in the flux, turbulence, and change of relationships. Statistically, this flux is seen in increasing divorce and remarriage rates. Escaping statistical analysis, but powerfully felt by many people nonetheless, are the fluctuations of love affairs, live-in relationships, and transient friendships. Given the high numbers of people experiencing forms of transition (both positive and negative) in their relationships, the demonstrable need for making sense of and coming to terms with these (that is, for becoming critical thinkers) is evident.

In many cases the participants involved will need to consult a skilled therapist or professional marital and family counselor. There is a limit to what self-analysis can achieve, or to what can be done even with the help of sympathetic friends who are willing to act as reflective mirrors for those seeking to understand their own, and their partner's, behaviors in relationships. But adaptations of the general techniques presented in Chapters Six and Seven are appropriate for developing critical thinking within intimate relationships. To begin to identify and challenge assumptions within a relationship, critical incident exercises and criteria analysis are perhaps the most relevant. Asking each other to describe the most significant critical incidents in which great satisfaction or frustration was experienced can be surprisingly revealing. Engaging in criteria analysis—asking each other, "When do you think this relationship is working best?"—can be a powerful way of revealing the privately held assumptions each partner has regarding his or her unquestioned expectations and assumptions about the relationship. These activities cannot be undertaken within the context of casual daily conversation; they need a period for deliberate reflection and interpretation of the results. But they can be accomplished without the presence of professional helpers such as therapists and counselors. In every relationship there are periods in which everyday pressures and requirements recede somewhat into the background, and it is during these times that criteria analysis can be done most effectively.

The processes of envisioning are easily adaptable to the second activity of critical thinking in relationships: exploring and imagining alternatives. Asking each other to invent ideal personal futures, and then comparing these, will indicate points of potential congruence and conflict in the development of the relationship. Engaging in the formulation of a shared preferred scenario has two benefits: it increases participants' understanding of each other's most deeply felt desires and longings, and it builds a shared commitment to those goals that are generated in common.

One final point needs to be made regarding how we might encourage critical thinking in our relationships. In seminars I have run on this topic, participants frequently ask me, "Why do you always stress change as necessary and positive in relationships?" "Aren't there situations when people are happy with their relationships and don't feel the need to change?" "Why do accounts of significant personal learning identify major traumas as the only triggers to personal change?" "Why should we be made to feel guilty if we're not engaged in a constant and upsetting process of renegotiating our relationships?" These questions are not posed by people who are evidently trying to avoid recognizing the need for change in their own lives. They make an excellent point: it is all too easy to accept uncritically a paradigm of personal relationships that sees these as characterized by continuously tortuous change.

It cannot be emphasized too strongly that change within relationships does not need to be constant or always radical and traumatic. Were this so, we would be continually ditching partners, seeking out new intimates, rejecting old contacts, and creating new networks. Daloz (1986, p. 144) emphasizes that personal change often involves a fusion of old and new, rather than a total abandonment of the old. Kegan (1982, p. 154) views personal transformation as a process of resolving old dichotomies by integrating the new with the old. Nonetheless, those involved in thinking critically about their relationships will be in an altered state regarding their beliefs and assumptions about how to behave within relationships. Instead of behaving in a habitually uncritical manner (for example, unthinkingly following parental prescriptions for appropriate marital conduct), they will have come to believe in the value of these prescriptions as a result of their own reflection. The end result of a period of reflection and critical scrutiny of assumptions and values may well be a reaffirmation of these same values and assumptions. The difference is that this commitment is informed, not unthinking. It has been reached after a process of critical reflection, not because of the insistence of some loved or feared external authority.

If one danger to be avoided is that of our coming to believe that critical reflection always leads to major alterations in the fabric of individual lives, another is that of presuming that the impetus for such changes is always negative. In intimate relationships there are always positive triggers for participants to reappraise their involvements. For example, the birth of a child will almost inevitably bring major changes in the relationship of marital partners or lovers, yet such alterations will be perceived as being caused by a joyful event. Again, falling in love is a process that causes those involved to question many aspects of their previous lives, most particularly their belief that past relationships were ''peak'' emotional experiences. When the new intimate holds beliefs contrary to those held by previous partners, or when he or she is involved in activities that are unfamiliar to the other partner, these beliefs and activities are not necessarily perceived as threats to the relationship; rather, they are frequently viewed as engaging and appealing. Exploring these unfamiliar beliefs seems to represent an exciting area for personal development. Participants in new relationships often speak of how the other's interests are broadening and developing them. They regard possibilities for future involvement as tantalizing, not irrelevant. They are challenged and intrigued by the prospect of sharing their new partner's interests.

Conclusion

Becoming critically aware of the ways in which we behave possessively and manipulatively within relationships is important if we wish to be involved in genuinely democratic, reciprocal relationships. Very few heterosexual relationships are entirely free from the stereotypical expectations regarding male and female roles that exist in the wider society. Very few families make a complete break with the habitual patterns of child rearing that have been passed down through the generations. But if we can be aware of the assumptions underlying our actions and of how these alter according to context, if we can imagine alternatives to the ways we currently behave in relationships, and if we are skeptical of any "final" solutions proposed to the ongoing problems of living in relationships, we stand a good chance of communicating clearly with those with whom we are involved. And in relationships in which communication is clear, those problems that *do* arise will be recognized earlier and will stand a better chance of being resolved than if we subscribe unthinkingly to beliefs and behaviors assimilated uncritically from external authorities.

❧ 12 ❧

Being a Skilled Facilitator
of Critical Thinking

Critical thinking is not an abstract, rarified academic process, observable only in college classrooms or undergraduate essays. It is an activity embedded in the vivid contexts of adult lives. As we struggle to build relationships, find meaning and satisfaction in work, and understand a political world portrayed through the distancing lens of the TV camera, we call upon our critical thinking faculties to help us in these tasks. Unfortunately, the literature on critical thinking is frequently so apparently specialized, or semantically impenetrable, that it is easy to conclude that the activity is of such a high order of cognitive complexity as to be beyond the reach of most "ordinary" people. Terms such as *double-loop learning* (Argyris, 1976) and *conscientization* (Freire, 1970b) are so specialized that they are beyond most people's immediate comprehension. Even less esoteric concepts, such as *reflective thinking* (Boud, Keogh, and Walker, 1985) and *action learning* (Morgan and Ramirez, 1983), are still part of the jargon of educational thinking rather than colloquial English. Add to this the connotations surrounding the activities of giving criticism (that it is a negative, hurtful, and arrogant activity) and of receiving criticism (that the receiver is found wanting or has failed in some way), and it is not hard to see why the

228

concept of critical thinking is unfamiliar to many people, even if the activity of critical thinking is one in which we frequently engage.

But engaging in an activity is not the same as doing it well. We have seen that critical thinking comprises two inter-related processes: identifying and challenging assumptions, and imagining and exploring alternatives. What frequently happens is that one process occurs without the other. On the one hand, we are critical of the assumptions under which we, or others, are operating, without being willing to suggest more valid or appropriate alternatives. On the other hand, we invent multiple alternatives of thinking and living, without stopping to analyze critically the assumptions underlying these. In the first case, we may appear to be unnecessarily cynical, ready to shoot down any alternative presented to us as somehow wanting. In the second case, we may seem unrealistically utopian, ready to dream up schemes aplenty without being careful to scrutinize their underlying assumptions for flaws or errors.

Another reason why critical thinking as a concept has been confined to the school or college classroom by most people is that *thinking* is interpreted as essentially a passive, armchair activity. American culture is one in which pragmatism and action are generally highly valued over such apparently unproductive activities as reflecting and thinking. Thinking is not seen as action, despite the fact that thinking is one of the most tiring activities in which we engage on a daily basis. People frequently talk of the stress of making crucial personal decisions (such as whether or not to take a certain job, whom or whether to marry, or whether to buy a particular house) as tiring or fatiguing them. But tell these same individuals that they are involved in critical thinking—in scrutinizing carefully the assumptions and reasons underlying the options open to them and in considering the benefits and negative consequences of following alternative courses of action—and they may find it difficult to see the connection.

If theorists, researchers, and teachers of critical thinking wish this concept to be taken more seriously outside the academic world, it is important that the action component of critical thinking be made explicit. Critical thinking is a continuous process composed of alternating phases of (1) reflecting on a problem or theme, (2) testing new solutions, strategies, or methods on the basis of that reflection, (3) reflecting on the success of these actions in particular contexts, and (4) further honing, refining, and adapting these actions according to alternative contexts. The action phases of critical thinking may be internal or external (that is to say, mental or behavioral). Mentally, we may consider and apply new perspectives to interpreting or reinterpreting familiar situations, problems, or habitual behaviors. Behaviorally, we may take some directly observable action in the world. The central point, however, is that thinking *is* action. That this point is coming to be appreciated in the most pragmatic and action-oriented of all spheres of American life—the world of business and industry—is evident in the widespread attention being devoted to Schön's concept of *reflective practitioners* (1983, 1987). His concern to make clear how practitioners think in action is echoed in Weick's (1983) analysis of managerial thinking in action.

A Theory in Use of Developing Critical Thinking

The concept of theories in use, introduced in Chapter Eight, was described as being composed of (1) the contextually grounded ideas about what approaches work well in particular contexts, (2) some explanations as to *why* they work well, and (3) a readiness to alter these practices according to changing contexts. Theories in use are the privately developed and proven ways of performing that practitioners know in their hearts to be true. Theories in use are derived inductively from reflecting on successful action. They are known intellectually and felt viscerally to be true. In this section, I wish to outline my own theory in use of developing critical thinking. This represents essentially the advice I would give to anyone who asked me for the "real" story of facilitating critical thinking, as contrasted with the fine-sounding and lofty (but basically unrealistic) prescriptions found in textbooks on the subject. The theory in use is divided into two sections, each of which contains five components. The first of these comprises a series of observations about how people think critically. These are derived from my own experiences, both personal and professional, with trying to get other people to think in this way. The second part comprises a set of guidelines I have evolved regarding the most effective ways to facilitate critical thinking. These guidelines are a mixture of warnings, advice, reminders, and specific suggestions about method.

Processes of Critical Thinking

My theory in use of how people engage in critical thinking is based on my observations of how people respond to tasks requiring them to undertake this very challenging activity. From their responses I have attempted, through inductive analysis, to identify some common processes involved. From this inductive effort, the following generalizations can be made. Because these generalizations are grounded in my own experience, they are likely to be disconfirmed or refuted by many readers' experiences, and will undoubtedly be altered many times in the future as I continually refine this theory in use.

1. Processes of critical thinking are person-specific.

How particular individuals respond to invitations to engage in critical thinking varies enormously. A great deal more thought and research are needed before we can predict with any likelihood of certainty how any one person will undertake to identify and challenge assumptions, or try to imagine alternatives to existing ways of thinking and living. People vary according to the capacities they inherit, the abilities they develop, and the experiences they undergo. Most significant, in my opinion, are the variables of personality and cultural background. Information about these two factors is the most important I can obtain before I try to make a person think critically about some aspect of life.

2. Emotions are central to critical thinking.

The processes involved in thinking critically are infused with a highly emotional dimension. Challenging unquestioned assumptions, looking skeptically at givens we have lived by, and trying to shake off habitual ideas and behaviors so that we can try out alternatives are emotionally potent activities. They may well produce anxiety, fear, resentment, and feelings of being threatened or intimidated. They may lead to emotional outbursts against the person who is prompting others to think critically. These activities can also be accompanied by feelings of liberation, release, relief, and the joy of abandoning internalized rules that we have perceived as constantly blocking our growth and development.

3. *Intrinsic and extrinsic reasons for thinking critically are both important.*
        Learning to think critically can be arduous. The people who are most likely to persist in this activity, and who are most likely to weather successfully periods of anxiety, self-doubt, blockage, and difficulty, are those who are driven by extrinsic as well as intrinsic motives. Hoping that some direct improvement in an area of their lives is likely to result from becoming critically alert is an important reason why people continue to struggle with difficult tasks and self-doubts.

4. *Critical insight often occurs unexpectedly.*
        The moments when people break through habitual ways of interpreting some idea, action, or social structure cannot be predicted in advance. It is not uncommon to be thinking about some aspect of one's life and experience a sudden flash of insight concerning an apparently unrelated area. Some of the most exciting experiences as a facilitator of critical thinking occur when learners depart from the ''script'' of an educational encounter to explore a concern that is of great personal significance but that had not been anticipated.

5. *Peer support is crucial to thinking critically.*
        Beginning to think critically is frequently a very tentative process. We may flirt privately with new and alternative ways of interpreting familiar ideas, behaviors, and social structures but lack the impetus to realize these in action. When people undertake critical thinking in groups, their private interpretations gain legitimacy as others venture similar interpretations and realizations. Realizing that others experience the discrepan-

cies, ambiguities, and contradictions we feel grants a degree of legitimacy to our own perceptions. As a consequence, we are more likely to follow through with our own processes of critical thinking.

Facilitating Critical Thinking

My theory in use of facilitating critical thinking derives from my experiences with trying to encourage such thinking in workshops, courses, and seminars given to a number of groups. The members of these groups represent diverse populations—school teachers, college faculty, trainers and human resource developers, counselors, therapists, community workers, staff developers, and health educators. Out of this experience I have evolved several rules of thumb that guide my actions, and several conclusions about the activity that I try to keep in mind as I act as a facilitator.

1. There is no standard model of facilitating critical thinking.

There is no Holy Grail of facilitating critical thinking and no one way to instructional enlightenment. Indeed, anyone who is critically alert will be immediately skeptical of standardized models that purport to be replicable in all possible situations. Different approaches will be called for depending on the characteristics of the particular audience and the demands of the context within which critical thinking is being developed. A degree of ambiguity should be expected as a constant feature of attempts to encourage critical thinking, given the complexity of variables present. The personalities of facilitators and learners, the contrasting expectations that people bring to any attempt to develop critical thinking, the range of abilities and past experiences evident in any group, and the particular institutional constraints concerned all affect significantly the extent to which any one model can be applied in a critical thinking effort.

2. Diversity in methods and materials is necessary.

Given that every group of people engaged in learning to think critically will exhibit a formidable diversity of abilities, experiences, and personalities, it follows that facilitators should be ready to try a range of different approaches. Some people learn visually, some think in a linear fashion, some can hold several related concepts in their minds at the same time and trace connections between them, some prefer a great deal of structure, some rebel against overdirection, some thrive on working independently, and some dislike working outside a group context. Given this diversity of learning styles, it is important that facilitators vary their methods, have a range of materials (visual and written) on hand, and make every effort to individualize their efforts where appropriate. This is a general principle of all attempts to facilitate learning, and it applies to encouraging critical thinking.

3. Perfection is impossible.

Nothing is more guaranteed to frustrate facilitators, and ultimately to hinder their efforts, than their seeking always to achieve some neatly predictable, perfect outcome of efforts to facilitate critical thinking. Nothing is more likely to prevent facilitators working in a relaxed but effective manner than their expectation that they must somehow exemplify the model of a "perfect" facilitator. As a facilitator you will never meet all the needs of your group members to their full satisfaction. You will never connect directly, simultaneously, and dramatically with each of your learners. While it is essential to have some clear purpose and rationale directing your efforts, you should avoid the mistake of crucifying yourself on the cross of perfection.

4. Learner satisfaction is not the sole aim of critical thinking.

One of the most frequent mistakes made in evaluating the worth of any educational endeavor is to judge its relative success by the indicator of participants' satisfaction. Most significant advances in people's ability to think critically arise out of periods of frustration and struggle. People may realize important insights long after they have left a workshop or course on critical thinking, and yet their realizations may be directly connected to their earlier participation in those activities. If we feel that we are successful only when people leave our workshops and courses feeling pleased with the activity, we may hold back from challenging learners and asking them to face some uncomfortable or confusing ambiguities.

5. Risk taking is important.

Good facilitators of critical thinking are ready and willing to take risks. In particular, they are eager to build on the excitement generated at those "teachable moments" when some serendipitous occurrence captures the imagination of group members. These emotionally charged periods can prompt some of the most memorable episodes in a facilitator's career. It is important to remember, however, that risk taking also entails the possibility of failure, or of only partial success, and facilitators need to be ready for their departures from a previously planned exercise to fall short of what they had hoped to achieve. They also need to remember that one less-than-successful venture in risk taking does not invalidate for the future all other attempts to build upon unexpected teachable moments.

The Facilitator as a Helper of Learning

Of central importance to developing critical thinking is the way in which the facilitators involved conceptualize their role. Perhaps the greatest mistake facilitators can make in this activity is to restrict their role to that of teachers. To many people, teachers are people who stand in front of classes and, through the force of their personalities, direct and control other people's learning activities. The winners of "teacher of the year" awards, in my experience, are those charismatic individuals who can hold a class on the edge of their seats, and who both inspire and entertain others through the sheer force of their personalities and through the enthusiasm and love of their subject that they radiate.

People like this are invaluable to learning and can be highly effective in motivating others to begin or persist in learning. But performing this activity of teaching in the way described does not cover the sum total of ways in which people can be helped to become critical thinkers. If people trying to develop critical thinking in others see themselves only as teachers needing to perform to some previously defined model of the ''good'' teacher, they run the risk of concentrating their energies on turning in stellar performances in workshops and courses. While these might be entertaining and highly enjoyable, they may have very little to do with participants actually developing any critical thinking skills.

The purpose of facilitation—the only reason facilitators are there—is to help people learn. The facilitator is, quite simply, a helper of learning. This very obvious truth is easily remembered and understood, and it has substantial implications for practice. When we gauge the success of our efforts by how far people have developed their own critical thinking proficiencies, then we focus our attentions on learners' development. We also avoid becoming fixated on the matter of our own performances. Simply remembering that a successful educational experience is one in which people are helped to learn is one of the most profound truths of education for critical thinking. Our performances as facilitators become almost irrelevant unless in some way they contribute directly to learners' critical thinking. This means that at every stage of their activities facilitators should be asking themselves, ''How does what I am doing contribute to my participants' becoming critical thinkers?'' If a convincing rationale cannot be produced as to how an activity does this, it should be stopped. The only reason for doing something is to help people understand or practice critical thinking. Whether or not an activity in some way contributes to the process of developing critical thinkers becomes the chief criterion to be applied when judging whether or not to try it out or to continue with it.

Conceiving of facilitators as helpers of learning means that range of abilities and exercises assumes equal importance alongside stellar classroom performance. For example, some of the most effective contributions toward developing critical thinking come through facilitators designing exercises or written materials that prompt participants to engage in this process without needing teachers standing over them directing their activities at each stage of the proceedings. If the exercises outlined throughout this book can be applied in different settings to help people think critically, I have made a contribution far greater than any I could make by speaking at conferences or running workshops. Facilitators of critical thinking need to remember that their success is not contingent on their possessing sparkling, winning personalities in the classroom. Their success is found in helping people think critically, and a well-designed exercise in which people are asked to confront and think through how they would resolve an ethical dilemma can do this very effectively.

Finally, on this point of the facilitator as a helper of learning, it has become increasingly evident over the years during which I have been trying to help people think critically that my own direct presence may sometimes actually hinder this activity. One of the most helpful things facilitators can do is remove themselves for a temporary period from the learners' presence. For example, in workshops on critical thinking I frequently require participants to form small groups and try out the criteria analysis exercise described in Chapter Six. When I first did this, I would dutifully visit each group to make sure that learners were "on target." Gradually it became apparent to me that my presence was actually distorting what was happening in these small groups. Before I visited them, some groups would be talking naturally and conversationally; upon my arrival this relaxed tone would disappear. Sometimes my presence would serve to numb group members into silence. Sometimes they would visibly change their behavior to show me what task-oriented, and therefore "good," group members they were. At other times it became obvious to me that they were trying to second-guess what they thought I wanted them to say, presuming that the criteria analysis exercise was supposed to lead to some "correct" answer. If I remained a quiet observer, people would be nervous because they felt they were on display before me and that I was checking their performance against some "correct" standard that I was keeping secret. If I participated as a group observer, whatever comments I made would receive disproportionate attention and consideration. People would listen carefully to see if they could discern in my contributions the "answers" to the exercise. These group reactions have happened in practically all groups, irrespective of the relative levels of educational sophistication of the members involved.

My tactic now is to leave small groups to themselves to conduct these exercises, and only to involve myself in their deliberations if and when I am asked by group members to participate. At the beginning of the exercise, I announce that I am available as a consultant to provide assistance, advice, or clarification on the purposes of the activity. I generally remove myself to a position far enough distanced from their activities that I cannot overhear what they are saying, but close enough that they can call on me for assistance when they feel they need it. The risk I run in doing this is that group members will chat about anything other than the stated exercise because they are either bored or intimidated by the activity. The advantage I gain is that my presence does not artificially distort group members' behaviors; they feel relaxed about being as truthful as they can about the matter under discussion. Additionally, by not standing over them and watching whether or not they are behaving like ''good' groups, I am sending them the message that I trust them enough to leave them to complete the exercise on their own. Being an effective helper of learning does not always require the physical presence of a teacher.

Developing Critical Thinking as a Learning Conversation

A useful metaphor for describing the process of developing critical thinking is that of a *learning conversation*. These two activities—having a good conversation and developing critical thinking—share three common features. They are reciprocal, they involve risk, surprise, and spontaneity, and they entail disagreement, diversity, and challenge.

1. Good conversations are reciprocal and involving.

In a good conversation, the participants are continually involved in the process; they are either talking or listening. In talking, they are doing such things as responding to previous comments, replying to questions posed, building on earlier arguments they have made, illustrating general ideas with particular examples, and initiating new areas for discussion. In listening, they are doing such things as processing the other's ideas, trying to understand the meaning of these, trying to interpret this meaning in the context of their own experience, and mentally rehearsing their next contribution. In a good conversation, both listening and contributing roles are essential. If one of these roles is not being performed, by definition it is not a good conversation. The most brilliant exposition means nothing if no one is listening. The most attentive listening is of little use if the other person is saying very little or repeating the same thing over and over again.

Developing critical thinking is a process in which listening and contributing are of equal importance. Many facilitators make the mistake of overemphasizing the contributing role, feeling that if they are not seen to be doing something all the time they are somehow shirking their pedagogic duty. Yet as the facilitator-as-helper-of-learning concept makes clear, listening well is as important to critical thinking as is contributing brilliantly. Unless facilitators listen attentively so that they gain a sense of participants' backgrounds, past experiences, frameworks of understanding, and habitual learning styles, how can they make informed judgments about what exercises, methods, and materials will be most likely to prompt critical thinking?

2. The course of good conversations cannot be anticipated.

One of the chief attractions of a good conversation is that it cannot be anticipated in advance. When we begin a conversation, we embark on a journey without knowing our final destination. Were we able to predict the exact course and ultimate outcome of the conversation, we would very soon become bored with the activity. When I am talking to someone and it becomes obvious very early on in the proceedings how the conversation is going to develop and where it will end, I try to extract myself from the activity as quickly as possible. Such conversations usually happen with people who repeat, firmly and fixedly, commonly accepted prejudices. They are so wedded to their points of view that contemplating any contrary arguments or admitting the legitimacy of other viewpoints becomes impossible for them.

Similarly, many elements in the process of developing critical thinking cannot be closely anticipated in advance. When we begin to ask people to identify assumptions underlying their habitual ways of thinking and learning, we do not know exactly how they are going to respond. When we ask them to consider alternatives, we do not know which of these will be considered seriously and which will be rejected out of hand. When people are presented with counterexamples that contradict their commonly held assumptions, when they are asked to explore unfamiliar ideas, and when they are asked to project themselves into unfamiliar situations and to describe how they would respond to these, we do not know exactly what will transpire. In good conversations, and in attempts to develop critical thinking, risk, surprise, and spontaneity are important and unavoidable. The impossibility of predicting the exact outcome of our efforts or the exact form of our activities means that we are constantly alert for new developments. This state of alertness is one characteristic of learners who are motivated to learn and is essential to the practice of critical thinking.

3. Good conversations entail diversity and disagreement.

A conversation in which one person agrees with everything the other person says is not really a conversation in the full sense of that word. When we are talking to someone who nods vigorously in agreement with everything we say, or who smiles pleasantly throughout our comments without offering any interpretations of these or any counterpoints, the chances are that our conversational partner is not really listening to anything we say. When people agree with everything we say, the experience is, initially at least, rather pleasant, since the rightness of our views and the correctness of our perceptions are confirmed. As the conversation proceeds, however, and the other person makes no attempt to interject with elaborations, interpretations, counterexamples, or additional points, the experience of talking to someone who seems so pliant and agreeable begins to sour.

The same applies to developing critical thinking. This process inevitably entails diversity of opinion, disagreement over "correct" interpretations of an idea, rule, or behavior, and challenges to existing ways of thinking and acting. A measure of diversity, disagreement, and challenge is central to helping people think critically. Unless we can accept that others have views very different from ours, and that a multiplicity of interpretations of practically every idea or action is possible, we will be unable to contemplate alternatives in our own thoughts and actions.

Conclusion

This book is, in one way, one part of a learning conversation. I hope that as you read it you have disagreed with much of it, that you have found examples that contradict my own, that you have been skeptical about any general rules or advice that I have offered, and that you have thought carefully about the applicability to your own life of any techniques I have presented. I do not presume to have all the answers to the question ''How can we develop critical thinkers?'' I doubt if anyone does. Indeed, as soon as anyone presented him- or herself as the guru of critical thinking, I would immediately become suspect of that person's real commitment to the process of critical thinking, since an element central to that process is becoming skeptical of any such claims to total truth.

The Risks and Rewards
of Helping Others Learn
to Think Critically

In Chapter Five the ways in which people can learn to think critically by observing role models of critical thinkers were described. In Chapter Eight the suggestion was made that the most fruitful approach to encouraging critical thinking at the workplace was that of using informal role models of critical thinking as consultants to other employees within their organizations. As a personal epilogue to this book, I want to present some of the ways in which I try to model critical thinking in my own work as an educator. In particular, I want to show how risk taking is essential in the process of critical thinking. We cannot hope to encourage other people to take the risk of probing previously unquestioned ideas, beliefs, and behaviors without being prepared to take risks ourselves in doing this. We cannot ask others to make public the assumptions underlying their actions, and to scrutinize these carefully for their fit with reality, unless we are willing to submit our own assumptions to the same public critical analysis.

These comments about my attempts to put into practice what I think about the importance of risk taking are an extension of the theory in use on how to develop critical thinking outlined in the previous chapter. The theory in use was presented as a general and generalizable set of recommendations about how best to foster critical thinking derived from my own context-specific experiences. In the current chapter, I want to flesh out the skeletal framework of this theory in use by providing some personal and concrete details of how I try to facilitate critical thinking in my own practice. The activities described are, of necessity, highly context-specific. However, my hope is that such a concretely detailed description of how I try to put into my own practice the principles of critical thinking discussed throughout this book will give readers a vivid illustration of how theoretical tenets can be translated into individual action.

Modeling Risk Taking

The first activity I wish to describe is how I try to encourage a sense of risk taking in my courses. It is my firm belief that critical processes are much more likely to flourish in an atmosphere in which those involved feel no sense of fear in trying out new ideas, testing tentative explanations, and offering widely diverging interpretations of events—in short, an atmosphere in which critical thinking is both valued and encouraged.

In my own work as a workshop leader, group facilitator, or professor, I frequently make an explicit virtue of departing from the written script of the encounter. This frequently confuses participants, particularly when (as happens regularly) the evaluation form handed out to participants at the end of a workshop or course asks them to rate my presentations on a five-point scale ranging from ''organized'' at one end to ''unorganized'' at the other. The assumption implicit in the form is evident: organized presentations (frequently interpreted as those that closely follow the previously prepared and distributed format) are characteristic of good professional educators. Unorganized presentations (frequently interpreted as those in which the instructor departs from the preordained sequence of activities and objectives, for whatever reasons) are characteristic of poorly prepared amateurs.

Participants faced with this form are frequently placed in a position of conflict. On the one hand, if they have enjoyed

the experience and gained something from it, they may wish
to give me a "good" rating. This would mean that they would
have to rate my presentations as "organized." On the other
hand, the aspect of the experience that made it enjoyable and
insightful may well have been my willingness to depart from
the planned script of activities and objectives so that as a group
we could follow up some line of inquiry, concern, or problem
perceived by a majority of group members as being of great
significance to them. This would mean they would have to rate
my presentations as "unorganized." Yet in so doing they would
implicitly be criticizing me. What frequently happens is that
participants give me a rating somewhere in the middle and then
write a comment to the effect that "not always being organized
can be good."

I regard the ability to make informed departures from
the script of a carefully planned encounter as one of the qualities
of a good helper or facilitator. Any learning network or community action group is a collection of idiosyncratic personalities,
all of whom bring to the group their own particular past experiences as well as their various current purposes and orientations. Group members are likely to exhibit different levels of
readiness for learning and varying learning styles. Each individual is a unique configuration of these personality traits, experiences, orientations, learning styles, and intentions. When
one considers the bewilderingly complex configuration of capacities represented in a group of individuals, it becomes evident that any closely prescribed pursuit of predetermined, standardized objectives is meaningless for anything other than closely
specified instrumental skill learning.

In terms of the development of critical capacities outlined
in this book, there is a real danger of specifying too closely be-
forehand the exact format for this process. It is certainly possible
to devise exercises and simulations that are intended to help
people become aware of internalized assumptions, scrutinize
these critically, and think of alternatives. It is likely, however,
that dramatic insights, revelations, and understanding of how
knowledge, behaviors, and values are culturally constructed will
frequently come unexpectedly to individuals. For example, it

is not at all uncommon for people to stumble on an insight regarding their own capacity for self-deception, or to come to a sudden realization of how they have been unthinkingly following behavioral and moral norms defined for them by someone else in a way that comes as a total surprise to them. Indeed, when I think about the most significant insights I have gained in these areas, they have invariably been the unanticipated, incidental outcomes of an activity in which I was involved for some other purpose.

The opportunity to model risk taking will vary, of course, from setting to setting. In institutions in which departures from standardized curricula and rigid formats are punished by informal or formal sanctions, the opportunity to do this will be limited. In other settings, such departures will not only be permitted, they will be the occasion and stimulus for significant learning and self-insight. When helpers and facilitators do depart from preset formats, however, they should make explicit their reasons for so doing. Whenever I abandon an exercise I had planned because a group discussion has captured people's imaginations and run well over the time allotted for it, I am careful to explain why I did not try to reign in group members' contributions and bring the discussion to an artificial close. When the supposed themes for consideration in a one-on-one consultation are superseded by the discussion of some unexpected concerns, I make sure that the other person involved is fully apprised of why I was willing to let that happen. Since one of the qualities of a good modeler is that of being a good communicator, it is obviously incumbent on me to explain and justify those actions that contradict my previously declared intentions.

Modeling Assumption Analysis

Critically analyzing assumptions is one of the most difficult of all capacities to model, since it entails a willingness to scrutinize one's existing givens—an activity that can frequently be threatening and anxiety-producing. In my own case, this difficulty is doubly compounded by my position of perceived authority in the institution within which I work. For example, I frequently require graduate students in my courses to undertake a critical examination of writers in the fields of education and psychology of learning. This is difficult, but not particularly traumatic for most people, until I ask them to undertake a critical analysis of my own writing. That brings students to a point of conflict. On the one hand, they may well have successfully proceeded through their previous undergraduate and graduate education by detecting their professors' assumptions and prejudices, and producing assignments that pander to these, sometimes in a very subtle manner. On the other hand, they are now being told that the very behavior for which they were previously rewarded (agreeing with professors) will be frowned upon, and the very behavior they had previously been most careful to avoid (disagreeing with professors) will gain them approval in my course.

Framing Critical Thinking in Terms Observers Understand. Although I am writing primarily from an educational perspective, my clients and learners are from a wide range of backgrounds (colleges, universities, business and industry, nonprofit organizations). In all my courses and workshops, my central purpose is to encourage participants to become critical thinkers. However, since this term is somewhat unfamiliar and possibly intimidating, I frame this purpose in terms participants will understand. For example, in workshops where managers and trainers from business and industry are the clientele, I speak of situational leadership, decision making, problem solving, and making good judgments about people. Central to these activities, of course, are certain activities of critical thinking—that is, becoming aware of how one's decisions are often strongly influenced by context (in this case, the corporate or organizational culture) and of how one's actions are affected by internalized and uncritically accepted assumptions and givens (about, for example, what motives colleagues are acting under) that may be inaccurate and inappropriate for the situation at hand.

The core of situational leadership, for example, is having a range of alternative management styles at your disposal and being able to make appropriate judgments and actions according to the context within which you are working. This is precisely what critical thinkers do; they are good at thinking contextually and flexible at adjusting assumptions, decisions, and behaviors according to the demands of the particular contexts involved. The term *situational leadership* is much more readily understood by trainers and managers than such phrases as *critical reflection* or *contextual thought*. These latter terms are alternately seen as unfamiliar, intimidating, or irrelevant—and are therefore ignored. Framing is all when it comes to being a good modeler of critical thinking. It is essential to use language and concepts readily understood by those whom you are seeking to influence.

Encouraging Critical Analysis of the Modeler's Work. If I am seeking to encourage people to become critically reflective about their own internalized assumptions and modes of behavior, it is important that I model this capacity in regard to my own work. There are three ways I do this: by making frequent public disavowals of my earlier ideas, by drawing attention to criticisms of my own work made by others, and by requiring critical analysis of my ideas by workshop and course participants. One of the capacities I have frequently observed and most admire in writers, teachers, and thinkers whom I use as my own role models is their readiness to admit when they are wrong and when their ideas, assumptions, and arguments have been shown to be poorly thought out, confusingly stated, or inaccurate. In my own classes and workshops, I try to be as open as possible about what I see as the shortcomings of my own past efforts. I will readily admit to being embarrassed at the apparent naiveté of some of my earlier writings. Very occasionally, I will actually put this into writing (Brookfield, 1987a), though I have to admit that this is harder for me to accomplish, given the informal norms surrounding the professional community. With the pressures of promotion, reappointment, and tenure, one is likely to think twice before publishing a piece disavowing ideas published earlier in a career, particularly if these publications were instrumental in getting one a job in the first place.

As an example of this kind of critical modeling, it might be useful to recount some of the doubts and uncertainties that I feel about this book. Although it has been four years in the writing, and has gone through four complete drafts, I still have nagging criticisms of my efforts to date. At times I feel the tone is too utopian, urging others to engage in activities that, in their own contexts, are unrealistic. Most people work and live within structures that are extremely hard to change, and I sometimes fall into the trap of presuming that it is easier to effect change than is actually the case. I also have a tendency to erect straw men so that I can then demolish them with elegance and style. This is little more than intellectual showing off and does very little to advance understanding or discussion of important issues. My style tends toward repetition, and I am aware of my tendency to beat readers over the head with an idea to a point that may sometimes be counterproductive.

My selection of examples undoubtedly reveals my own biases—especially my selection of events from the political world, where my opposition to conservative ideas and policies comes through clearly. I tend to emphasize the mistakes of the right and minimize or ignore those of the left (witness my discussions of Republican and Democratic politics or the British Conservative and Labour parties). At times these biases are even concealed in "objective," empirical fact. In draft form this manuscript was criticized for being too political by some, and for not being political enough by others. Some have criticized its emphasis on transforming social structures; others have said that this theme is not dealt with enough.

The important thing to realize, I think, is that books are not static, once-and-for-all-time universal statements of an author's ideas. Authors change their ideas, they become more knowledgeable, informed, or sophisticated, and their works improve. Books are just as contextually and historically specific as other external forms of thought, such as speeches or even conversations. Books are also, ultimately, personal statements. How we write, what we choose to write about, what examples we select to prove our case or disprove that of our opponents, what we emphasize, what we ignore, what we deride, and what we approve are all reflections of our own personalities. Books should be regarded as elements in an ongoing dialogue—invitations to further reaction and discussion and not the last word on the matters discussed.

Academic settings are not the only ones in which recognizing one's faults can be difficult. The unwillingness to admit to error for fear of others' perceiving us as somehow inadequate is perhaps even more pervasive in the world of business and industry than elsewhere. As anyone who has attended workshops on leadership, problem solving, or decision making knows, it is very rare that participants will admit publicly to doubts about their effectiveness or abilities. Acknowledging that one is having problems functioning effectively in a particular work environment can be a highly threatening public admission to make. The fear is that such an admission might start rumors about one's supposed incompetence that will do considerable career damage. The only way that employees and managers will be willing to admit publicly to error, doubt, and anxiety, and be willing to ask for the assistance of colleagues in scrutinizing their actions critically, is if such behaviors are modeled by those in positions of considerable power. It is naive in the extreme for trainers or outside consultants to presume that they can enter an organization and conduct a one-day or weekend workshop on critical thinking or trust building that will transform how people behave at work. Only if this openness and trust are evident in how people in power behave toward those beneath them will the climate for success in such a workshop be established.

Drawing attention to others' criticisms of my work is accomplished by my photocopying reviews critical of my ideas and including these in readings and resource packages distributed in the course or workshop I am leading. For example, my ideas on self-directed learning have been criticized by Brockett (1985) and Smith (1986) as being too selective in citing relevant studies, too dismissive of the use of quantitative instruments, conceptually ambiguous, and overly philosophical. In workshops and classes where I am exploring self-directed learning, I include these two pieces as accompaniments to my own published works on this topic. By encouraging participants to read these critiques along with my own works, I hope that I am sending a clear and unequivocal message that criticism of self and others is perfectly acceptable and appropriate in my sessions.

Encouraging public critical analysis of my ideas among workshop participants or group members is pursued through my setting small-group exercises in which this is required. For example, an exercise I frequently require asks participants to read three or four interpretations (one of which would be mine) of the same idea or concept. Within small groups, participants are asked to summarize briefly the central arguments of each piece, to select those elements that they feel have some validity, to identify ambiguous, confusing, and poorly presented arguments, and to choose those ideas that participants find to be contradicted by their own experiences. I set the same requirements for course members' written work. After they have shown briefly that they have understood the central ideas in a body of written work (my own work included), I ask that a critical analysis of these ideas be undertaken. Typically, the written instructions for one of these assignments ask learners to:

1. Identify the hidden assumptions underlying writers' central ideas.
2. Identify any ethical questions that have not been addressed by these writers.
3. Highlight ambiguities, fallacious reasoning, and lack of clarity in these writers' expressions of their ideas.
4. Identify contradictions in these writers' works.
5. Examine whether or not these writers' ideas take account of the practical realities of facilitating learning that have become evident in course members' own experiences.

Such an assignment has a dual function: it encourages critical analysis of experts' ideas, and it emphasizes the validity of participants' own experiences. It is important when setting such an assignment to stress that critical analysis involves elements of positive as well as negative appraisal. This makes it considerably easier for some people to engage in criticism; they can balance what they see as negative comments with positive ones. This helps to ease their fears that they will be perceived by the authority figure concerned as being engaged in demolition of "expert" work.

Encouraging Self-Evaluation. A central aim of modeling critical thinking for others is to prompt them to apply habits

of critical analysis to their own lives. Sometimes modeling these behaviors is not enough, and the modeler has to be more directive in encouraging the kinds of behaviors desired. In my own work, for example, I try to go beyond simply demonstrating the kinds of critical thinking I feel are important; I also require learners and workshop participants to analyze critically their own activities. At a minimum, all assignments in my courses include a self-assessment section, in which participants are asked to evaluate their own work. On a more sophisticated level, I use learning contracts in the majority of my courses. Learning contracts (Berte, 1975; Knowles, 1986) are a means by which learners can assume individual control over their learning. At the heart of using learning contracts is the idea that learners specify their own evaluative criteria and indicators. In workshops and courses where I use learning contracts as the chief mode of assessment, there are several things I typically require:

1. A title for the project.
2. A statement of purposes and objectives.
3. A description of resources (for example, experts, colleagues, books, videos, computer software).
4. A summary of methods (for example, literature reviews, interviews, questionnaires, observations).
5. A specification of criteria for assessment.
6. A specification of indicators for judging whether or not these criteria have been met.
7. A description of data collection techniques by which evaluative evidence will be collected.
8. A self-evaluation.

Learning contracts can frequently be intimidating to learners—particularly the requirement that they specify their own evaluative criteria, indicators, and methods so that they can conduct a self-evaluation. Evaluation is concerned, ultimately, with values and questions of power. The greatest threat to educational institutional authority is when decisions regarding quality and assessment are in the hands of learners rather than teachers. To many learners, the experience of evaluating their own efforts is so unfamiliar that they cannot believe their judgments are really going to be accepted as valid by experts and authority figures. As Rogers (1980, p. 273) writes, "Students have been 'conned' for so long that a teacher who is real with them is usually seen for a time as simply exhibiting a new brand of phoniness."

Modeling Openness

Building an atmosphere of trust between helpers and participants in any kind of educational or training setting will only happen if the helper models openness, honesty, and integrity, if participants sense that the leader's word can be relied upon and that he or she is not attempting to keep from them information about informal organizational norms or private leader prejudices. Organizations frequently operate according to a mix of publicly declared values (enshrined in such things as mission statements) and informal norms or private knowledge (on such things as appropriate conduct to superiors and inferiors or the "pecking order" submerged within the official institutional hierarchy). This is why it is frequently so difficult for educators, trainers, counselors, and other facilitators of critical thinking to build an atmosphere of genuine trust and honesty within an organizational setting. In informal networks (such as professional development exchanges, gay and lesbian networks, and student groups for divestment from South Africa), self-help support groups (such as Alcoholics Anonymous and the British single-parent Gingerbread groups), and community action groups (such as tenant organizations), the problems posed by official organizational hierarchies and the informal norms or private knowledge submerged within these are largely avoided. Those norms, informal hierachies, and rivalries certainly exist within these groups, but in a much more public way. They can be addressed directly by members.

For helpers working within organizational settings, there will be many times when there is no option but to admit publicly to clients, trainees, and learners that they are caught at the nexus of several contradictory and conflicting pressures. People will generally be responsive and understanding of leaders who admit openly that they are constrained by organizational givens and institutional structures. In my own work, I am quite willing to describe how my freedom of action is limited by organizational constraints and how my frustration at this affects my own morale. If I am asked for information that is deemed confidential within the institution, I will tell people that this is the case rather than trying to pretend that I do not have access to it.

Being open and honest with oneself and others is arguably the most difficult interpersonal task of adult life. It entails psychological, political, and economic risks to one's self-esteem and livelihood. Daloz (1986) speculates that being open and honest comes more easily to female than male helpers, and it may well be that men's cultural conditioning makes it more difficult, embarrassing, or threatening for them to be open about their feelings, situations, doubts, pleasures, and anxieties. Although women may talk openly about their feelings, Belenky, Clinchy, Goldberger, and Tarule (1986) argue that they find it harder than men to be critical. These writers assert that very few women find reasoned critical discourse a congenial form of conversation among friends, and that "although it may be difficult for men, many women find it easier to believe than to doubt" (p. 113). In other words, women appear to be more open and trusting than men when it comes to considering other people's ideas and less ready to be critically skeptical. The gender specificity of such components of critical thinking as reflective skepticism is an area of important future inquiry.

Irrespective of the gender of those involved, openness is essential to educators' and helping professionals' actions. Thinking critically is precarious and uncertain. Only if those trying to encourage people to become critical thinkers are themselves honest about the assumptions they hold dearest, and the contextuality of these assumptions, will clients, trainees, and learners take them seriously. Only if educators and helpers apply the same reflective skepticism to their own ideas that they expect from others will people be ready to question the universal applicability of "quick fixes." Only if helpers and educators are willing to admit to alternative interpretations on matters they care deeply about will people be willing to consider alternatives in their own lives. In these attempts to be open to other ways of thinking about our personal and public worlds, we see the spirit of critical thinking.

Conclusion

Taking the risk to think critically, and to realize in our actions the insights we gain through this, is one of the most powerful activities of adult life. The reason we persist in doing this, even when it seems to produce only frustration, perplexity, and anxiety, is the rewards it produces. As critical thinkers we are engaged in a continual process of creating and re-creating our personal, work, and political lives. We do not take our identities as settled; rather, we are aware of the scope for development in all areas of life. We see the future as open to our influence. We regard the world as changeable through our own individual actions and through collective action in concert with others who share our commitment to broader political and social changes. We do not accept the idea that because things are the way they are now, they must always be this way. And we do not think that we (or anyone else) have the ultimate answer to life's ambiguities and problems. But we do have confidence in knowing that those things in which we believe, and the actions we take arising out of these beliefs, spring from a process of careful analysis and testing against reality—in other words, from critical thinking.

References

Adams, F. *Making Production, Making Democracy: A Case Study of Teaching in the Workplace.* Chapel Hill, N.C.: Twin Streams Educational Center, 1982.

Adams, J. L. *Conceptual Blockbusting: A Guide to Better Ideas.* (2nd ed.) New York: Norton, 1979.

Allport, C. W. *Becoming: Basic Considerations for a Psychology of Personality.* New Haven, Conn.: Yale University Press, 1955.

Altheide, D. L. *Creating Reality: How TV News Distorts Events.* Beverly Hills, Calif.: Sage, 1976.

Altheide, D. L. *Media Power.* Beverly Hills, Calif.: Sage, 1985.

Apple, M. W. *Ideology and Curriculum.* London: Routledge & Kegan Paul, 1981.

Apple, M. W. (ed.). *Cultural and Economic Reproduction in Education: Essays on Class, Ideology, and the State.* London: Routledge & Kegan Paul, 1982a.

Apple, M. W. *Education and Power.* London: Routledge & Kegan Paul, 1982b.

Apps, J. W. *Improving Practice in Continuing Education: Modern Approaches for Understanding the Field and Determining Priorities.* San Francisco: Jossey-Bass, 1985.

Argyris, C. *Increasing Leadership Effectiveness.* New York: Wiley-Interscience, 1976.

Argyris, C. *Reasoning, Learning, and Action: Individual and Organizational.* San Francisco: Jossey-Bass, 1982.

Argyris, C., Putnam, R., and Smith, D. M. *Action Science: Concepts, Methods, and Skills for Research and Intervention.* San Francisco: Jossey-Bass, 1985.

Argyris, C., and Schön, D. A. *Theory in Practice: Increasing Professional Effectiveness.* San Francisco: Jossey-Bass, 1974.

Argyris, C., and Schön, D. A. *Organizational Learning: A Theory of Action Perspective.* Reading, Mass.: Addison-Wesley, 1978.

Armstrong, R. "Towards the Study of Community Action." *Adult Education* (U.K.), 1972, *45* (1), 21–25.

Armstrong, R., and Davies, C. T. "Community Action, Pressure Groups and Education." *Adult Education* (U.K.), 1977, *50* (3), 149–154.

Arnold, R., and Burke, B. *A Popular Education Handbook: An Educational Experience Taken from Central America and Adapted to the Canadian Context.* Toronto: CUSO-Development Education and Department of Adult ·Education, Ontario Institute for Studies in Adult Education, 1983.

Aronowitz, S., and Giroux, H. A. *Education Under Siege: The Conservative, Liberal, and Radical Debate over Schooling.* South Hadley, Mass.: Bergin & Garvey, 1985.

Back, K. W. *Beyond Words: The Story of Sensitivity Training and the Encounter Movement.* New York: Russell Sage Foundation, 1972.

Barber, B. *Strong Democracy: Participatory Politics for a New Age.* Berkeley: University of California Press, 1984.

Barndt, D., Cristall, F., and Marino, D. *Getting There: Images of Women's Journeys to Equality.* Toronto: Between the Lines, 1983.

Basseches, M. *Dialectical Thinking and Adult Development.* Norwood, N. J.: Ablex Publishing Corporation, 1984.

Beidler, P. G. (ed.). *Distinguished Teachers on Effective Teaching.* New Directions for Teaching and Learning, no. 28. San Francisco: Jossey-Bass, 1986.

Belenky, M. F., Clinchy, B. M., Goldberger, N. R., and Tarule, J. M. *Women's Ways of Knowing: The Development of Self, Voice, and Mind.* New York: Basic Books, 1986.

Benne, K. D., Bradford, L. P., Gibb, J. R., and Lippitt, R. O. *The Laboratory Method of Changing and Learning: Theory and Application.* Palo Alto, Calif.: Science and Behavior Books, 1975.

Bennis, W. "The Artform of Leadership." In S. Srivastva and Associates, *The Executive Mind: New Insights on Managerial Thought and Action.* San Francisco: Jossey-Bass, 1983.

Berger, P. L., and Kellner, H. *Sociology Reinterpreted: An Essay on Method and Vocation.* Garden City, N.Y.: Anchor Press, 1981.

Bernstein, B. *Class, Codes, and Control.* Vol. 3: *Towards a Theory of Educational Transmission.* (2nd ed.) London: Routledge & Kegan Paul, 1977.

Bernstein, P. *Workplace Democratization: Its Internal Dynamics.* New Brunswick, N.J.: Transaction Books, 1980.

Berte, N. R. (ed.). *Individualizing Education by Learning Contracts.* New Directions for Higher Education, no. 10. San Francisco: Jossey-Bass, 1975.

Boshier, R. *Toward a Learning Society.* Vancouver, Canada: Learning Press, 1980.

Boshier, R. "Beyond Ambulance Driving: A Conceptual and Empirical Perspective on Adult Education Program Planning Theory." *Proceedings of the Adult Education Research Conference,* no. 25. Raleigh: North Carolina State University, 1984.

Boshier, R. *Toward a Learning Society.* Vancouver, Canada: Learning Press, 1986.

Botkin, J. W., Elmandjra, M., and Malitza, M. *No Limits to Learning: Bridging the Human Gap.* Oxford, England: Pergamon Press, 1979.

Boud, D., Keogh, R., and Walker, D. *Reflection: Turning Experience into Learning.* London: Kogan Page, 1985.

Boulding, E. "Learning to Image the Future." In W. G. Bennis, K. D. Benne, R. Chin, and K. E. Corey (eds.), *The Planning of Change.* (4th ed.) New York: Holt, Rinehart & Winston, 1976.

Bourdieu, P., and Passerson, J. *Reproduction in Education, Society, and Culture.* Beverly Hills, Calif.: Sage, 1977.

Bowles, S. B., and Gintis, H. *Schooling in a Capitalist Society: Educational Reform and the Contradictions of Economic Life.* New York: Basic Books, 1976.

Bowles, S. B., and Gintis, H. *Democracy and Capitalism*. New York: Basic Books, 1986.

Boyd, E. M., and Fales, A. W. "Reflective Learning: Key to Learning from Experience." *Journal of Humanistic Psychology*, 1983, *23* (2), 99–117.

Bradford, L. P., Gibb, J. R., and Benne, K. D. *T-Group Theory and Laboratory Method: Innovation in Re-education*. New York: Wiley, 1964.

Bramner, L. M., and Abrego, P. J. "Intervention Strategies for Coping with Transitions." *The Counseling Psychologist*, 1981, *9* (2), 19–36.

Brightman, S. "Bamboozled Electorate Needs Help from Adult Educators." *Adult and Continuing Education Today*, 1984, *14* (23), 106, 111.

Brockett, R. G. "A Response to Brookfield's Critical Paradigm of Self-Directed Learning." *Adult Education Quarterly*, 1985, *36* (1), 55–59.

Brook, L., and Garforth, T. " 'Issues': An Exercise in Adult Political Education." *Adult Education* (U.K.), 1986, *58* (4), 318–321.

Brooke, P. (ed.). *Report of the Citizenship Education Symposium*. Occasional Papers in Continuing Education, no. 23. Vancouver, Canada: Centre for Continuing Education, University of British Columbia, 1983.

Brookfield, S. D. *Independent Adult Learning*. Unpublished doctoral dissertation, Department of Adult Education, University of Leicester, 1980.

Brookfield, S. D. *Adult Learners, Adult Education, and the Community*. New York: Teachers College Press; Milton Keynes, England: Open University Press, 1984.

Brookfield, S. D. *Self-Directed Learning: From Theory to Practice*. New Directions for Continuing Education, no. 25. San Francisco: Jossey-Bass, 1985.

Brookfield, S. D. "Media Power and the Development of Media Literacy: An Adult Educational Interpretation." *Harvard Educational Review*, 1986a, *56* (2), 151–170.

Brookfield, S. D. *Understanding and Facilitating Adult Learning: A Comprehensive Analysis of Principles and Effective Practices*. San Francisco: Jossey-Bass; Milton Keynes, England: Open University Press, 1986b.

Brookfield, S. D. "Conceptual, Methodological, and Practical Ambiguities in Self-Directed Learning." In H. B. Long and R. M. Smith (eds.), *Self-Directed Learning: Application and Theory.* Athens, Ga.: Department of Adult Education, University of Georgia, 1987a.

Brookfield, S. D. (ed.). *Learning Democracy: Eduard Lindeman on Adult Education and Social Change.* London: Croom Helm, 1987b.

Broughton, J. "Beyond Formal Operations: Theoretical Thought in Adolescence." *Teachers College Record,* 1977, *79* (1), 87–97.

Brown, H. W. "Lateral Thinking and Andragogy: Improving Problem Solving in Adulthood." *Lifelong Learning: An Omnibus of Practice and Research,* 1985, *8* (7), 22–25, 27.

Browning, D. S. *Generative Man: Psychoanalytic Perspectives.* Philadelphia: Westminster Press, 1972.

Bryson, L. *Adult Education.* New York: American Book Company, 1936.

Burgoyne, J., and Hodgson, V. "Natural Learning and Managerial Action: A Phenomenological Study in the Field Setting." *Journal of Management Studies,* 1983, *2* (3), 387–399.

Business–Higher Education Forum. *America's Business Schools: Priorities for Change.* Washington, D.C.: Association of American Colleges, 1983.

Butts, R. F. *The Revival of Civic Learning: A Rationale for Citizenship Education in American Schools.* Phi Delta Kappa Educational Foundation, 1980.

Callaway, H. "Women's Perspectives: Research as Re-Vision." *Convergence,* 1981, *14* (4), 34–43.

Cameron, S. W. "The Perry Scheme: A New Perspective on Adult Learners." *Proceedings of the Adult Education Research Conference,* no. 24. Montreal: Concordia University–University of Montreal, 1983.

Candy, P. C. *Mirrors of the Mind: Personal Construct Theory in the Training of Adult Educators.* Manchester Monographs, no. 16. Manchester, England: Department of Adult and Higher Education, University of Manchester, 1981.

Carkhuff, R. R., and Berenson, B. G. *Beyond Counseling and Therapy*. (2nd ed.) New York: Holt, Rinehart & Winston, 1977.

Carnoy, M., and Levin, H. M. *Schooling and the Democratic State*. Stanford, Calif.: Stanford University Press, 1985.

Carr, W., and Kemmis, S. *Becoming Critical: Knowing Through Action Research*. Deakin, Australia: Deakin University Press, 1983.

Cohen, B. "Rights Education." *Adult Education* (U.K.), 1976, *49* (4), 234–239.

Cohen-Rosenthal, E. "Participation as Pedagogy: Quality of Working Life and Adult Education." *Convergence*, 1982, *15* (1), 5–16.

Collins, M. "Jurgen Habermas's Concept of Communicative Action and Its Implications for the Adult Learning Process." *Proceedings of the Adult Education Research Conference*, no. 26. Tempe: Arizona State University, 1985.

Combs, A. W., Avila, D. L., and Purkey, W. W. *Helping Relationships: Basic Concepts for the Helping Professions*. Newton, Mass.: Allyn & Bacon, 1971.

Corey, G. *Theory and Practice of Group Counseling*. (2nd ed.) Monterey, Calif.: Brooks/Cole, 1985.

Corey, G., and Corey, M. S. *Groups: Process and Practice*. (2nd ed.) Monterey, Calif.: Brooks/Cole, 1982.

Corrigan, P. *Schooling the Smash Street Kids*. London: Macmillan, 1979.

Crabtree, J. "A Vision of Greatness." *Adult Leadership*, 1963, *12* (6), 162–164, 189–190.

Crick, B., and Porter, A. (eds.). *Political Education and Political Literacy*. Harlow, England: Longman, 1978.

Cronen, V. E., Pearce, W. B., and Tomm, K. "A Dialectical View of Personal Change." In K. J. Gergen and K. E. Davis (eds.), *The Social Construction of the Person*. New York: Springer-Verlag, 1985.

Daloz, L. *Effective Teaching and Mentoring: Realizing the Transformational Power of Adult Learning Experiences*. San Francisco: Jossey-Bass, 1986.

D'Andrea, A. L. "Teachers and Reflection: A Description and

Analysis of the Reflective Process Which Teachers Use in Their Experiential Learning." Unpublished doctoral dissertation, Department of Education, Ontario Institute for Studies in Education, 1986.

D'Angelo, E. *The Teaching of Critical Thinking*. Amsterdam: B. R. Gruner, 1971.

De Bono, E. *Lateral Thinking: Creativity Step by Step*. New York: Harper & Row, 1970.

Deshler, D. "Moral Faith and Cognitive Development: Aspects of Critical Awareness on the Part of Professors of Adult Education." Paper presented to the Commission of Professors of Adult Education Conference, Milwaukee, Nov. 5, 1985.

Dewey, J. *Democracy and Education*. New York: Free Press, 1916.

Dewey, J. *How We Think: A Restatement of the Relation of Reflective Thinking to the Educative Process*. Chicago: Henry Regnery Co., 1933.

Diamond, E., and Bates, S. *The Spot: The Rise of Political Advertising on Television*. Cambridge, Mass.: MIT Press, 1984.

Dobbert, M. L. *Ethnographic Research: Theory and Application for Modern Schools and Societies*. New York: Praeger, 1982.

Dowling, M., Goodman, J., Gotting, D., and Hyman, J. "Shop Stewards and Employee Participation: Is There a Special Training Need?" *The Industrial Tutor*, 1984, *3* (10), 20–29.

Drake, J. *Teaching Critical Thinking*. Danville, Ill.: Interstate Publishers, 1976.

Duck, S., and Perlman, D. (eds.). *Understanding Personal Relationships*. Beverly Hills, Calif.: Sage, 1985.

Eble, K. E. *The Aims of College Teaching*. San Francisco: Jossey-Bass, 1983.

Egan, G. *The Skilled Helper: A Systematic Approach to Effective Helping*. (3rd ed.) Monterey, Calif.: Brooks/Cole, 1986.

Ehrenhalt, S. H. "No Golden Age for College Graduates." *Challenge*, 1983, *26*, 42–50.

Eiger, N. "Tocqueville, Participation, and Workplace Democracy as an Educative Force." In R. Hoghielm (ed.), *Rekindling Commitment in Adult Education*. Stockholm: Department of Educational Research, Stockholm Institute of Education, 1985.

Elbow, P. *Writing Without Teachers*. London: Oxford University Press, 1973.

Elias, J. L. *Psychology and Religious Education*. Malabar, Fla.: Robert E. Krieger, 1983.

Ellison, A. "Political Literacy and Adult Education." *Adult and Continuing Education Today*, 1984, *14* (28), 109.

Ennis, R. H. "A Concept of Critical Thinking." *Harvard Educational Review*, 1962, *32* (1), 81–111.

Erikson, E. H. *Childhood and Society*. New York: Norton, 1950.

Evans, S. M., and Boyte, H. C. *Free Spaces: The Sources of Democratic Change in America*. New York: Harper & Row, 1986.

Everhart, R. *Reading, Writing and Resistance*. London: Routledge & Kegan Paul, 1983.

Ewert, D. M. "Involving Adult Learners in Program Planning." In S. B. Merriam (ed.), *Linking Philosophy and Practice*. New Directions for Continuing Education, no. 15. San Francisco: Jossey-Bass, 1982.

Farquhar, E. C., and Dawson, K. S. *Citizen Education Today: Developing Civic Competencies*. Washington, D.C.: Office of Education, U.S. Department of Health, Education, and Welfare, n.d.

Faure, E., and others. *Learning to Be: The World of Education Today and Tomorrow*. Paris: UNESCO Press, 1972.

Fay, B. *Social Theory and Social Practice*. London: Allen & Unwin, 1975.

Ferraro, G., and Francke, L. B. *Geraldine Ferraro*. New York: Bantam Books, 1985.

Field, J. "Peace Studies: A Report on Two Evening Classes." *Adult Education* (U.K.), 1983, *56* (2), 132–136.

Fiske, J., and Hartley, J. *Reading Television*. London: Methuen, 1978.

Flanagan, J. C. "The Critical Incident Technique." *Psychological Bulletin*, 1954, *51* (4), 327–358.

Fowler, J. W. *Stages of Faith: The Psychology of Human Development and the Quest for Meaning*. San Francisco: Harper & Row, 1981.

Fowler, J. W. *Becoming Adult, Becoming Christian: Adult Development and Christian Faith*. San Francisco: Harper & Row, 1984.

Fox, J., Lippitt, G. G., and Schindler-Rainman, E. *The Humanized Future: Some New Images.* La Jolla, Calif.: University Associates, 1976.

Freire, P. *Cultural Action for Freedom.* Cambridge, Mass.: Harvard Educational Review and Center for the Study of Development and Social Change, 1970a.

Freire, P. *Pedagogy of the Oppressed.* New York: Continuum, 1970b.

Freire, P. *Education for Critical Consciousness.* New York: Continuum, 1973.

Freire, P. *The Politics of Education.* South Hadley, Mass.: Bergin & Garvey, 1985.

Freire, P. "Keynote Address." Presented at Workshop on Worker Education, City College of New York Center for Worker Education, New York, Feb. 8, 1986.

Friedan, B. *The Feminine Mystique.* New York: Simon & Schuster, 1963.

Friedlander, F. "Patterns of Individual and Organizational Learning." In S. Srivastva and Associates, *The Executive Mind: New Insights on Managerial Thought and Action.* San Francisco: Jossey-Bass, 1983.

Fromm, E. *Escape from Freedom.* New York: Holt, Rinehart & Winston, 1941.

Fromm, E. *Man for Himself: An Inquiry into the Psychology of Ethics.* New York: Holt, Rinehart & Winston, 1947.

Fromm, E. *The Art of Loving.* New York: Harper & Row, 1956.

Fromm, E. *To Have or to Be?* New York: Harper & Row, 1976.

Gamson, Z. F., and Associates. *Liberating Education.* San Francisco: Jossey-Bass, 1984.

Gardell, B. *Worker Participation and Autonomy.* Report no. 31, Research Unit for Social Psychology of Work. Stockholm: University of Stockholm, 1982.

Garfinkel, H. *Studies in Ethnomethodology.* Englewood Cliffs, N.J.: Prentice-Hall, 1967.

GATT-Fly. *AH-HAH! A New Approach to Popular Education.* Toronto: Between the Lines, 1983.

Gayfer, M. "Women Speaking and Learning for Ourselves." *Convergence,* 1980, *13* (1, 2), 1–13.

Gelpi, E. *A Future for Lifelong Education.* 2 vols. Manchester,

England: Department of Adult and Higher Education, University of Manchester, 1979.

Gelpi, E. *Lifelong Education and International Relations.* London: Croom Helm, 1985.

Gergen, K. J., and Davis, K. E. (eds.). *The Social Construction of the Person.* New York: Springer-Verlag, 1985.

Gibbons, I., and West, P. "Adult Education and Political Education." *Adult Education* (U.K.), 1984, *57* (2), 148-149.

Gilligan, C. "Woman's Place in Man's Life Cycle." *Harvard Educational Review,* 1979, *49* (4), 431-446.

Gilligan, C. *In a Different Voice: Psychological Theory and Women's Development.* Cambridge, Mass.: Harvard University Press, 1982.

Gilligan, C. "Marital Dialogues." In V. Rogers (ed.), *Adult Development Through Relationships.* New York: Praeger, 1984.

Giroux, H. A. *Ideology, Culture, and the Process of Schooling.* Philadelphia: Temple University Press, 1981.

Giroux, H. A. *Theory and Resistance in Education: A Pedagogy for the Opposition.* South Hadley, Mass.: Bergin & Garvey, 1983.

Gitlin, T. *Inside Prime Time.* New York: Pantheon Books, 1983.

Glaser, E. M. "Critical Thinking: Educating for Responsible Citizenship in a Democracy." *National Forum,* 1985, *65* (1), 24-27.

Glasgow University Media Group. *Bad News.* London: Routledge & Kegan Paul, 1976.

Glasgow University Media Group. *More Bad News.* London: Routledge & Kegan Paul, 1980.

Glasgow University Media Group. *Really Bad News.* London: Writers and Readers Cooperative, 1982.

Glasgow University Media Group. *War and Peace News.* Milton Keynes, England: Open University Press, 1985.

Gould, R. L. *Transformations: Growth and Change in Adult Life.* New York: Simon & Schuster, 1978.

Gould, R. L. "Transformations During Early and Middle Adult Years." In N. J. Smelser and E. H. Erikson (eds.), *Themes of Work and Love in Adulthood.* Cambridge, Mass.: Harvard University Press, 1980.

Gould, R. L. "Recovering from Childhood: Distortions of the

Past on the Present." In V. Rogers (ed.), *Adult Development Through Relationships.* New York: Praeger, 1984.

Graber, D. A. *Processing the News: How People Tame the Information Tide.* New York: Longman, 1984.

Greenberg, E. S. *Workplace Democracy: The Political Effects of Participation.* Ithaca, N.Y.: Cornell University Press, 1986.

Greenberg, I. A. (ed.). *Psychodrama: Theory and Therapy.* New York: Behavioral Publications, 1974.

Greene, M. "In Search of a Critical Pedagogy." *Harvard Educational Review,* 1986, *56* (4), 427–441.

Guba, E. G., and Lincoln, Y. S. *Effective Evaluation: Improving the Usefulness of Evaluation Results Through Responsive and Naturalistic Approaches.* San Francisco: Jossey-Bass, 1981.

Guglielmino, L. M. "Development of the Self-Directed Learning Readiness Scale." Unpublished doctoral dissertation, Department of Adult Education, University of Georgia, 1977.

Guildford, J. P. "The Structure of Intellect." *Psychological Bulletin,* 1956, *53* (4), 267–293.

Habermas, J. *Communication and the Evolution of Society.* Boston: Beacon Press, 1979.

Hall, R. H. *Dimensions of Work.* Beverly Hills, Calif.: Sage, 1986.

Hall, S. "Encoding/Decoding." In S. Hall, D. Hobson, A. Lowe, and P. Willis (eds.), *Culture, Media, Language.* London: Hutchinson, 1980.

Hallet, G. L. *Logic for the Labyrinth: A Guide to Critical Thinking.* Washington, D.C.: University Press of America, 1984.

Halpern, D. F. *Thought and Knowledge: An Introduction to Critical Thinking.* Hillsdale, N.J.: Erlbaum, 1984.

Handron, D. "Critical Reflectivity in Action: An Observational Analysis of the Donahue Show." Unpublished paper, Department of Higher and Adult Education, Teachers College, Columbia University, 1985.

Hansen, D. A. *An Invitation to Critical Sociology: Involvement, Criticism, Exploration.* New York: Free Press, 1976.

Harris, W. J. A. *Comparative Adult Education: Practice, Purpose, and Theory.* Harlow, England: Longman, 1980.

Hart, M. "Thematization of Power, the Search for Common

Interests, and Self-Reflection: Towards a Comprehensive Concept of Emancipatory Education." *International Journal of Lifelong Education,* 1985, *4* (2), 119–134.

Havighurst, R. J. *Human Development and Education.* New York: Longmans, Green, 1953.

Healy, G. M. "The Building of a Civically Literate Society: Implications for Policy and Practice Related to the Education of Adults." *Proceedings of the Adult Education Research Conference,* no. 20. Ann Arbor, Mich.: 1979.

Heaney, T. "Material for Learning and Acting." In J. P. Wilson (ed.), *Materials for Teaching Adults: Selection, Development, and Use.* New Directions in Continuing Education, no. 17. San Francisco: Jossey-Bass, 1983.

Hechinger, F. M. "Thinking Critically." *New York Times,* Feb. 24, 1987, p. 27.

Henderson, E. S. "Theoretical Perspectives on Adult Education." In E. S. Henderson and M. B. Nathenson (eds.), *Independent Learning in Higher Education.* Englewood Cliffs, N.J.: Educational Technology Publications, 1984.

H. M. Stationery Office. *Adult Education: A Plan for Development.* London: H. M. Stationery Office, 1973.

Herring, J. W. "Adult Education: Senior Partner to Democracy." *Adult Education,* 1953, *3* (2), 53–59.

Hoggart, R. Chairman's Preface to *Political Education for Adults.* Leicester, England: Advisory Council for Adult and Continuing Education, 1983.

Hopson, B., and Adams, J. *Transition: Understanding and Managing Personal Change.* Montclair, N.J.: Allenhald & Osmund, 1977.

Hostler, J. "The Education of Adults." *Studies in Adult Education,* 1977, *9* (1), 58–64.

Houle, C. O. *The Design of Education.* San Francisco: Jossey-Bass, 1972.

Hoy, J. M. "Executive Women's Learning in Organizational Settings." Unpublished doctoral dissertation, Department of Higher and Adult Education, Teachers College, Columbia University, 1987.

Hudson, L. *Contrary Imaginations: A Psychological Study of the English Schoolboy.* London: Methuen, 1966.

Hudson, L. *Frames of Mind: Ability, Perception, and Self-Perception in the Arts and Sciences.* London: Methuen, 1968.

Hullfish, H. G., and Smith, P. G. *Reflective Thinking: The Method of Education.* Westport, Conn.: Greenwood Press, 1961.

Hutchins, D. E., and Cole, C. G. *Helping Relationships and Strategies.* Monterey, Calif.: Brooks/Cole, 1986.

Ilsley, P. J. "The Relevance of the Future in Adult Education: A Phenomenological Analysis of Images of the Future." *Proceedings of the Adult Education Research Conference,* no. 24. Montreal: Concordia University–University of Montreal, 1984.

International League for Social Commitment in Adult Education. Announcement of Third Annual Conference: "The Art of the Oppressed: Learning About Power and Powerlessness." Folkhighschool, Bergen, Netherlands, June 28–July 3, 1987.

Isenberg, D. J. "The Structure and Process of Understanding: Implications for Managerial Action." In S. Srivastva and Associates, *The Executive Mind: New Insights on Managerial Thought and Action.* San Francisco: Jossey-Bass, 1983.

Jacques, D. *Learning in Groups.* London: Croom Helm, 1984.

Jacques, E. "The Midlife Crisis." In S. I. Greenspan and G. H. Pollock (eds.), *The Course of Life: Psychoanalytic Contributions Toward Understanding Personality Development.* Vol. 3: *Adulthood and the Aging Process.* Bethesda, Md.: National Institute of Mental Health, 1980.

Jarvis, P. "Thinking Critically in an Information Society." *Lifelong Learning: An Omnibus of Practice and Research,* 1985, *8* (6), 11–14.

Johnston, J. S., Jr., and Associates. *Educating Managers: Executive Effectiveness Through Liberal Learning.* San Francisco: Jossey-Bass, 1986.

Jones, A. H. *Civic Learning for Teachers: Capstone for Educational Reform.* Ann Arbor, Mich.: Prakken Publications, 1985.

Jones, B. "The Teaching of Controversial Issues in Adult Education." *Studies in Adult Education,* 1986, *18* (1), 3–10.

Kanter, R. M. *Men and Women of the Corporation.* New York: Basic Books, 1983.

Kauffman, D. L. *Teaching the Future: A Guide to Future-Oriented Education.* Palm Springs, Calif.: ETC Publications, 1976.

Keddie, N. "Adult Education: An Ideology of Individualism." In J. L. Thompson (ed.), *Adult Education for a Change.* London: Hutchinson, 1980.

Kegan, R. *The Evolving Self: Problem and Process in Human Development.* Cambridge, Mass.: Harvard University Press, 1982.

Kellner, D. "TV, Ideology, and Emancipatory Popular Culture." *Socialist Review,* 1979, *9* (3), 13–53.

Kelly, G. A. *The Psychology of Personal Constructs.* Vols. 1 and 2. New York: Norton, 1955.

Kennedy, W. B. "Toward an Understanding of 'Reception' as a Factor in the Influence of Mass Media." Unpublished paper, Union Theological Seminary, New York, 1984.

King, P. M., Kitchener, K. S., and Wood, P. K. "The Development of Intellect and Character: A Longitudinal-Sequential Study of Intellectual and Moral Development in Young Adults." *Moral Education Forum,* 1985, *10* (1), 1–13.

Kinney, J. J. "Why Bother? The Importance of Critical Thinking." In R. E. Young (ed.), *Fostering Critical Thinking.* New Directions for Teaching and Learning, no. 3. San Francisco: Jossey-Bass, 1980.

Kitchener, K. S. "The Reflective Judgment Model: Characteristics, Evidence, and Measurement." In R. A. Mines and K. S. Kitchener (eds.), *Adult Cognitive Development: Methods and Models.* New York: Praeger, 1986.

Knowles, M. S. *The Modern Practice of Adult Education: From Pedagogy to Andragogy.* (2nd ed.) New York: Cambridge Books, 1980.

Knowles, M. S. *Using Learning Contracts: Practical Approaches to Individualizing and Structuring Learning.* San Francisco: Jossey-Bass, 1986.

Knowles, M. S., and Klevins, C. "Historical and Philosophical Perspectives." In C. Klevins (ed.), *Materials and Methods in Adult and Continuing Education.* Canoga Park, Calif.: Klevens Publications, 1982.

Knox, A. B. *Adult Development and Learning: A Handbook on Indi-*

vidual Growth and Competence in the Adult Years. San Francisco: Jossey-Bass, 1977.

Knox, A. B. *Helping Adults Learn: A Guide to Planning, Implementing, and Conducting Programs.* San Francisco: Jossey-Bass, 1986.

Kohlberg, L. *The Philosophy of Moral Development.* San Francisco: Harper & Row, 1981.

Kolb, D. A. *The Adaptive Style Inventory.* Form B481. Cleveland, Ohio: David Kolb, 1980.

Kretovics, J. R. "Critical Literacy: Challenging the Assumptions of the Mainstream." *Journal of Education,* 1985, *167* (2), 50–62.

Labouvie-Vief, G. "Adult Cognitive Development: In Search of Alternative Interpretations." *Merrill-Palmer Quarterly,* 1977, *23* (4), 227–263.

Labouvie-Vief, G. "Beyond Formal Operations: Uses and Limits of Pure Logic in Life-Span Development." *Human Development,* 1980, *23,* 141–161.

Lakin, M. *Interpersonal Encounter: Theory and Practice in Sensitivity Training.* New York: McGraw-Hill, 1972.

Lang, G. E., and Lang, K. *Politics and Television Re-Viewed.* Beverly Hills, Calif.: Sage, 1984.

Lasker, H., and Moore, J. "Current Studies of Adult Development: Implications for Education." In H. Lasker, J. Moore, and E. L. Simpson, *Adult Development and Approaches to Learning.* Washington, D.C.: National Institute of Education, 1980.

Lawson, K. H. *Philosophical Concepts and Values in Adult Education.* Milton Keynes, England: Open University Press, 1979.

Levinson, D. J. *The Seasons of a Man's Life.* New York: Knopf, 1978.

Lewis, L. "Theater: A Catalyst for Dialogue and Action." In L. H. Lewis (ed.), *Experiential and Simulation Techniques for Teaching Adults.* New Directions for Continuing Education, no. 30. San Francisco: Jossey-Bass, 1986.

Lieberman, M. A., Borman, L. D., and Associates. *Self-Help Groups for Coping with Crisis.* San Francisco: Jossey-Bass, 1979.

Lindeman, E. C. "New Needs for Adult Education." *Annals of the American Academy of Political and Social Sciences,* 1944, *231,* 115–122.

Lindeman, E. C. "The Sociology of Adult Education." *Journal of Educational Sociology,* 1945, *19* (1), 144–149.

Lindeman, E. C. *The Meaning of Adult Education.* Montreal: Harvest House, 1961.(Originally published 1926.)

Lippitt, G. L. *Visualizing Change: Model Building and the Change Process.* Fairfax, Va.: NTL Learning Resources Corporation, 1973.

Lipsky, M. *Street-Level Bureaucracy: Dilemmas of the Individual in Public Services.* New York: Russell Sage Foundation, 1980.

Livingstone, D. W. (ed.). *Critical Pedagogy and Cultural Power.* South Hadley, Mass.: Bergin & Garvey, 1987.

Loevinger, J. *Ego Development: Conceptions and Theories.* San Francisco: Jossey-Bass, 1976.

Long, H. B. *Adult Learning: Research and Practice.* New York: Cambridge Books, 1983.

Lovett, T. *Adult Education, Community Development, and the Working Class.* London: Ward Lock Educational, 1975.

Lovett, T., Clarke, C., and Kilmurray, A. *Adult Education and Community Action.* London: Croom Helm, 1983.

Lowy, A., Kelleher, D., and Finestone, P. "Management Learning: Beyond Program Design." *Training and Development Journal,* 1986, *40* (6), 34–37.

McGivney, V., and Sims, D. *Adult Education and the Challenge of Unemployment.* Milton Keynes, England: Open University Press, 1986.

McKenzie, L. *Adult Education and the Burden of the Future.* Washington, D.C.: University Press of America, 1978.

McPeck, J. E. *Critical Thinking and Education.* New York: St. Martin's Press, 1981.

McRobbie, A., and McCabe, T. (eds.). *Feminism for Girls: An Adventure Story.* London: Routledge & Kegan Paul, 1981.

Mager, R. F. *Developing Attitude Toward Learning.* Belmont, Calif.: Fearon, 1968.

Mager, R. F. *Preparing Instructional Objectives.* (2nd ed.) Belmont, Calif.: Fearon, 1975.

Mager, R. F., and Beach, K. M. *Developing Vocational Instruction.* Belmont, Calif.: Fearon, 1972.

Mahrer, A. R. *Experiential Psychotherapy: Basic Practices.* New York: Brunner/Mazel, 1983.

Marcuse, H. "Repressive Tolerance." In R. P. Wolff, B. Moore, and H. Marcuse (eds.), *A Critique of Pure Tolerance.* Boston: Beacon Press, 1965.

Margolis, M. *Viable Democracy.* Harmondsworth, England: Penguin Books, 1979.

Marshall, E. K., Kurtz, P. D., and Associates. *Interpersonal Helping Skills: A Guide to Training Methods, Programs, and Resources.* San Francisco: Jossey-Bass, 1982.

Marsick, V. *Learning in the Workplace: Theory and Practice.* London: Croom Helm, 1987.

Maslow, A. *Motivation and Personality.* New York: Harper & Row, 1970.

Masterman, L. *Teaching About Television.* London: Macmillan, 1980.

Masterman, L. "Television Literacy and Adult Education." In M. Tight (ed.), *Opportunities for Adult Education.* London: Croom Helm, 1983.

Mathews, D. "Civic Intelligence." *Social Education,* 1985, *49* (8), 678–681.

Merriam, S. B. "Male Middle Age in Modern Fiction." In A. B. Knox (ed.), *Programming for Adults Facing Mid-Life Change.* New Directions for Continuing Education, no. 2. San Francisco: Jossey-Bass, 1979.

Merriam, S. B. "Mentors and Protégés: A Critical Review of the Literature." *Adult Education Quarterly,* 1983a, *33* (3), 161–173.

Merriam, S. B. (ed.). *Themes of Adulthood Through Literature.* New York: Teachers College Press, 1983b.

Merriam, S. B. *Adult Development: Implications for Adult Education.* Columbus, Ohio: ERIC Clearinghouse on Adult, Career, and Vocational Education, Information Series no. 282, 1984.

Meyers, C. *Teaching Students to Think Critically: A Guide for Faculty in All Disciplines.* San Francisco: Jossey-Bass, 1986.

Mezirow, J. "Perspective Transformation." *Studies in Adult Education,* 1977, *9* (2), 153–164.

Mezirow, J. "A Critical Theory of Adult Learning and Education." *Adult Education,* 1981, *32* (1), 3–27.

Mezirow, J. "Transformations in Adult Learning." Paper

presented at Annual Conference of the American Association
for Adult and Continuing Education, Philadelphia, Nov. 29,
1983.

Mezirow, J. "Concept and Action in Adult Education." *Adult Education Quarterly,* 1985a, *35* (3), 142–151.

Mezirow, J. "A Critical Theory of Self-Directed Learning." In S. D. Brookfield (ed.), *Self-Directed Learning: From Theory to Practice.* New Directions for Continuing Education, no. 25. San Francisco: Jossey-Bass, 1985b.

Midwinter, E. *Patterns of Community Education.* London: Ward Lock Educational, 1973.

Mills, C. W. *Mass Society and Liberal Education.* Chicago: Center for the Study of Liberal Education for Adults, 1954.

Mills, C. W. *The Sociological Imagination.* Oxford, England: Oxford University Press, 1959.

Moran, G. *Education Toward Adulthood.* New York: Paulist Press, 1979.

Moreno, J. L. *Psychodrama.* Vol. 1. (Rev. ed.) Beacon, N.Y.: Beacon House, 1946.

Morgan, G. *Images of Organizations.* Beverly Hills, Calif.: Sage, 1986.

Morgan, G., and Ramirez, R. "Action Learning: A Holographic Metaphor for Guiding Social Change." *Human Relations,* 1983, *37* (1), 1–28.

Morino, D. "Re-framing: Hegemony and Adult Education Practice." Paper presented at the Standing Conference on University Teaching and Research in the Education of Adults (SCUTREA), Sheffield University, England, July 1985.

Morley, D. *The "Nationwide" Audience: Structure and Decoding.* British Film Institute Monograph no. 12. London: British Film Institute, 1980.

Musgrove, F. *Margins of the Mind.* London: Methuen, 1977.

Myers, I. B., and Myers, P. B. *Gifts Differing.* Palo Alto, Calif.: Consulting Psychologists Press, 1980.

Naisbitt, J. *Megatrends: Ten New Directions Transforming Our Lives.* New York: Warner Books, 1982.

National Commission on Excellence in Education. *A Nation at Risk: The Imperative for Educational Reform.* Washington, D.C.: U.S. Department of Education, 1983.

National Institute of Education. *Involvement in Learning: Realizing the Potential of American Higher Education*. Washington, D.C.: U.S. Department of Education, 1984.

Nelson, J. N. "Television and Its Audiences as Dimensions of Being: Critical Theory and Phenomenology." *Human Studies,* 1986, *9* (1), 55–69.

Neugarten, B. L., and Associates (eds.). *Personality in Middle and Later Life*. New York: Atherton, 1964.

Neumann, A. "Critical Thinking Skills: A Framework of Definitions and Applications to Management and Organizational Studies." Unpublished paper, Department of Higher and Adult Education, Teachers College, Columbia University, 1986.

Newman, F. *Higher Education and the American Resurgence*. Princeton, N.J.: Carnegie Foundation for the Advancement of Teaching, 1985.

O'Neill, T. *Censorship—Opposing Views*. St. Paul, Minn.: Greenhaven Press, 1985.

Osborn, A. *Applied Imagination: Principles and Procedures of Creative Problem Solving*. New York: Scribner's, 1963.

Osborne, K. Q. "Informal Learning and Public Policy Issues." In H. W. Stubblefield (ed.), *Continuing Education for Community Leadership*. New Directions for Continuing Education, no. 11. San Francisco: Jossey-Bass, 1981.

O'Sullivan, D. "Socialization, Social Change and Ideology in Adult Education." *Adult Education* (U.K.), 1980, *52* (5), 318–323.

Ouchi, W. G. *Theory Z*. Reading, Mass.: Addison-Wesley, 1981.

Pascale, R. T., and Athos, A. G. *The Art of Japanese Management*. New York: Warner Books, 1981.

Pask, G. *Conversation, Cognition and Learning: A Cybernetic Theory and Methodology*. Amsterdam: Elsevier Publications, 1975.

Paterson, J. W. "Learning in Social Action Settings: Implications for Program Development." Unpublished doctoral dissertation, Department of Higher and Adult Education, Teachers College, Columbia University, 1985.

Paterson, R. W. K. *Values, Education, and the Adult*. London: Routledge & Kegan Paul, 1979.

Patton, M. Q. *Qualitative Evaluation Methods*. Beverly Hills, Calif.: Sage, 1980.

Perlman, D., and Duck, S. (eds.). *Intimate Relationships: Development, Dynamics, and Deterioration.* Beverly Hills, Calif.: Sage, 1986.

Perry, W. G. *Forms of Intellectual and Ethical Development in the College Years: A Scheme.* New York: Holt, Rinehart & Winston, 1970.

Perry, W. G. "Growth in the Making of Meaning." In A. W. Chickering (ed.), *The Modern American College.* San Francisco: Jossey-Bass, 1981.

Peters, T. J., and Waterman, R. H. *In Search of Excellence: Lessons from America's Best-Run Companies.* New York: Harper & Row, 1982.

Piaget, J. *The Psychology of the Child.* New York: Harper & Row, 1969.

Polyani, M. *Personal Knowledge: Towards a Post-Critical Philosophy.* Chicago: University of Chicago Press, 1962.

Postman, N. S. *Amusing Ourselves to Death.* New York: Viking Penguin, 1986.

Powell, J. W. *Learning Comes of Age.* New York: Association Press, 1956.

Prince, G. M. *The Practice of Creativity.* New York: Macmillan, 1970.

Quarrey, M., Blasi, J., and Rosen, C. *Taking Stock: Employee Ownership at Work.* New York: Ballinger, 1986.

Ranney, A. *Channels of Power: The Impact of Television on American Politics.* New York: Basic Books, 1983.

Ridley, F. F. "What Adults, What Politics?" In Advisory Council for Adult and Continuing Education, *Political Education for Adults.* Leicester, England: Advisory Council for Adult and Continuing Education, 1983.

Riegel, K. F. "Dialectic Operations: The Final Period of Cognitive Development." *Human Development,* 1973, *16,* 346–370.

Robinson, J. P., and Levy, M. R. *The Main Source: Learning from Television News.* Beverly Hills, Calif.: Sage, 1986.

Robinson, R. S. "Television Literacy for Adults." *Media and Adult Learning,* 1986, *9* (1), 13–16.

Roche, G. "Much Ado About Mentors." *Harvard Business Review,* 1979, *20* (3), 14–16, 20, 24, 26–28.

Rogers, C. R. *On Becoming a Person: A Therapist's View of Psychotherapy.* Boston: Houghton Mifflin, 1961.

Rogers, C. R. *A Way of Being.* Boston: Houghton Mifflin, 1980.

Rogers, D. *The Adult Years: An Introduction to Aging.* (2nd ed.) Englewood Cliffs, N.J.: Prentice-Hall, 1982.

Rogers, V. (ed.). *Adult Development Through Relationships.* New York: Praeger, 1984.

Rubin, L. B. *Worlds of Pain: Life in the Working Class Family.* New York: Basic Books, 1976.

Ruggiero, V. R. *Beyond Feelings: A Guide to Critical Thinking.* Palo Alto, Calif.: Mayfield Publications, 1975.

Schaie, K. W., and Geiwitz, J. *Adult Development and Aging.* Boston: Little, Brown, 1982.

Schein, E. *Organizational Culture and Leadership: A Dynamic View.* San Francisco: Jossey-Bass, 1985.

Schlossberg, N. K. "A Model for Analyzing Human Adaptation to Transition." *The Counseling Psychologist,* 1981, *9* (2), 2–18.

Schlossberg, N. K. *Counseling Adults in Transition: Linking Practice with Theory.* New York: Springer, 1984.

Schön, D. A. *The Reflective Practitioner: How Professionals Think in Action.* New York: Basic Books, 1983.

Schön, D. A. *Educating the Reflective Practitioner: Toward a New Design for Teaching and Learning in the Professions.* San Francisco: Jossey-Bass, 1987.

Scriven, M. *Reasoning.* New York: McGraw-Hill, 1976.

Scriven, M. "Critical for Survival." *National Forum,* 1985, *65* (1), 43–46.

Sennett, R., and Cobb, J. *The Hidden Injuries of Class.* New York: Knopf, 1972.

Shor, I. *Critical Teaching and Everyday Life.* Boston: South End Press, 1980.

Simmons, J., and Mares, W. *Working Together: Employee Participation in Action.* New York: Columbia University Press, 1985.

Smelser, N. J., and Erikson, E. H. (eds.). *Themes of Work and Love in Adulthood.* Cambridge, Mass.: Harvard University Press, 1980.

Smith, D. G. "College Classroom Interactions and Critical

Thinking." *Journal of Educational Psychology,* 1977, *69* (2), 180–190.

Smith, R. M. *Learning How to Learn: Applied Theory for Adults.* New York: Cambridge Books, 1982.

Smith, R. M. *Helping Adults Learn How to Learn.* New Directions for Continuing Education, no. 19. San Francisco: Jossey-Bass, 1983.

Smith, R. M. "Review of *Self-Directed Learning: From Theory to Practice,* S. D. Brookfield (ed.)." *Adult Education Quarterly,* 1986, *36* (4), 244–247.

Smith, T. V., and Lindeman, E. C. *The Democratic Way of Life.* New York: Mentor Books, 1951.

Snow, C. P. *Corridors of Power.* New York: Scribner's, 1951.

Snow, C. P. *The Masters.* New York: Scribner's, 1964.

Snow, C. P. *Last Things.* New York: Scribner's, 1970.

Spender, D. "Learning to Create Our Own Knowledge." *Convergence,* 1980, *13* (1, 2), 14–23.

Spradley, J. P. *The Ethnographic Interview.* New York: Holt, Rinehart & Winston, 1979.

Srivastva, S., and Associates. *The Executive Mind: New Insights on Managerial Thought and Action.* San Francisco: Jossey-Bass, 1983.

Sternberg, R. J. "Teaching Critical Thinking; Part 1: Are We Making Critical Mistakes?" *Phi Delta Kappan,* 1985, *67* (3), 194–198.

Stewart, D. "Politics Is Not a Four-Letter Word." *Continuum,* 1981, *56* (1), 63–66.

Stewart, D. *Adult Learning in America: Eduard Lindeman and His Agenda for Lifelong Education.* Melbourne, Fla.: Robert Krieger, 1987.

Stice, J. (ed.). *Developing Critical Thinking and Problem-Solving Abilities.* New Directions for Teaching and Learning, no. 30. San Francisco: Jossey-Bass, 1987.

Stirling, J., and Mellor, M. "Worker Co-operatives: Passé or Panacea?" *The Industrial Tutor,* 1984, *3* (10), 12–19.

Stock, A. "Role-Playing and Simulation Techniques." In M. D. Stephens and G. W. Roderick (eds.), *Teaching Techniques in Adult Education.* Newton Abbot, England: David and Charles, 1971.

Stokes, K. (ed.). *Faith Development in the Life Cycle*. New York: W. H. Sadlier, 1982.

Stonewater, J. K. "Strategies for Problem Solving." In R. E. Young (ed.), *Fostering Critical Thinking*. New Directions for Teaching and Learning, no. 3. San Francisco: Jossey-Bass, 1980.

Storr, A. *The Integration of the Personality*. Harmondsworth, England: Penguin Books, 1965.

Sullivan, E. *A Critical Psychology: Interpretation of the Personal World*. New York: Plenum, 1984.

Svinicki, M. D., and Kraemer, R. H. "Critical Thinking: Some Views from the Front Line." In R. E. Young (ed.), *Fostering Critical Thinking*. New Directions for Teaching and Learning, no. 3. San Francisco: Jossey-Bass, 1980.

Swindler, A. "Love and Adulthood in American Culture." In N. J. Smelser and E. H. Erikson (eds.), *Themes of Work and Love in Adulthood*. Cambridge, Mass.: Harvard University Press, 1980.

Taylor, R. "Current Developments in Peace Studies in Adult Continuing Education." *Adult Education* (U.K.), 1984, *57* (19), 17–22.

Taylor, S. J., and Bogdan, R. *Introduction to Qualitative Research Methods: The Search for Meanings*. New York: Wiley, 1984.

Thiel, J. P. "Successful Self-Directed Learners' Learning Styles." *Proceedings of the Adult Education Research Conference*, no. 25. Raleigh: North Carolina State University, 1984.

Thompson, E. P. *The Making of the English Working Class*. Harmondsworth, England: Penguin Books, 1968.

Thompson, J. L. *Learning Liberation: Women's Response to Men's Education*. London: Croom Helm, 1983.

Toffler, A. *Future Shock*. New York: Random House, 1970.

Tough, A. M. *The Adult's Learning Projects: A Fresh Approach to Theory and Practice in Adult Learning*. (2nd ed.) Toronto: Ontario Institute for Studies in Education, 1979.

Tuchman, G. *Making News: A Study in the Construction of Reality*. New York: Free Press, 1978.

Tuckett, A. "The Place of Political Education in Adult Education in Britain." *The Political Papers*, no. 10. London: Adult Education Training Unit, The City Literary Institute, n.d.

Tyler, L. E. *Thinking Creatively: A New Approach to Psychology and Individual Lives.* San Francisco: Jossey-Bass, 1983.

Usher, R. S. "Political Education: Process or Product." *Studies in Adult Education,* 1981, *13* (1), 45–54.

Van Hoose, W. H., and Worth, M. R. *Adulthood in the Life Cycle.* Dubuque, Iowa: W. M. C. Brown, 1982.

Van Maanen, J. V. (ed.). *Qualitative Methodology.* Beverly Hills, Calif.: Sage, 1983.

Walter, G. A., and Marks, S. E. *Experiential Learning and Change.* New York: Wiley, 1981.

Weathersby, R. P., and Tarule, J. M. *Adult Development: Implications for Higher Education.* AAHE-ERIC Higher Education Research Report, no. 4. Washington, D.C.: American Association for Higher Education, 1980.

Weick, K. E. "Managerial Thought in the Context of Action." In S. Srivastva and Associates, *The Executive Mind: New Insights on Managerial Thought and Action.* San Francisco: Jossey-Bass, 1983.

Werner, H. D. *Cognitive Therapy: A Humanistic Approach.* New York: Free Press, 1982.

Wexler, P. *Critical Social Psychology.* London: Routledge & Kegan Paul, 1983.

White, R. A. "Mass Communication and Culture: Transition to a New Paradigm." *Journal of Communications,* 1983, *33* (3), 279–301.

Wieseltier, L. "What Went Wrong: An Analysis of Reagan's Foreign Policy." *New York Times,* Dec. 7, 1986, p. 45.

Williams, R. *Marxism and Literature.* Oxford, England: Oxford University Press, 1977.

Williamson, J. *Decoding Advertizements: Ideology and Meaning in Advertizing.* London: Marion Boyars Publishing, 1978.

Willis, P. *Learning to Labour.* Westmead, England: Saxon House, 1977.

Witkin, H. A. "The Nature and Importance of Individual Differences in Perception." *Journal of Personality,* 1949, *18,* 145–170.

Witkin, H. A. "Individual Differences in Ease of Perception of Embedded Figures." *Journal of Personality,* 1950, *19,* 1–15.

Wlodkowski, R. J. *Enhancing Adult Motivation to Learn: A Guide to Improving Instruction and Increasing Learner Achievement.* San Francisco: Jossey-Bass, 1985.

Woodworth, W., Meek, C., and Whyte, W. F. (eds.). *Industrial Democracy: Strategies for Community Revitalization.* Beverly Hills, Calif.: Sage, 1985.

Wright, J. "Community Learning." In R. D. Boyd, J. W. Apps, and Associates, *Redefining the Discipline of Adult Education.* San Francisco: Jossey-Bass, 1980.

Wright, T. "A Political Literacy Campaign?" *Adult Education* (U.K.), 1980, *53* (1), 6–12.

Yankelovich, D. "Bringing the Public to the Table." Speech to the 1983 National Conference of the Domestic Policy Association. New York: Public Agenda Foundation, 1983.

Yinger, R. J. "Can We Really Teach Them to Think?" In R. E. Young (ed.), *Fostering Critical Thinking.* New Directions for Teaching and Learning, no. 3. San Francisco: Jossey-Bass, 1980.

Young, R. E. (ed.). *Fostering Critical Thinking.* New Directions for Teaching and Learning, no. 3. San Francisco: Jossey-Bass, 1980.

Zachary, L. "An Analysis of the Relevance of the Perry Scheme of Intellectual and Ethical Development to the Practice of Adult Education." Unpublished doctoral dissertation, Department of Higher and Adult Education, Teachers College, Columbia University, 1985.

Zander, A. *Making Groups Effective.* San Francisco: Jossey-Bass, 1982.

Zander, A. *The Purposes of Groups and Organizations.* San Francisco: Jossey-Bass, 1985.

Ziegler, W. L. *On Civic Literacy.* Syracuse, N.Y.: Syracuse University Research Corporation, 1975.

Ziegler, W. L. "The Life of the Public and the Life of Learning: Notes Towards a Social Philosophy for Adult Education." *Adult Leadership,* 1976, *24* (8), 254–256, 281–284.

Ziegler, W. L., Healy, G. M., and Ellsworth, J. H. "Civic Literacy." In C. Klevins (ed.), *Materials and Methods in Continuing Education.* Canoga Park, Calif.: Klevens Publications, 1978.

Zimmerman, J. F. *Participatory Democracy: Populism Revised.* New York: Praeger, 1986.

Zinn, H. *A People's History of the United States.* New York: Harper & Row, 1980.

Zweig, F. *The Quest for Fellowship.* London: Heinmann, 1965.

Zwerdling, D. *Workplace Democracy: A Guide to Workplace Ownership, Participation, and Self-Management Experiments in the United States and Europe.* New York: Harper & Row, 1984.

Name Index

281

Subject Index